Windows XP for Seniors

Addo Stuur

Windows XP
for Seniors

For everyone who wants to learn to use the computer at a later age

This book has been written using the Visual Steps™ method.
Translated by Lorri Granger and Grayson Morris
Edited by Ria Beentjes and Marleen Vermeij
© 2008 Visual Steps B.V.
Cover design by Studio Willemien Haagsma bNO

Seventh printing: January 2008
ISBN-13: 978 90 5905 044 0
ISBN-10: 90 5905 044 4

Do you have questions or suggestions?
E-mail: info@visualsteps.com

Would you like more information?
www.visualsteps.com

Website for this book:
www.visualsteps.com/winxp
Here you can register your book.

Register your book
We will keep you aware of any important changes that are necessary to you as a user of the book. You can also take advantage of our periodic newsletter informing you of our product releases, company news, tips & tricks, special offers, etc.

Table of Contents

Foreword

I wrote this book in order to introduce seniors to the computer. I'll
show you the basics of the operating system *Windows XP*, step by
step. Use this book right next to your computer as you work through
each chapter at your own pace. You'll be amazed how easy it is to
learn this way. When you've finished this book, you'll know how to
start programs, how to write a letter, how to surf the Internet and how
to send an e-mail. This book was written based on the Visual
Steps™ method, which was specifically developed for adults with no
prior computer experience. A number of people have helped me in
developing this method. I would especially like to thank
Dr. Hans van der Meij.

I hope you will enjoy reading this book!

Addo Stuur

P.S.
After you've finished this book, you'll know how to send an e-mail.
Your comments and suggestions are most welcome. My e-mail
address is: info@visualsteps.com

Introduction to Visual Steps™

The Visual Steps manuals and handbooks offer the best instructions on the computer expressway. Nowhere else in the world will you find better support while getting to know the computer, the Internet, *Windows* and other computer programs.

Visual Steps manuals are special because of their:

- **Content**
  Your way of learning, your needs, your desires and your know-how and skills have been taken into account.
- **Structure**
  You can get straight to work. No lengthy explanations. What is more, the chapters are organized in such a way that you can skip a chapter or redo a chapter without worry. The small steps taken in Visual Steps also make it easy to follow the instructions.
- **Illustrations**
  There are many, many illustrations of computer screens. These will help you to find the right buttons or menus, and will quickly show you whether you are still on the right track.
- **Format**
  A sizable format and pleasantly large letters enhance readability.

In short, these are manuals that I believe will be excellent guides.

Dr. H. van der Meij

Faculty of Applied Education, Department of Instruction Technology, University of Twente, the Netherlands

What You'll Need

In order to work through this book, you'll need a number of things on your computer.

The primary requirement for working with this book is having the US version of **Windows XP** on your computer. You can check this yourself by turning on your computer and looking at the welcome screen.

If you have *Windows XP* on your computer, usually the following things will also already be on your computer.

Accessories

Wordpad

Paint

Calculator

Games

Solitaire

In *Windows XP*, the group *Desktop Accessories* will have been installed with the following programs:
- *WordPad*
- *Paint*
- *Calculator*

You should also see the group *Games*, in which you'll find the program:
- *Solitaire*

Internet Options

A functioning **Internet connection** is needed for the two chapters about the Internet.
For the settings for your Internet connection, please see the software and information supplied by your Internet provider.
(Chapters 9 and 10)

E-mail
Outlook Express

Internet
Internet Explorer

The following programs need to be installed on your computer, before you can work through this book:
- *Outlook Express* 6
- *Internet Explorer* 7

Internet Explorer version 7 was released in January 2007 by *Microsoft* via Automatic Update to all *Windows XP* Service Pack 2 users.

Are you still running *Internet Explorer* version 6 on your computer? Then you will first need to download and install version 7 on your computer. This can be a rather daunting task for the beginning computer user. You may want to seek help by going to your computer dealer or by requesting assistance from someone you know who has experience with computers.
On the webpage **www.visualsteps.com/ie7install** you will find instructions for downloading and installing *Internet Explorer 7*. On page 220 you can read how to find out which version of *Internet Explorer* is running on your computer.

- Are you missing some of the things listed above?
- Do you want to customize your computer to suit your own wishes?

If so, you will need the *Microsoft Windows XP* CD-ROM.
This was included when you received your computer.
No? Don't worry, it's probably already on your computer.

The following things are useful. But it isn't a problem if you don't have them. Simply skip over the relevant pages.

An empty diskette ("floppy disk") or USB memory stick for saving files. (Chapter 6)

A printer is recommended for some of the exercises. If you don't have a printer, don't worry. Simply skip these exercises. (Chapter 4)

A music CD.
(Chapter 11)

How This Book Is Organized

This book is set up in such a way that you don't necessarily have to work through it from the beginning to the end.

The Basics

- Be sure to read and work carefully through Chapters 1 and 2 first. These discuss the basics in *Windows XP*.
- Then you can continue with chapters 3, 4 and 5. These chapters introduce the keyboard and the mouse, as well as word processing. These are skills that every computer user must master. The objective of these chapters is being able to write a letter.

Once you've mastered the basics, you can choose from the following topics:

Optional Subjects

- **File management**
  You can choose to work with files and folders in Chapter 6. This chapter can be worked through separately.
- **Text layout**
  Or you can choose to layout text and work with illustrations in chapters 7 and 8. The objective in the exercises in these chapters is to make driving instructions with a map.
- **Internet**
  If you want to learn how to use the Internet, read Chapters 9 and 10. You'll need a functioning Internet connection, however. The objective of the exercises in these chapters is to send the driving instructions with a card by e-mail.
- **Customizing computer settings**
  In a chapter that can be used separately, Chapter 11, you can learn how to customize your computer settings to suit your individual needs or desires.

The Screen Shots

The screen shots in this book were made on a computer running *Windows XP* with *Service Pack 2*. *Service Pack 2* is an extension to *Windows XP* provided by *Microsoft*. If you don't (yet) have *Service Pack 2* on your computer, some of the images may differ from what you see on your screen.

How To Use This Book

This book was written using the Visual Steps™ method. It's important that you work through the book **step by step.** If you carefully follow all of the steps, you won't encounter any surprises.

There are various icons used in this Visual Steps™ book. This is what they mean:

Actions
These icons indicate that something must be done:

🖱	The miniature mouse indicates that you must do something with the mouse.
⌨	The mini-keyboard means that you must type something using the keyboard.
☞	The little hand indicates that you must do something else, such as putting a CD-ROM into the computer.

In addition to these actions, in some spots in the book **extra assistance** is given so that you can successfully work through the book.

Help
Extra assistance can be found by looking for the following icons:

⇨	The arrow gives a warning.
�	The bandage offers assistance if something goes wrong.
✓	The check mark is used with the exercises. These exercises at the end of each chapter will let you independently repeat the actions.
👣1.1	Have you forgotten how to perform an action? Use the number beside the footsteps to look it up in the back of the book in the section *How Do I Do That Again?*

This book also contains general information and tips about computers and *Windows XP*. This information is given in separate boxes.

Extra Information
These boxes are marked with the following icons:

	The small book marks extra background information that you can take your time reading. You do not actually need this information to work through the book.
	The light bulb indicates an extra tip that can be useful when using *Windows XP*.

Test Your Knowledge

Have you finished reading this book? Test your knowledge then with the test *Windows XP*. Visit the website: **www.ccforseniors.com**

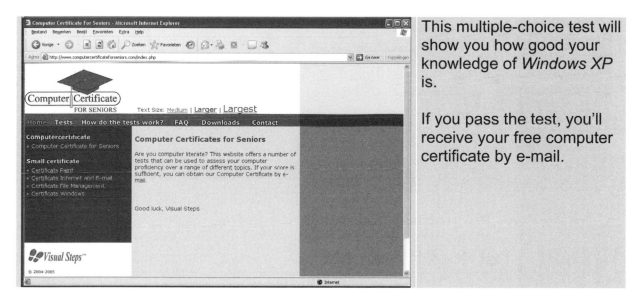

This multiple-choice test will show you how good your knowledge of *Windows XP* is.

If you pass the test, you'll receive your free computer certificate by e-mail.

For Teachers

This book is designed as a self-study guide. It is also well suited for use in a group or a classroom setting. For this purpose, we offer a free teacher's manual containing information about how to prepare for the course (including didactic teaching methods) and testing materials. You can download this teacher's manual (PDF file) from the website which accompanies this book: **www.visualsteps.com/winxp**

Register Your Book

You can register your book. We will keep you aware of any important changes that are necessary to you as a user of the book. You can also take advantage of:
Our periodic newsletter informing you of our product releases, company news, tips & tricks, special offers, etc.
You can find information on how to register your book in chapter 9: *Surfing the Internet.*

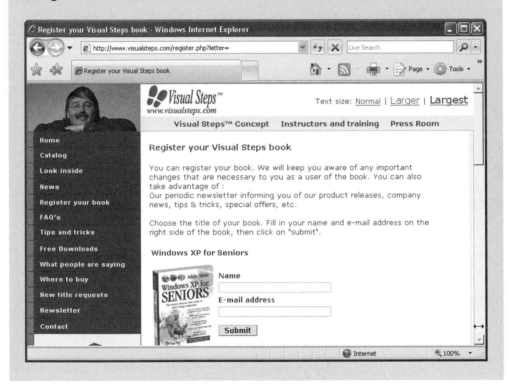

Visual Steps Newsletter

The free Visual Steps Newsletter will inform you of our product releases, free tips & tricks, special offers, free guides, etc.
It is sent to you periodically by e-mail. Please rest assured that we will not use your e-mail address for any purpose other than sending you the information you have requested and we will not share this address with any third-party. Each newsletter contains a clickable link to unsubscribe from our newsletter.

1. Starting and Stopping in Windows XP

The computer you're sitting in front of is also called a *PC*. This is an abbreviation for *Personal Computer*. In the past twenty years, the PC has conquered the world, marching from the office to the home. Nowadays nearly everyone has heard of *Windows*. But it was not all that long ago - 1993 in fact - that *Windows* was used on PCs for the first time. Since then, *Windows* has marched along with the PC.
But what exactly is *Windows?* It's a system you can use to operate your computer. Before *Windows* came along, computers were operated by typing a variety of complicated commands. But with *Windows* you can perform most operations by using the mouse. After reading this chapter, you'll understand why this operating system is called *Windows.* You'll see that nearly everything that happens is displayed in "window panes" on your screen.

In this chapter, you'll learn how to:

- start and stop *Windows XP*
- point and click with the mouse
- enter commands
- start and stop programs
- minimize and maximize a window
- use the taskbar

⇨ Please note:

This book assumes that you are working with a computer mouse. If you are working on a laptop with touchpad, you may want to purchase an external mouse in order to more easily follow the steps in this book. It is good idea to become familiar with a computer mouse. You will then be able to work on a desktop computer later on.

💡 Tip

Take your laptop with you when you go to buy a computer mouse at the computer store. The sales representative can then show you how to connect your new mouse to your laptop. Then when you get home you can get started right away.
Later on, if you want to learn more about using the touchpad to operate your laptop, surf to the website www.visualsteps.com/winxp/news and read the Tip *Working with a touchpad*.

Starting Windows XP

Windows XP is automatically started when you turn on your computer. If you are using a desktop computer, the power button is often located on the front of the case. On a laptop, the power button is most likely found on the keyboard. You can easily identify this button by this symbol: ⏻. Take a look:

☞ **Press the power button**

⇨ **Please note:**

With many desktop computers, the monitor or screen will also be automatically started. With other computers, you must do this yourself.
The screen of a laptop does not need to be turned on separately.

☞ **Press the power button**

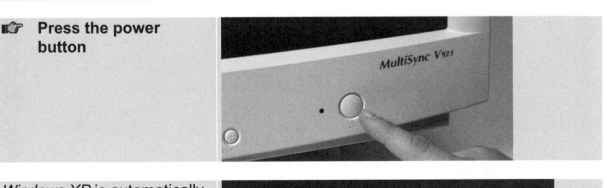

Windows XP is automatically started when you turn on your computer.

Sometimes you see a screen that looks like this:

In that case: ask someone to help you because you will have to click on the username you want to use:

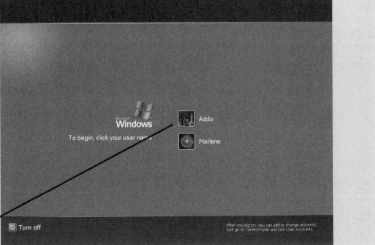

After a moment this screen, called the *Desktop*, appears:

➡️ **Please note:**

The screen illustrations used in this book were made with the *Windows XP* standard settings. However, these may differ significantly from what you see on your screen. The settings in *Windows XP* can be changed in many ways.

Using the Mouse

You will operate the computer almost entirely using the mouse. The first few times that you use the mouse, it will seem unfamiliar. Just remember that everyone, even children, had to learn how to use a mouse. No one simply knew how: it's matter of practicing. The more you use the mouse, the more proficient you'll become.

You can do **five different things** with the mouse:

- point
- click
- double-click
- drag
- right-click

You'll learn how to point and click in this chapter.

💡 Tip

What's the best way to hold the mouse?

Not like this: **But like this:**

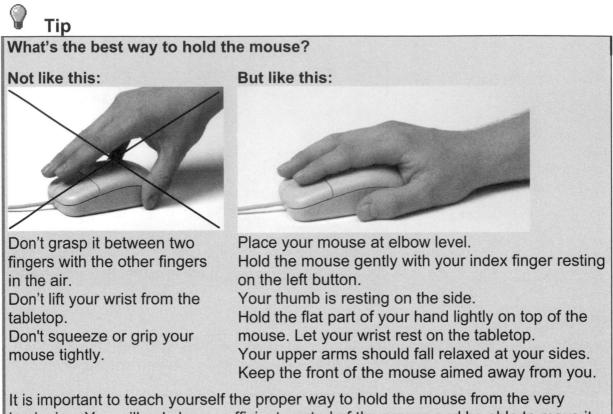

Don't grasp it between two   Place your mouse at elbow level.
fingers with the other fingers   Hold the mouse gently with your index finger resting
in the air.   on the left button.
Don't lift your wrist from the   Your thumb is resting on the side.
tabletop.   Hold the flat part of your hand lightly on top of the
Don't squeeze or grip your   mouse. Let your wrist rest on the tabletop.
mouse tightly.   Your upper arms should fall relaxed at your sides.
                                                    Keep the front of the mouse aimed away from you.

It is important to teach yourself the proper way to hold the mouse from the very
beginning. You will only have sufficient control of the mouse and be able to move it
precisely if you keep it in the palm of your hand.

Pointing

The first thing you need to know is how to point at things with the pointer on the
screen.

Somewhere on the screen
you can see a pointer ₭ :

⊕ **Move the mouse over
the tabletop**

The pointer moves with it.

The pointer on the screen is also called the *mouse pointer.* You can use the mouse pointer to point at things on the screen.

Sometimes things will appear on the screen when you point to something. Try it:

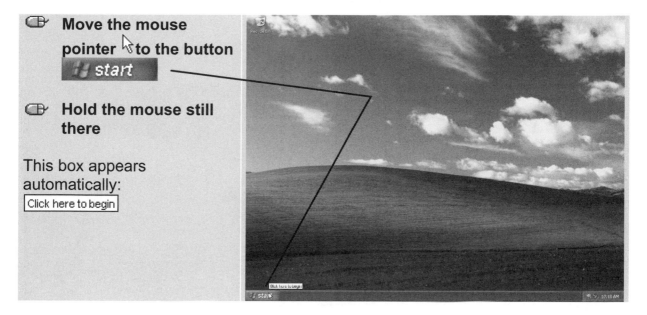

☞ **Move the mouse pointer ⬉ to the button**

☞ **Hold the mouse still there**

This box appears automatically:

Click here to begin

The Mouse Buttons

Computer mice are available in a wide variety of types and colors. And yet they are all similar: every mouse has at least two buttons.

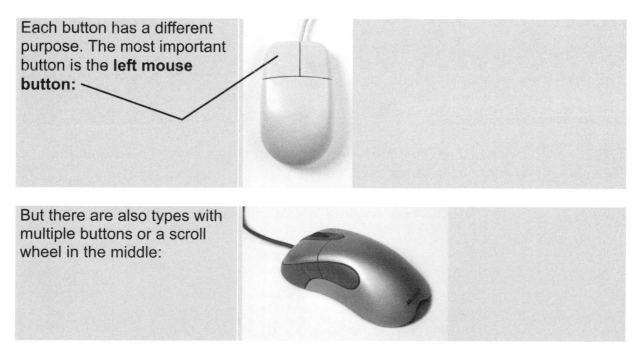

Each button has a different purpose. The most important button is the **left mouse button:**

But there are also types with multiple buttons or a scroll wheel in the middle:

Clicking

Clicking is the mouse action that you'll use the most. You click to start a program, for example.

Clicking is done like this:

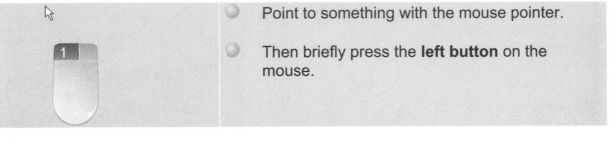

○ Point to something with the mouse pointer.

○ Then briefly press the **left button** on the mouse.

Try it:

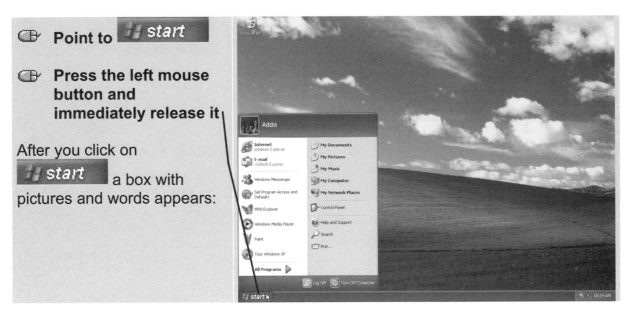

☞ **Point to** ⊞ start

☞ **Press the left mouse button and immediately release it**

After you click on ⊞ start a box with pictures and words appears:

This is called a **menu**, like a menu in a restaurant with a variety of choices. In this case, the menu contains commands.

You can also point to things on the menu:

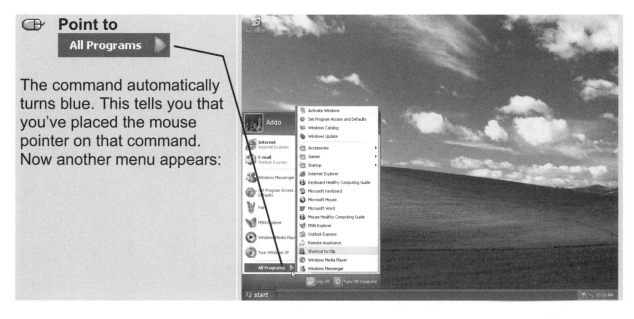

Point to

All Programs

The command automatically turns blue. This tells you that you've placed the mouse pointer on that command. Now another menu appears:

Each command with a small triangle ▶ next to it has a new menu. Take a look:

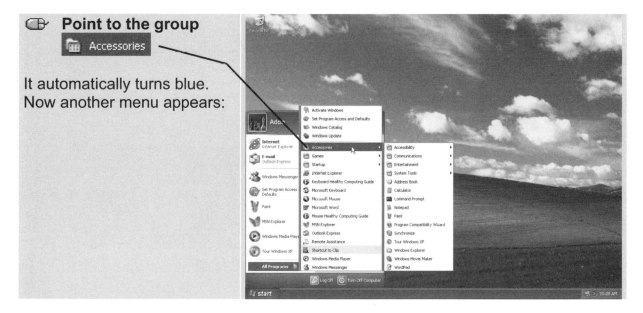

Point to the group

Accessories

It automatically turns blue. Now another menu appears:

HELP! The wrong menu appears.

Did you accidentally click on something else?

Esc

At the top left of your keyboard, press
The menu disappears.

Now you can tell the computer to start the program *Calculator:*

👈 **Click on**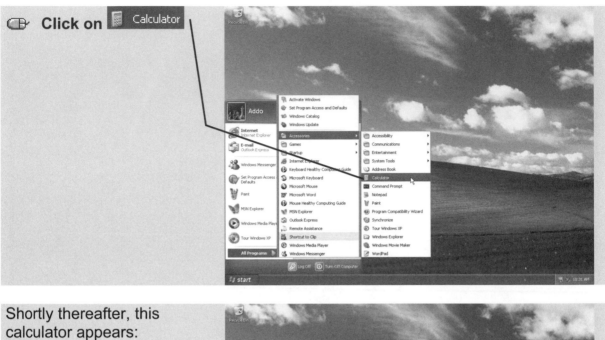

Shortly thereafter, this calculator appears:

🩹 HELP! I clicked on the wrong word.

Can you still see the menu, but the wrong word has been selected?
👈 **Click on the right word**

🩹 HELP! I clicked on the wrong program.

Did you accidentally start a different program?

👈 **At the top right of the wrong program, click on** ☒
☞ **Now go back through the steps above to start the** *Calculator*

Entering Commands

You've told the computer to start the Calculator program. That has now been done.

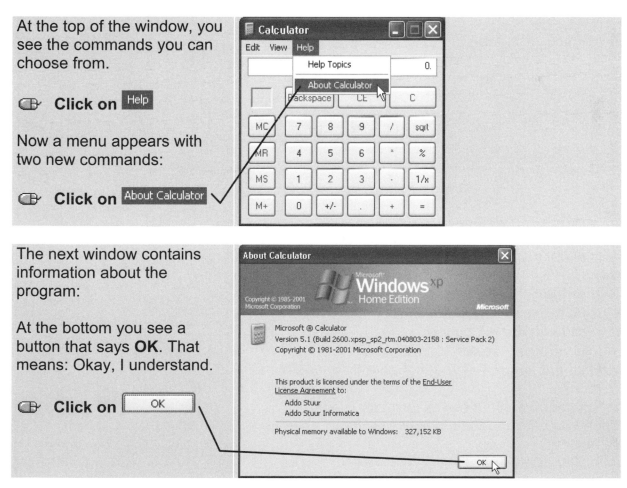

You see a frame around the calculator:

This frame is called a *window frame* or *window*. All of the programs in *Windows XP* are displayed in a frame of this type, and they all work in virtually the same way. This makes them easy to use.

At the top of the window, you see the commands you can choose from.

☞ **Click on** Help

Now a menu appears with two new commands:

☞ **Click on** About Calculator

The next window contains information about the program:

At the bottom you see a button that says **OK**. That means: Okay, I understand.

☞ **Click on** OK

Calculating by Clicking

Naturally, the *Calculator* works just like a real calculator, except that instead of pressing the buttons, you click on them with the mouse:

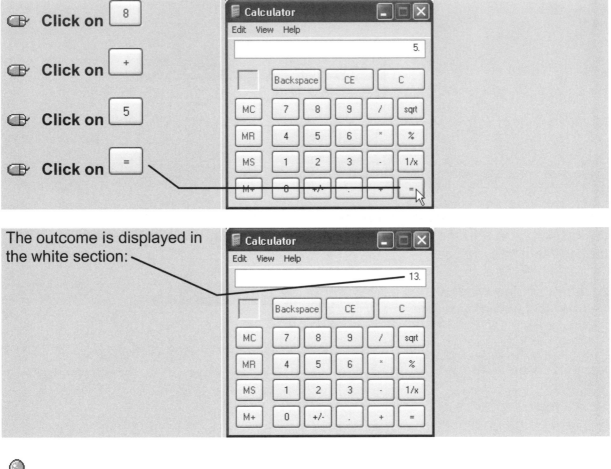

☞ **Click on** 8

☞ **Click on** +

☞ **Click on** 5

☞ **Click on** =

The outcome is displayed in the white section:

Is it difficult to click on the right spot?
This usually means that you have moved the mouse after pointing and before clicking.
Remember:
• Hold the mouse gently with your index finger resting on the left button.
• Your thumb is resting on the side.
• Hold the flat part of your hand lightly on top of the mouse.
• Let your wrist rest on the tabletop.
Then you won't need to look at your hand when you click.
☞ **Try again**

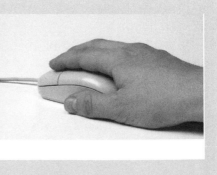

Minimizing a Window

A window can be changed in various ways. You can temporarily make the window small, for example. This is called *minimizing*. This can be useful if you want to work with a different program for a while.

You don't have to stop the program; you can simply temporarily minimize the window. You can do this with the *window buttons* at the top right.

☞ **Click on** ■

The window is minimized and disappears from the screen.

Next to **start** you now see the *Calculator* button:

You didn't stop the *Calculator*; you simply put the window "away" for a while at the bottom of your screen.

Starting Another Program

In *Windows XP*, you can easily start various programs one after the other. Take a look:

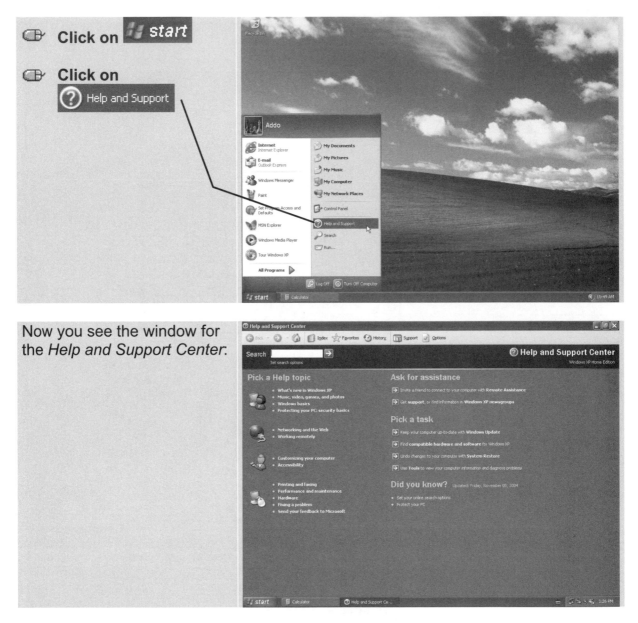

You didn't receive a manual with *Windows XP*. All of the information you need is contained in this digital Help system. We'll discuss this in more detail later.

Maximizing and Minimizing

The window *Help and Support Center* fills the entire screen. There's a button 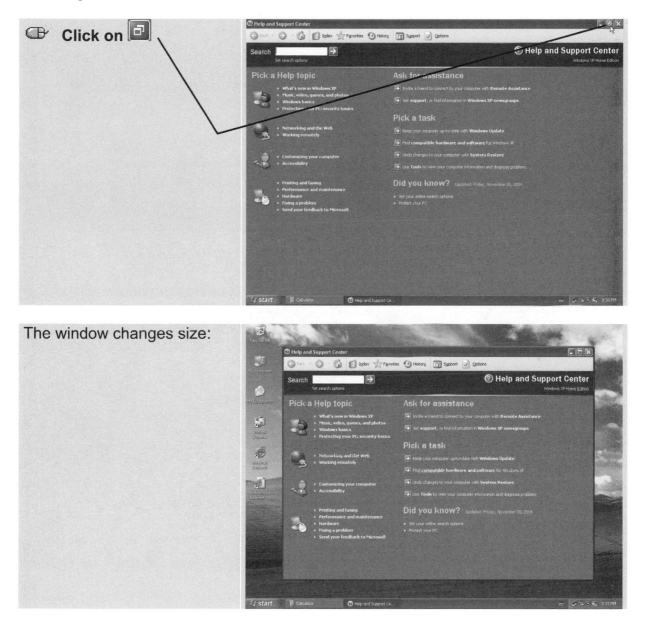 for reducing the window to a different, smaller size.

☞ **Click on**

The window changes size:

Nearly every window can be maximized to fill the entire screen. This is how:

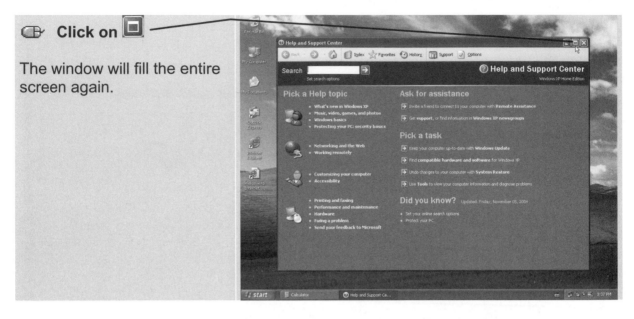

Click on ☐

The window will fill the entire screen again.

The *Help and Support Center* window can also be "put away" (minimized).

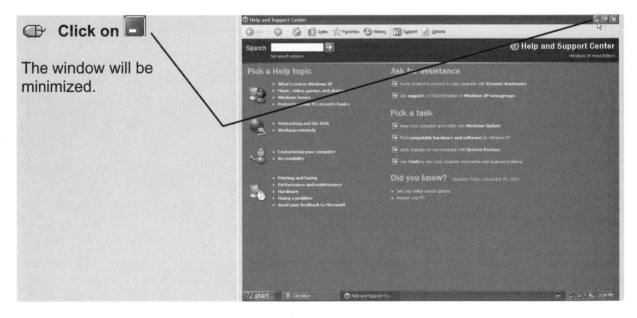

Click on ☐

The window will be minimized.

Now you've started two programs: the *Calculator* and the *Help and Support Center*.

Both are now minimized and have a button at the bottom:

The blue bar next to ![start] is called the **taskbar**. This bar always contains buttons for the programs that you're working with.

Opening a Window with the Taskbar

You can quickly reopen a window with the taskbar:

👉 **Click on**
   📟 Calculator

The window for the *Calculator* will be reopened.

Stopping a Program

A window can also be definitively **closed**. The program is then stopped. You can do this with another window button:

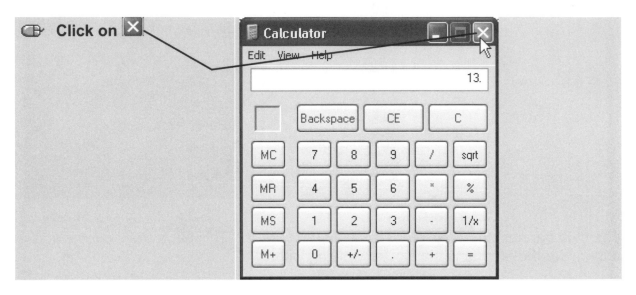

The window will be closed and the button *Calculator* will no longer be displayed in the taskbar. The program has stopped.

Click on ❌

The window *Help and Support Center* will be closed.

Help and Support Center has now also been closed and is no longer shown in the taskbar.

Stopping Windows XP

So far you've learned some important things about *Windows XP*. It's also handy to know one more thing: how to stop *Windows XP*. As silly as it seems, this is done using the *Start* button:

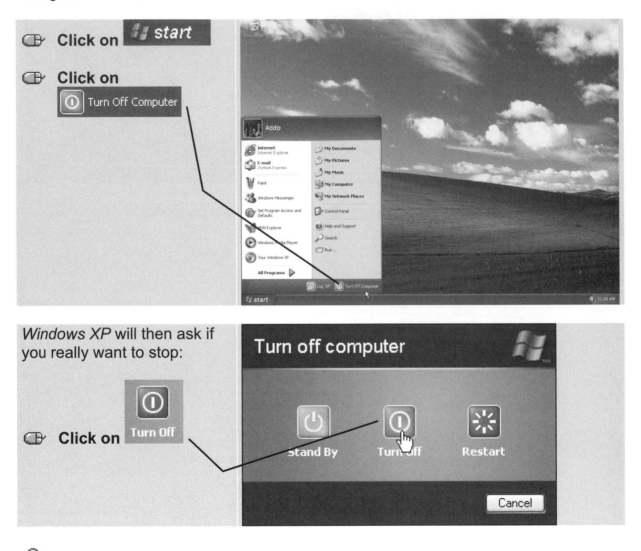

Tip
If you click on ⬚ Cancel , *Windows XP* will not be stopped. You can use this button if you change your mind and want to continue.

Exercises

The following exercises will help you master what you've just learned. Have you forgotten how to do something? Use the number beside the footsteps to look it up in the appendix *How Do I Do That Again?*

Exercise: Starting and Stopping

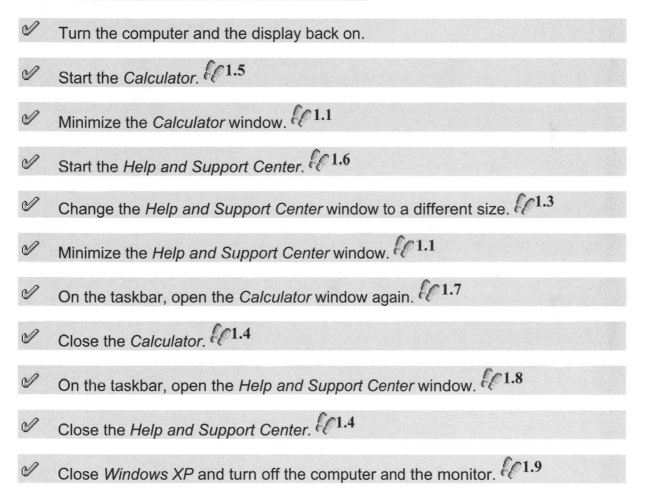

✔ Turn the computer and the display back on.

✔ Start the *Calculator*. 🐾1.5

✔ Minimize the *Calculator* window. 🐾1.1

✔ Start the *Help and Support Center*. 🐾1.6

✔ Change the *Help and Support Center* window to a different size. 🐾1.3

✔ Minimize the *Help and Support Center* window. 🐾1.1

✔ On the taskbar, open the *Calculator* window again. 🐾1.7

✔ Close the *Calculator*. 🐾1.4

✔ On the taskbar, open the *Help and Support Center* window. 🐾1.8

✔ Close the *Help and Support Center*. 🐾1.4

✔ Close *Windows XP* and turn off the computer and the monitor. 🐾1.9

When you've practiced enough, you can read the background information and tips on the next page. If you would rather keep working with your computer, you can go on to Chapter 2. The background information and tips can be read another time.

Background Information

When should you turn off the computer?
In general, computer technicians will agree that frequently turning the computer on and off isn't good for it. Computers are built to be left on for many thousands of hours. There's virtually no wear, especially if your computer is on *standby*. Modern computers and displays also use very little electricity, and that usage is minimized when the computer is on *standby*.
Are you working with your computer and you want to do something else, then come back in an hour or so? Just leave the computer on. That's better than turning it off and on.

Your computer is "asleep": standby
Most models of computers and displays have a variety of options for conserving energy. The display is put on **standby**, just like your television. The hard disk on your computer can also be temporarily stopped. You can activate this type of energy-conserving measure in *Windows XP*. You can set, for example, the period of time after which these options are automatically activated if the computer isn't being used. You'll read how to set the *standby* mode in Chapter 11.

What are the various parts of *Windows XP* called?

Window:
A frame containing a program or information.

Icon *My Computer*:
Here you can see everything that's on your computer.

Icon *Recycle Bin*:
Saves all of the things you've deleted so that you can retrieve them later.

Start menu:
Menu used to start programs.

Icons:
Small pictures that you can click on to open a program or section of the computer, for example.

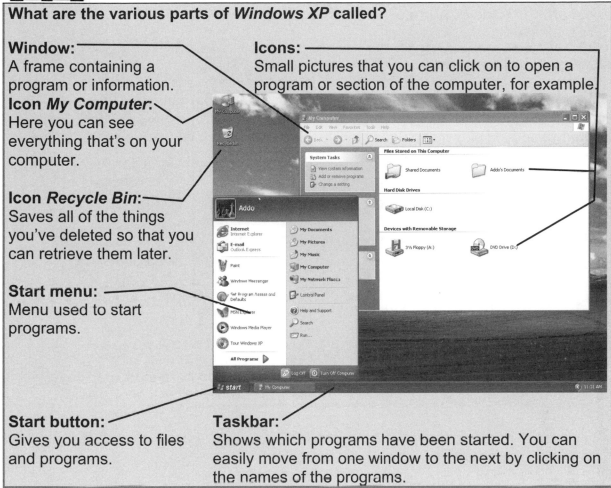

Start button:
Gives you access to files and programs.

Taskbar:
Shows which programs have been started. You can easily move from one window to the next by clicking on the names of the programs.

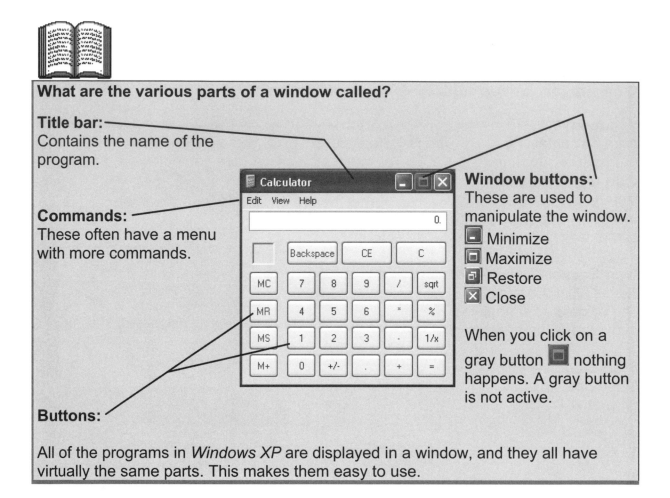

What are the various parts of a window called?

Title bar:
Contains the name of the
program.

Commands:
These often have a menu
with more commands.

Buttons:

Window buttons:
These are used to
manipulate the window.

Minimize

Maximize

Restore

Close

When you click on a
gray button nothing
happens. A gray button
is not active.

All of the programs in *Windows XP* are displayed in a window, and they all have
virtually the same parts. This makes them easy to use.

Windows
Every two or three years, a new version of *Windows* is released. This is necessary in
order to keep up with developments in computer technology.
Since *Windows* was
introduced, six major
versions have been
released: *Windows 3.1*, *95*,
98, Me, XP and *Vista*.
There's also a *Windows*
version called *Windows
2000*. This version is not
really intended for use in
the home, but more for
corporate networks.

Tips

 ## HELP! My computer has switched off.

Did you not use your computer for a while and does it appear to be switched off?

The computer and the monitor have automatically switched to the *standby* mode. You can see that the lights on the display and computer have changed from green to yellow or orange.

☞ **You can 'wake up' your computer by pressing a key on the keyboard or by slightly moving the mouse**

 ## HELP! I see something else all of a sudden.

Has another image suddenly appeared on your screen?

A moving illustration such as this, perhaps:

This means that your computer's **screen saver** has been activated. The screen saver prevents your screen from "burn-in". Burn-in can happen when the same, motionless image is on your screen for a long period of time while you're not using the computer. You can change the settings for the screen saver in *Windows XP* to suit your taste. For example, you can set the number of minutes that the image has to remain motionless before the screen saver is activated. You can also turn the screen saver off.

☞ **You can remove the screen saver from your screen by pressing a key on the keyboard or by slightly moving the mouse**

💡 Tip

An hourglass?

Has your mouse pointer ⍨ changed into an hourglass ⧗?

That means your computer is busy doing something.

☞ **Simply wait patiently until your computer is done and the hourglass has disappeared**

💡 Tip

Restart or turn off?

The window *Turn off computer* can also be used to restart the computer or to put it in the standby mode:

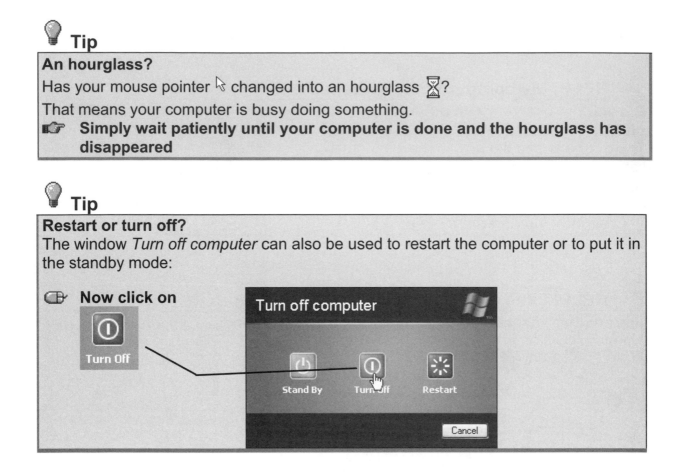

2. More Use of the Mouse in Windows XP

The mouse has become an essential part of the computer. But it's actually a relatively new addition. The mouse didn't become a standard part of PCs until *Windows* was introduced. Before then, only computers made by *Apple* had a mouse, and it had only one button. It quickly became evident that operating a PC had to be made easier so that a wider group could use it. This is why the software became increasingly *graphic*: pictures and buttons replaced complicated commands. *Windows XP* is an excellent example of this. The most important commands can be carried out by using the mouse. Various aspects of *Windows XP* were developed to make it easier and easier to use – there are various kinds of buttons in many sizes on the screen: buttons to press, on and off buttons, buttons that turn and scrollbars. The mouse has also been given more and more functions. In this chapter, you'll learn how to utilize those functions. Maybe someday in the future the mouse will become less important, if computers can "listen" and accept verbal commands. Until then, however, the mouse has center stage in *Windows XP*.

In this chapter, you'll learn how to:

- drag with the mouse
- use a scrollbar
- use the *Help and Support Center*
- double-click with the mouse
- change the size of a window
- right-click with the mouse

Getting Ready

Before you can start:

☞ **Turn the computer and the monitor on**

☞ **Start the *Calculator* 1.5**

The *Calculator* window is opened:

The Next Three Mouse Actions

In the previous chapter, you learned that there are five different things you can do with the mouse:

- point
- click
- drag
- double-click
- right-click

You learned the first two of these in the previous chapter. In this chapter, you'll learn how to do the last three.

Dragging

You can move things on the screen by dragging them.

Dragging is done like this:

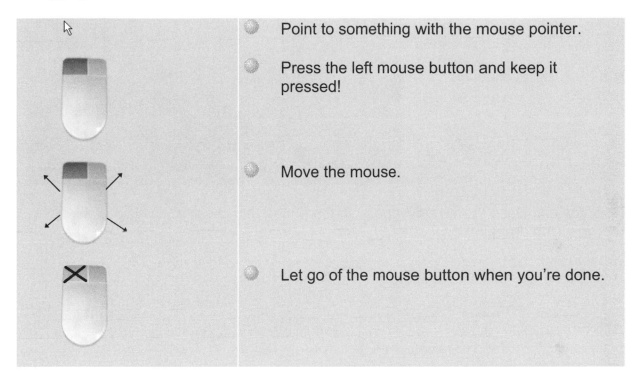

Point to something with the mouse pointer.

Press the left mouse button and keep it pressed!

Move the mouse.

Let go of the mouse button when you're done.

By dragging with the mouse you can move the *Calculator* window, for example. Try it:

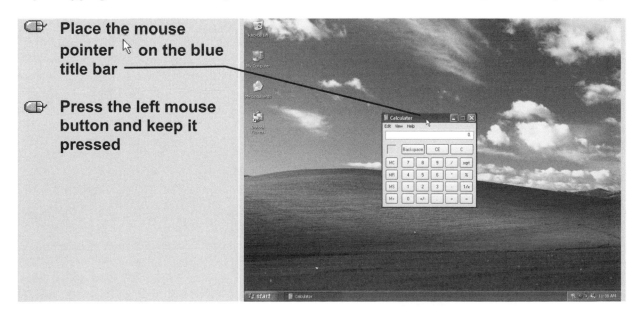

Place the mouse pointer ↖ on the blue title bar

Press the left mouse button and keep it pressed

Keep pressing the mouse button and slide the mouse over the tabletop

The calculator slides with the mouse pointer.

Now you can close the window again. At the end of this chapter you'll find exercises for practicing dragging.

Close the *Calculator* window 𝓁𝓁1.4

Tip

Dragging in Solitaire

To continue to practice dragging, I recommend that you play the popular card game *Solitaire* on the computer. It's the perfect, handy way to learn to use the mouse.

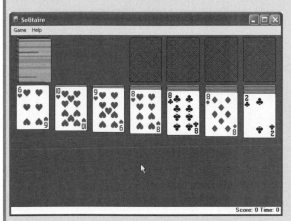

This *Solitaire* program comes with *Windows XP* and it has probably already been installed on your computer. In Appendix A at the back of this book you can read how to start this program and play the game.

Dragging with a Scrollbar

There are many situations in *Windows* in which you must drag. You can practice these using the window for the *Help and Support Center*.

☞ **Start *Help and Support Center*** 📖1.6

🖱 **Click on**
  • **Customizing your computer**

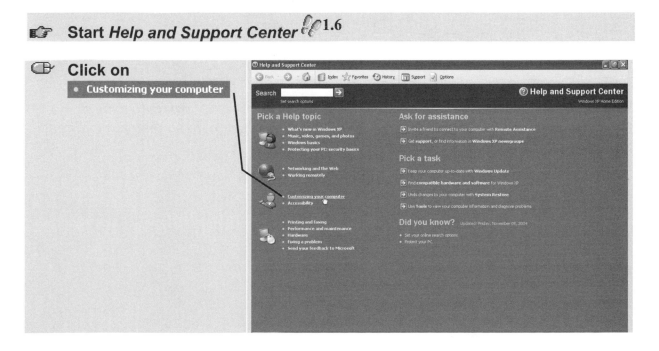

One way to drag is by using **scrollbars**. Take a look:

In the right-hand side of the left window, you see a vertical bar with two pointers:

This bar is called a *scrollbar*.

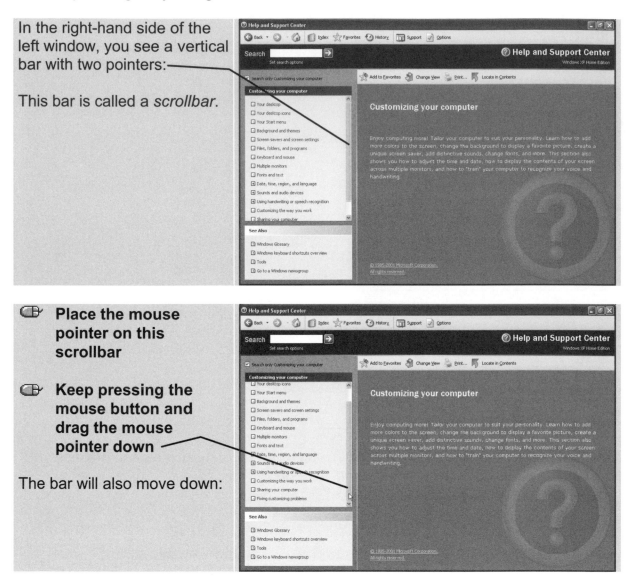

Place the mouse pointer on this scrollbar

Keep pressing the mouse button and drag the mouse pointer down

The bar will also move down:

You can use the scrollbar to scroll down the contents of a window, in this case, the topics listed under *Customizing your computer*. These scroll up so that you can read through to the last lines in the list.

Enlarging and Reducing a Window

By dragging with the mouse, you can also change the size of a window.

The window currently fills the screen:

First change the window to its previous size.

☞ **Click on** 🗗

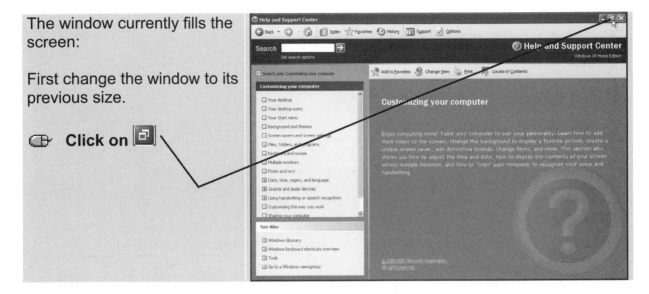

The window is now smaller and has a frame around it.

☞ **Place the mouse
pointer precisely on
the right edge of the
window's frame**

The mouse pointer changes
into a double arrow ↔:

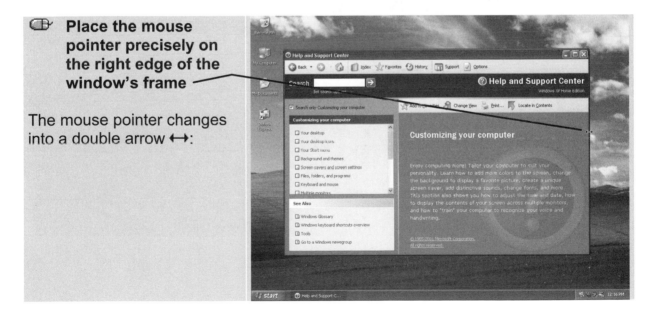

Keep pressing the mouse button and drag the mouse to the left

You will see the size of the window reduce. The text automatically adjusts to fit:

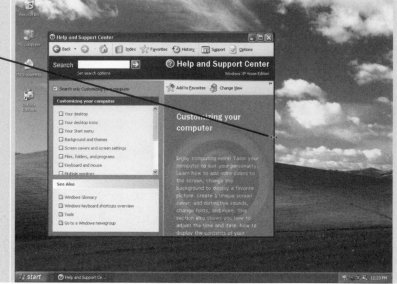

By dragging with the mouse, you can also change the height of a window:

Place the mouse pointer precisely on the bottom edge of the window's frame

The mouse pointer changes into a double arrow $\updownarrow$:

Keep pressing the mouse button and move the mouse upward

You will see the window reduce in size:

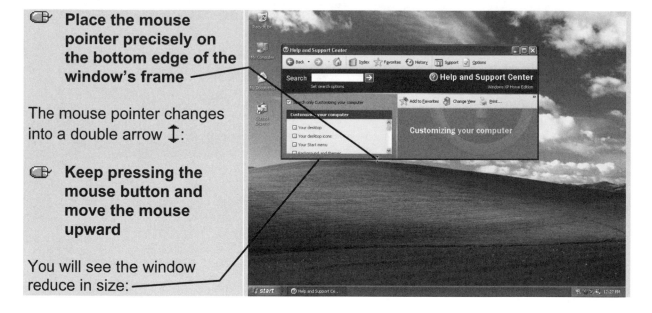

For the next few steps, it's handy to change the window back so that it fills the screen:

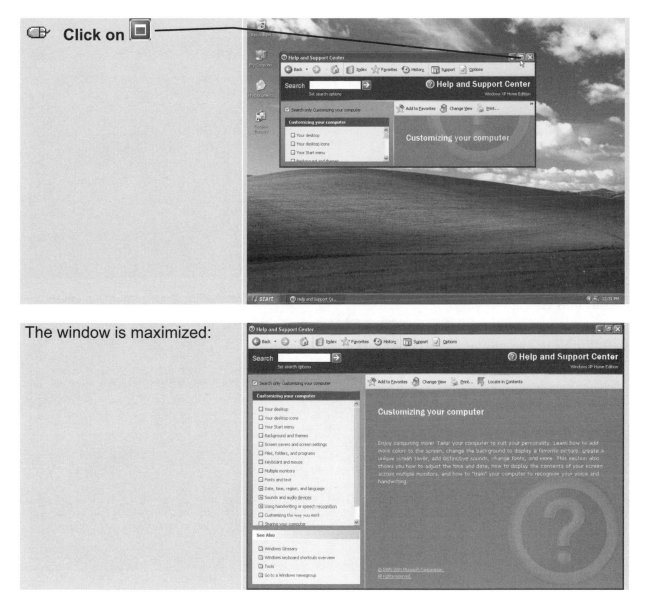

Click on ▫ —

The window is maximized:

Because you already have the *Help and Support Center* on, you can take a closer look at how this program works.

Back to the Beginning

It's easy to go back to the previous screen:

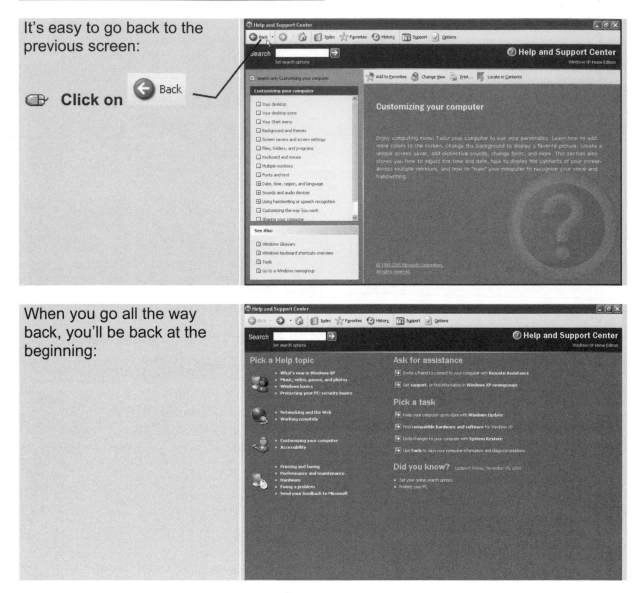

🖰 **Click on** 🔙 Back

When you go all the way back, you'll be back at the beginning:

Using the Help and Support Center

The *Help and Support Center* is an extensive digital manual for *Windows XP*. Just like paper manuals, it has a table of contents. You can see the table of contents on the left.

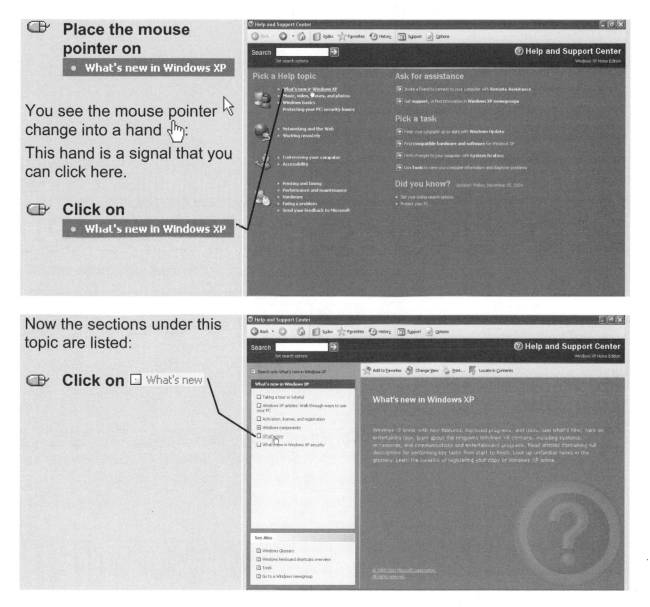

☞ **Place the mouse pointer on**
- **What's new in Windows XP**

You see the mouse pointer change into a hand:
This hand is a signal that you can click here.

☞ **Click on**
- **What's new in Windows XP**

Now the sections under this topic are listed:

☞ **Click on** ☐ What's new

The relevant information is now displayed in the frame on the right:

By clicking on the topics and sections that are underlined, you can find the information you need. You can read this information by clicking in the frame on the right.

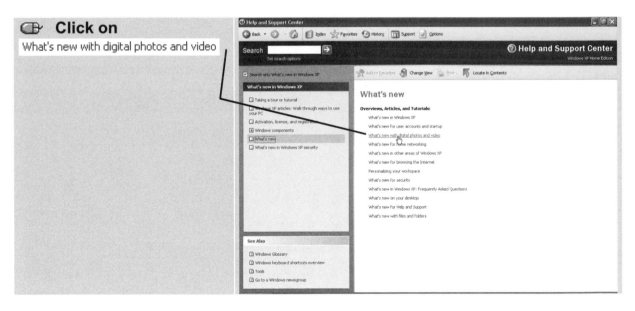

In the frame on the right, you can read information about the new digital media:

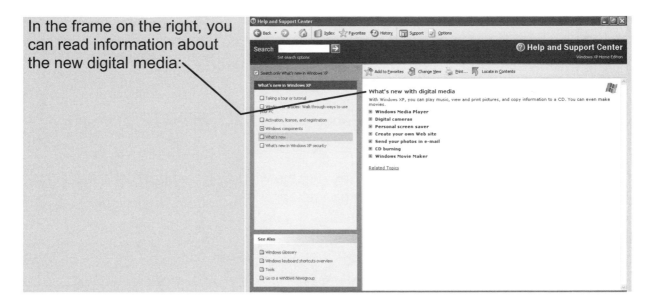

Now you can close the *Help and Support Center* window.

☞ **Close the *Help and Support Center* window** 🐾 1.4

Now you once again see the *Desktop* for *Windows XP*:

💡 Tip

The previous size of the *Help and Support Center* window

Windows XP "remembers" the size that you gave to the *Help and Support Center* window.

When you start the *Help and Support Center* program, the window will automatically be maximized.

However, if you click on the button 🗗 *Restore,* the window will appear in the size that you gave it the last time you used it, for example:

Double-Clicking

Until now, you've clicked only once on a word, a command or a button. However, in *Windows XP* you sometimes need to *double-click* on things, such as the icons on the screen shown below:

This is how to double-click:

	⚪ Point to something with the mouse pointer.
	⚪ Press the left mouse button **two times in rapid succession**.

A program can be quickly started with an icon. Try to double-click on one:

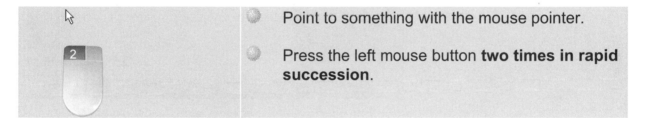

☞ **Double-click on the**

Recycle Bin

Now you see this window:

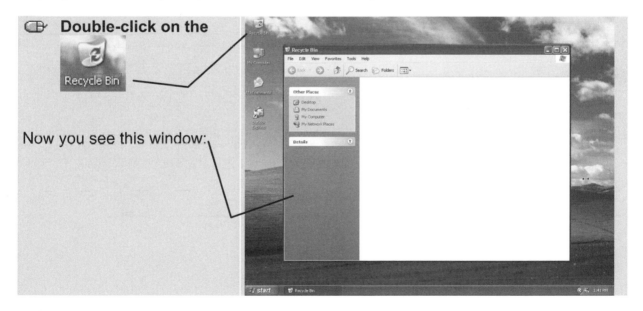

💡 **Tip**

When double-clicking, it's important that you **do not move the mouse** between the two clicks. When you do, *Windows* interprets this as two single clicks on two different spots. You might need to try a few times before double-clicking works.

☞ **Close the *Recycle Bin* window again** ✍1.4

You can also open another window by double-clicking on it, for example the window *My Computer*.

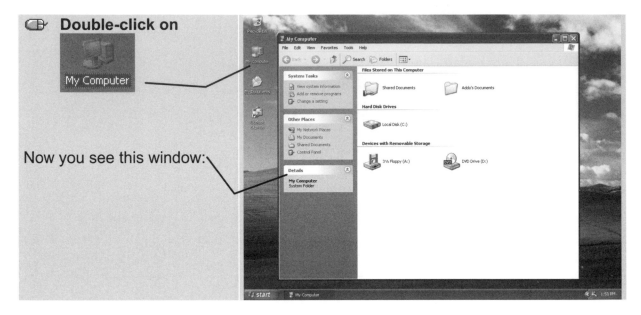

Double-click on

Now you see this window:

This window shows the various parts of your computer.

HELP! Double-clicking won't work.

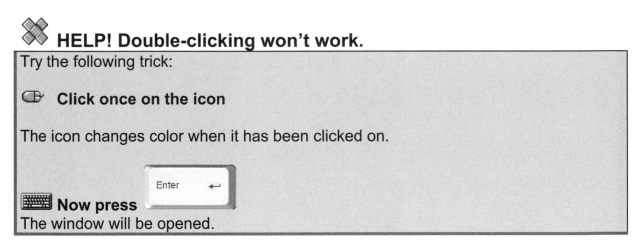

Try the following trick:

Click once on the icon

The icon changes color when it has been clicked on.

Now press Enter ⏎

The window will be opened.

The Many Faces of a Window

You've probably noticed that the screen illustrations in this book sometimes differ from what you see on your screen. This is in part due to the fact that *Windows XP* can be customized. You can change the window *My Computer*, for example:

Click on View

You now see this menu:

Some of the commands have a check mark ✔, others have a dot ●.

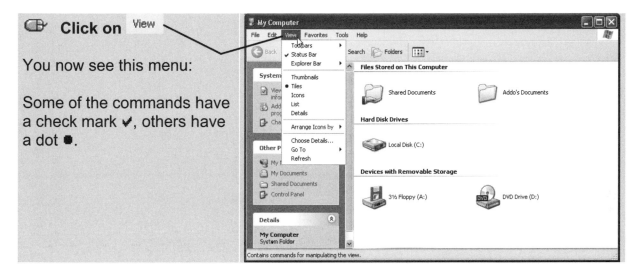

Commands with a Check Mark

A command with a check mark ✔ is a command that can be switched on or off. You can give the window a different appearance, for example. Try it:

Click on View

Click on Toolbars

Check to see if there's a check mark ✔ by Standard Buttons

Is there a check mark?
Then click on Standard Buttons

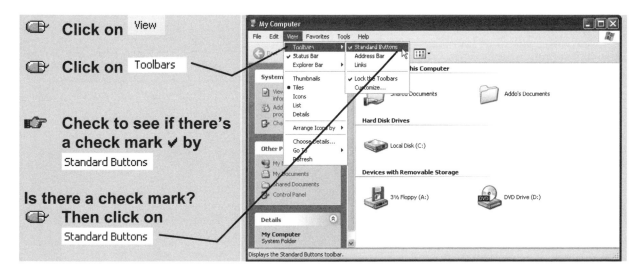

✖ HELP!

Is there <u>no</u> check mark?

☞ **Then don't do anything**

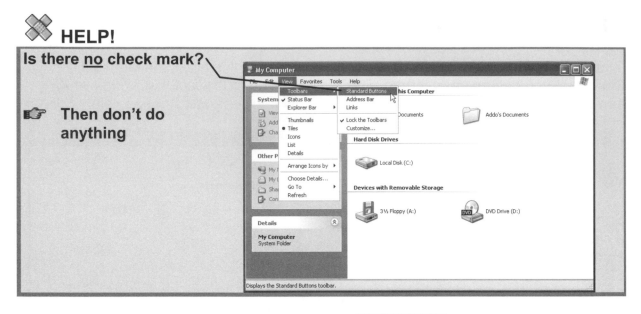

The check mark is removed and the command Standard Buttons has been switched off.

Now the window has no buttons:

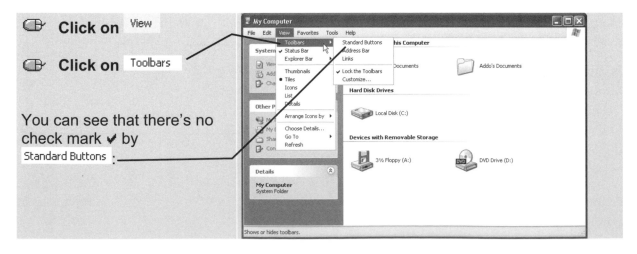

The check mark for the command Standard Buttons is gone now – take a look:

🖰 **Click on** View

🖰 **Click on** Toolbars

You can see that there's no check mark ✔ by Standard Buttons :

You can switch the command Standard Buttons back on:

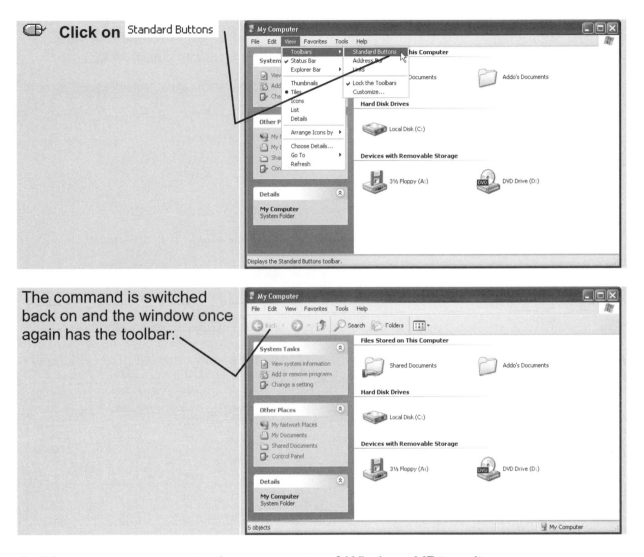

Click on Standard Buttons

The command is switched back on and the window once again has the toolbar:

In this way, you can customize many parts of *Windows XP* to suit your own preferences. In general, the settings are simple and can be switched on or off. Feel free to experiment: any changes you make can always be undone.

Selecting from a List

There is another type of command that can be switched on and off, except with a difference: you must always select one command from a group. Take a look:

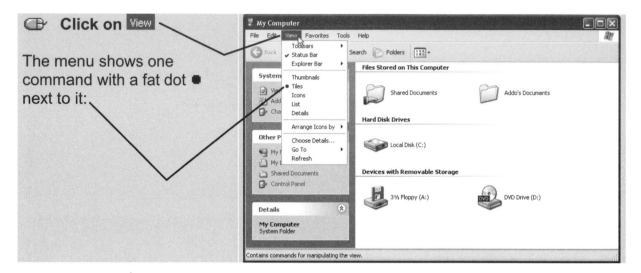

Click on View

The menu shows one command with a fat dot ● next to it:

A command with a fat dot in front of it works slightly differently than simply switching on and off with the check mark. Take a look:

These five commands go together. One of these commands will always be active:

Here, for example, the command ● Tiles is active, as you can see because it has the dot next to it.

Try selecting a different command, for example the command List .

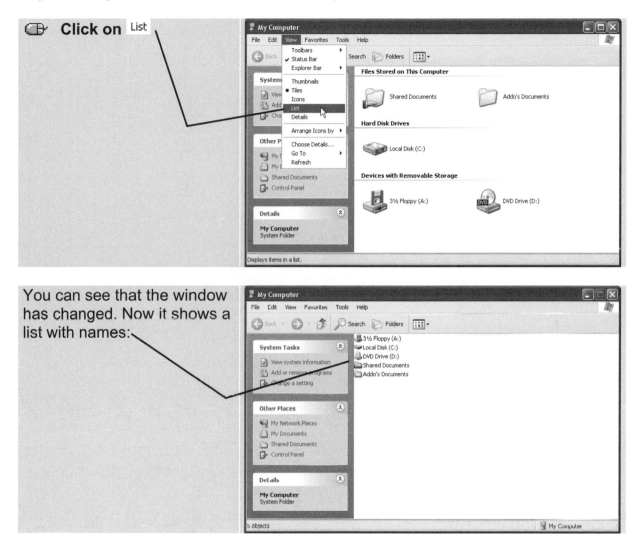

Click on List

You can see that the window has changed. Now it shows a list with names:

It's easy to make the window look the way it did before, with icons.

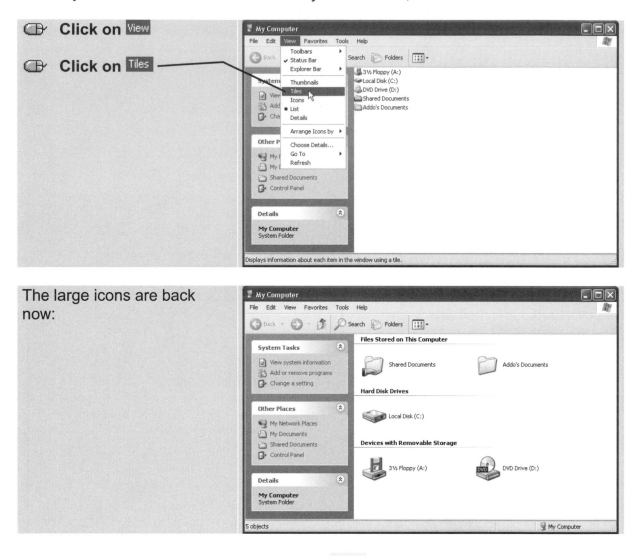

Nearly every *Windows* window has a menu View with which its appearance can be changed. You can use this to choose the appearance that you like best.

Right-Clicking

The last topic we'll discuss in this chapter is the fifth mouse action: *right-clicking.*
After all, there's a reason why the mouse has two buttons.
Right-clicking is done like this:

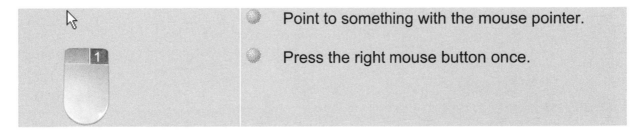

Point to something with the mouse pointer.

Press the right mouse button once.

This is the same action as the regular click, but with the right mouse button.
However, the right mouse button has an entirely different function, as you'll see:

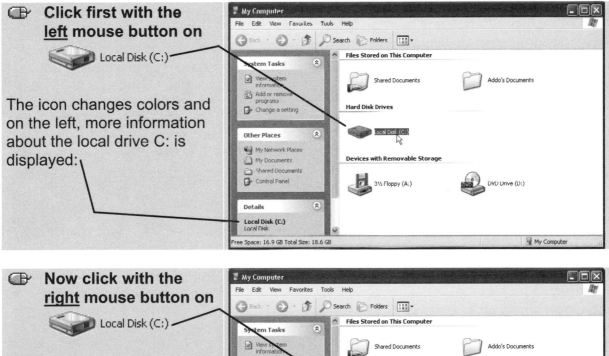

Click first with the left mouse button on

Local Disk (C:)

The icon changes colors and on the left, more information about the local drive C: is displayed:

Now click with the right mouse button on

Local Disk (C:)

Now you see a menu next to the mouse pointer with various commands:

This is how to make this menu disappear:

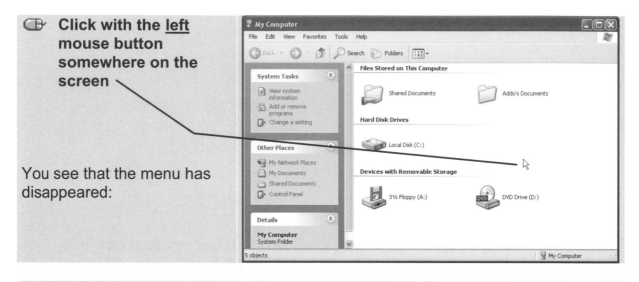

☞ **Click with the left mouse button somewhere on the screen**

You see that the menu has disappeared:

☞ **Close the window** *My Computer* 📖 1.4

You can right-click on many parts of *Windows XP.* This will always make a menu appear. These menus can be used to enter commands that are related to the part you clicked on. You can right-click on the *Desktop*, for example:

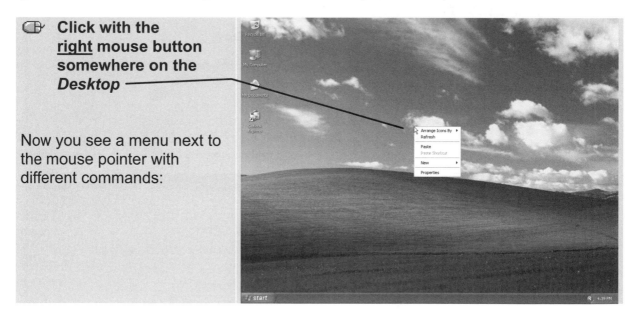

☞ **Click with the right mouse button somewhere on the Desktop**

Now you see a menu next to the mouse pointer with different commands:

If you want to select a command from a menu of this type, you must use the left mouse button.

**Click with the
left mouse button on**
Properties

Now a new window appears. You can use this window to change various settings for your screen. Now you can close the window again.

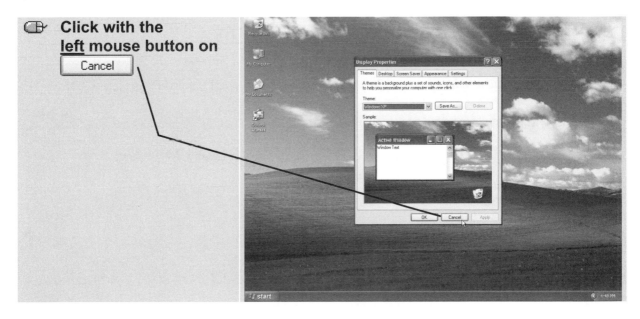

**Click with the
left mouse button on**
Cancel

The *Display Properties* window has now disappeared.

We've introduced you to all five mouse actions. You've also seen various parts of *Windows XP*, such as using the check marks and dots next to commands. You can practice what you've learned with the following exercises.

Exercises

The following exercises will help you master what you've just learned. Have you forgotten how to do something? Use the number beside the footsteps to look it up in the appendix *How Do I Do That Again?*

Exercise: Dragging a Window

✔ Start the *Calculator*. 𝒷1.5

✔ Drag the *Calculator* window to the top left. 𝒷1.11

✔ Drag the *Calculator* window to the bottom right. 𝒷1.11

✔ Now drag the *Calculator* window to the middle. 𝒷1.11

✔ Close the *Calculator* window. 𝒷1.4

Exercise: Double-Clicking and Dragging

✔ Open the window *My Computer*. 𝒷1.10

✔ Drag the window to the top left of the screen. 𝒷1.11

✔ Drag the window to the bottom right of the screen. 𝒷1.11

✔ Close the window *My Computer*. 𝒷1.4

✔ Start the program *Help and Support Center*. 𝒷1.6

✔ Change the *Help and Support Center* window to a different size: the previous size. 𝒷1.3

✔ Shorten the length of the *Help and Support Center* window. 𝒷1.12

✔ Scroll through the text in the *Help and Support Center* window using the scrollbar 𝒷1.13

✔ Now close the *Help and Support Center* window. 𝒷1.4

Exercise: Using the Help and Support Center

✓   Start the program *Help and Support Center*. ✎1.6

✓   Look at the index: ✎1.30

Index

Type in the keyword to find:

```
[                                    ]
```

```
* characters                              ▲
? characters
   click ? to get Help
   foreign language characters
   searching with wildcard characters
12 or 24 hours, how your computer displays time
256 colors
3-dimensional
   DirectX
   visual effects of Windows
abbreviations in days or months
acceleration of mouse pointers
accessibility resources (for people with disabilities
   overview
   administrators, managing Accessibility programs
   blind persons
   blind persons -- High Contrast
   blind persons -- Magnifier
   blind persons -- Narrator
   blind persons -- ToggleKeys
   customizing Windows for accessibility
   deaf persons
   deaf persons -- ShowSounds              ▼
```

[Display]

✓   Look at the information about wildcard characters: ✎1.31

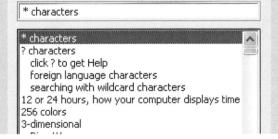

```
* characters                              
```

```
* characters                              ▲
? characters
   click ? to get Help
   foreign language characters
   searching with wildcard characters
12 or 24 hours, how your computer displays time
256 colors
3-dimensional
```

✓ Read the information about wildcard characters: 🦶1.23

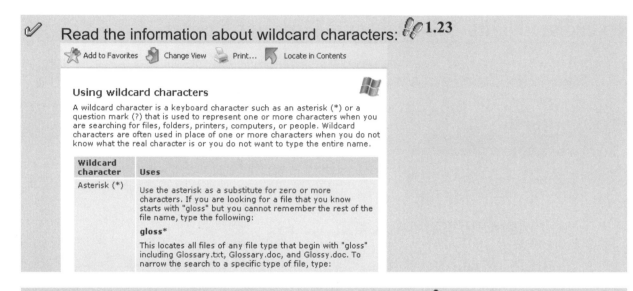

⭐ Add to Favorites   🔖 Change View   🖨 Print...   ▶ Locate in Contents

Using wildcard characters

A wildcard character is a keyboard character such as an asterisk (*) or a question mark (?) that is used to represent one or more characters when you are searching for files, folders, printers, computers, or people. Wildcard characters are often used in place of one or more characters when you do not know what the real character is or you do not want to type the entire name.

Wildcard character	Uses
Asterisk (*)	Use the asterisk as a substitute for zero or more characters. If you are looking for a file that you know starts with "gloss" but you cannot remember the rest of the file name, type the following: **gloss*** This locates all files of any file type that begin with "gloss" including Glossary.txt, Glossary.doc, and Glossy.doc. To narrow the search to a specific type of file, type:

✓ Go back to the *Help and Support Center* start page: 🦶1.32

⊘ Help and Support Center

◀ Back ▾ ⊙ ▾ ⌂ | 📖 Index ⭐ Favorites 🕐 History | Support ✓ Options

Search [   ] ➡   ⊘ **Help and Support Center**
Set search options   Windows XP Home Edition

Pick a Help topic   **Ask for assistance**

• What's new in Windows XP   → Invite a friend to connect to your computer with **Remote Assistance**
• Music, video, games, and photos
• Windows basics   → Get **support**, or find information in **Windows XP newsgroups**
• Protecting your PC: security basics

• Networking and the Web   **Pick a task**
• Working remotely
                                     → Keep your computer up-to-date with **Windows Update**
• Customizing your computer   → Find **compatible hardware and software** for Windows XP
• Accessibility
                                     → Undo changes to your computer with **System Restore**
                                     → Use **Tools** to view your computer information and diagnose problems
• Printing and faxing
• Performance and maintenance   **Did you know?**   Updated: Wednesday, June 23, 2004
• Hardware
• Fixing a problem   • Description of a Personal Firewall
• Send your feedback to Microsoft   • How to turn on and turn off System Restore in Windows XP
                                     • How to restore the operating system to a previous state in Windows XP
                                     • How to Determine If Hardware or Software Is Compatible with Windows XP
                                     • Information About Hardware Device Drivers for Windows XP
                                     • Support WebCasts

✓ Read the information about *Networking:* 🦶1.31

Networking and the Web

⊞ E-mail and the Web

⊞ Home and small office networking

⊡ Sharing files, printers, and other resources

⊡ Passwords and security

⊞ Networking

⊡ Fixing networking or Web problems

✓ Close the *Help and Support Center* window. 🦶1.4

Exercise: Left- and Right-Clicking

✔ Click with the **right** mouse button somewhere on the *Desktop*.

✔ Click with the **left** mouse button on Properties.

✔ Click with the **left** mouse button on Cancel.

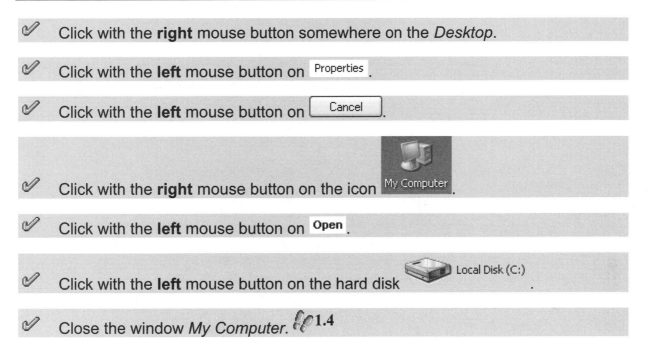

✔ Click with the **right** mouse button on the icon My Computer.

✔ Click with the **left** mouse button on Open.

✔ Click with the **left** mouse button on the hard disk Local Disk (C:).

✔ Close the window *My Computer*. 1.4

Background Information

What are the various parts of a window called?

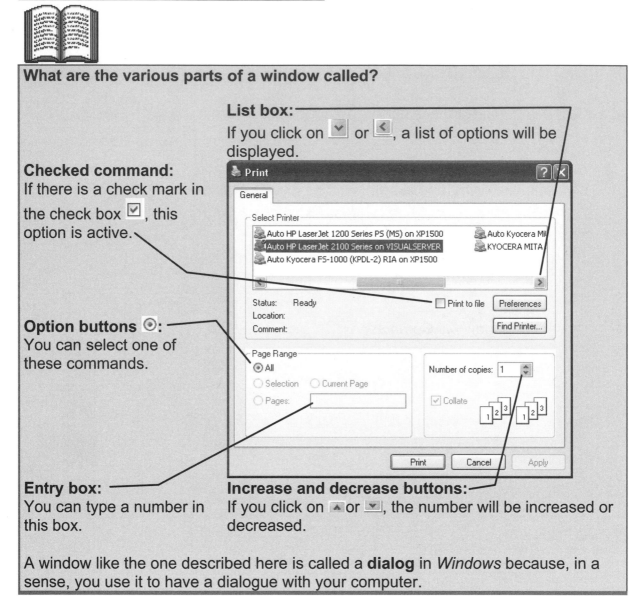

List box:
If you click on ⌄ or ◂, a list of options will be displayed.

Checked command:
If there is a check mark in the check box ☑, this option is active.

Option buttons ◉:
You can select one of these commands.

Entry box:
You can type a number in this box.

Increase and decrease buttons:
If you click on ▲ or ▼, the number will be increased or decreased.

A window like the one described here is called a **dialog** in *Windows* because, in a sense, you use it to have a dialogue with your computer.

Hardware and Software
The distinction between these two terms is sometimes difficult to make. In any case, "hard" and "soft" are not really correct. Both of these are collective terms. *Hardware* is actually anything related to the computer that you can hold onto or screw open. *Software* is not tangible: it's a computer program, a data file or a computer game. You cannot hold onto software and remove it from the computer using your hands. It's distributed on a CD-ROM or disk, or perhaps using an "intangible" network, such as the Internet.

Hardware: The Parts of the Computer

The large container that holds the computer itself is called the *system cabinet.* The system cabinet holds the computer's memory and the processor chip that makes everything work. This cabinet also holds the disk drive and, if you have one, the CD-ROM drive and/or DVD player.

System cabinet

Every computer has a monitor. The quality of the screen is much better than that of a regular television. Letters and graphic elements are therefore extremely sharp and easy to read.
The size of the computer screen is expressed in *inches*. The standard size of a computer screen these days is 17 inches. Larger screens measuring 19 or 21 inches are popular among people who are employed to work with computers. A larger display always enhances the legibility of small elements.

Computer screen

There are two kinds of monitors: the CRT monitor and the flat TFT monitor.

Other hardware elements are the keyboard, the mouse and the speakers.

TFT monitor

Hardware
A portable computer or *laptop* is a complete system. The system cabinet, the keyboard, the mouse, and the display are integrated into a single unit. The surface size is about the same as that of a sheet of writing paper. The flat display is flipped up when the laptop is being used. Although laptops are much smaller than a regular PC, they're usually just as powerful.

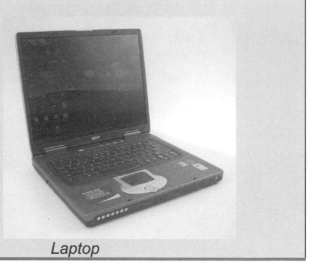

Laptop

How does a traditional mouse work?
The standard mouse is actually relatively simple in terms of technology. Turn the mouse over.
You can see a little ball that rolls as the mouse is moved over the tabletop.

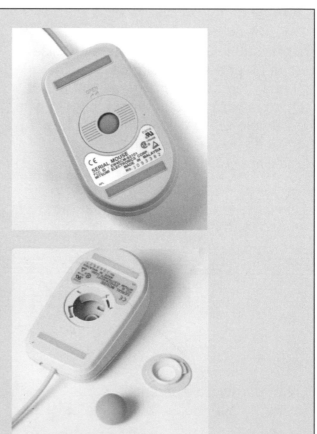

If you take the ball out, you can see three little wheels inside that register the movements of the ball and transmit these to the computer. When the mouse slides, the ball rolls and the wheels on the inside move.

A modern variation on this mouse uses an infrared light (LED) or laser light instead of a ball.

Tips

💡 Tip

Proper Mouse Placement
Sometimes the mouse will be too far from you on the tabletop or located at the edge of the mouse mat.

Then it's difficult to work with the mouse. It's almost as if the mouse is trying to get away! It's important then to put the mouse back in the right place on the tabletop. This is how:

☞ **First move the mouse pointer to the middle of the screen**

☞ **Now pick up the mouse**

☞ **Put the mouse in the right place**

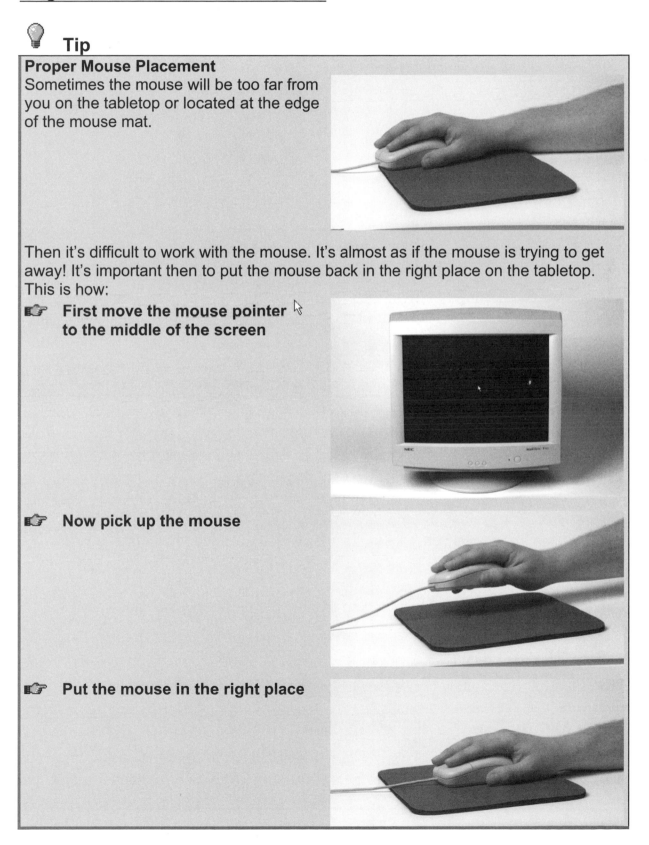

💡 Tip

Are you left-handed?
Then use the mouse with your left hand. You can switch the settings for the mouse buttons to make your mouse more suitable for left-handed users.

You'll read how to change the mouse settings in Chapter 11.

💡 Tip

Using the *Windows Help* System
There are many different ways to activate the *Help* system. Many programs have a help function that can explain things.

⚪   In some windows you will see a button with a question mark at the top right:

First click on this button [?] and then on the part of the window that you want information about.

⚪   With other windows, you'll see a menu at the top:

This menu [Help] gives you access to a Help system that contains various types of information about the program.

3. Keyboard Skills

Word processing is the application that made the *Personal Computer* (PC) so popular. It is also the most widely-used application. The typewriter era is long gone, in part thanks to how easy computers have made it to write and produce texts.
As a computer user, it's handy to have good word processing skills. These skills are not only needed for writing letters or e-mail messages, for example, but also for various other things. A certain amount of keyboard skill is needed if you're to become handy in using the computer, because not everything can be done with the mouse.
Windows XP has a simple word processing program that you can use to practice.
The program is called *WordPad* and was installed on your computer together with *Windows XP*.

In this chapter, you'll learn how to:

- start *WordPad*
- type using the keyboard
- correct a typing error
- type capital letters
- make a new line
- type various special characters
- move the cursor
- start a new text
- stop *WordPad*

Starting WordPad

WordPad is the word processing program used in this chapter. You can start it using the *Start* button:

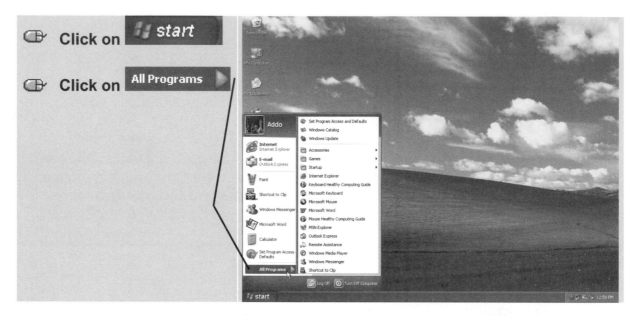

The *WordPad* program is located in the folder 📂 named *Accessories*:

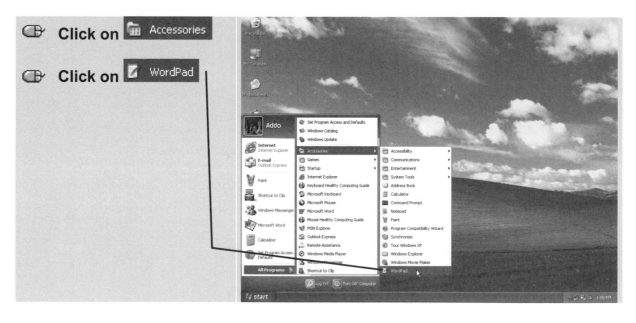

Now you see the empty *WordPad* screen:

The text you type will appear in the big white box. This box is like a blank sheet of paper.

At the top left, you'll see a short blinking line. This is called the **cursor**.

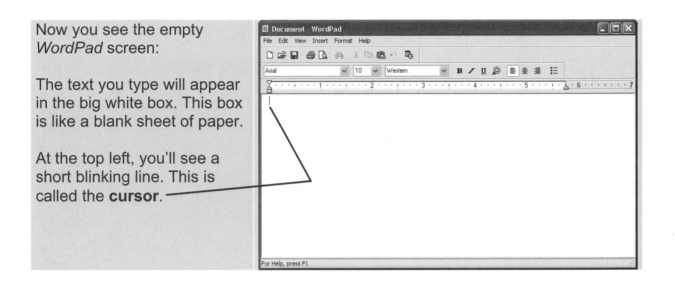

The Keyboard

A computer keyboard has more than one hundred keys. That's much more than the old-fashioned typewriter. When you look at the keyboard, you'll see keys for letters and numbers, as well as various other keys. You'll learn to use many of these keys with this book.

The position of the letters and punctuation marks is still the same as on a typewriter:

At the bottom you see a large white key. This is called the space bar:

The space bar is used to type spaces (white space) between words.

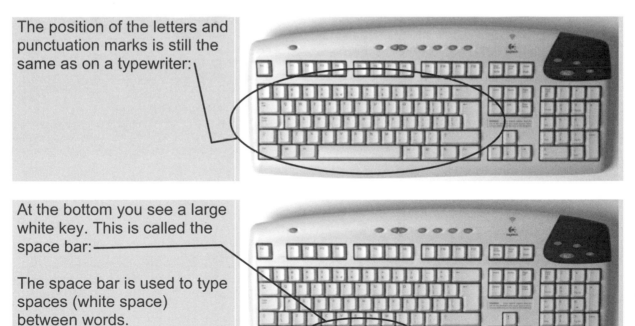

Now you can start typing. The letters will appear where the cursor is:

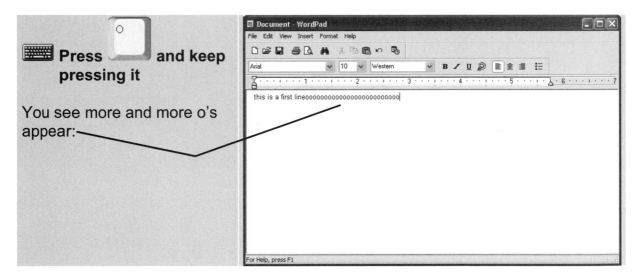

Type:
this is a first
line

Repeat Keys

The keys on a computer keyboard are repeat keys. This means that if you keep pressing a key, you'll automatically see multiple letters appear on the screen. Try it:

Press [o] **and keep pressing it**

You see more and more o's appear:

Luckily, it's also easy to remove letters you don't need.

A Typing Error?

In this case, you typed the wrong letters o on purpose, but it will not be uncommon for you to accidentally press the wrong key. You can remove a wrong letter by pressing the Backspace key.

That's a big key, sometimes with only an arrow pointing to the left:

The Backspace key is usually located at the top right of the keyboard:

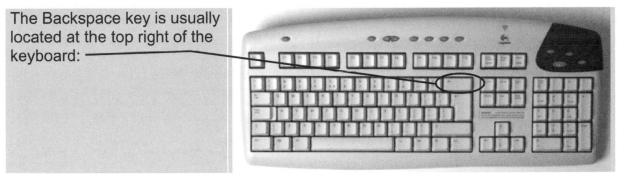

The Backspace key is used to remove the letter to the left of the cursor. You can use it to remove the letters o that you don't need, for example:

Press [← Backspace] **as many times as necessary to remove all of the o's**

You see that all of the o's have disappeared:

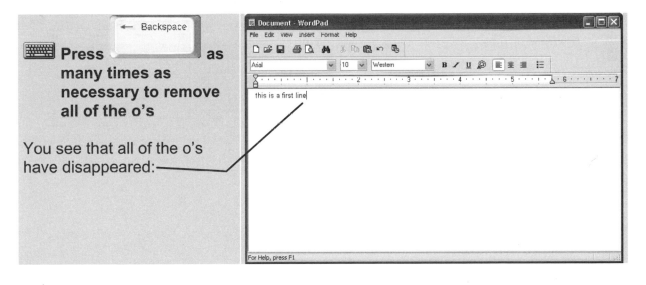

➡ **Please note:**

The Backspace key itself is also a repeat key. Don't press it too long or you'll have to retype the text.

Capital Letters

Until now, you've only typed lower-case letters. But you can also type capital letters.

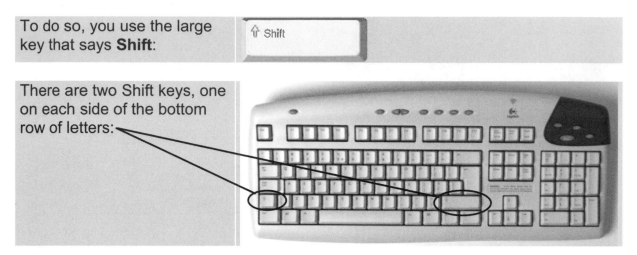

To do so, you use the large
key that says **Shift**:

⇧ Shift

There are two Shift keys, one
on each side of the bottom
row of letters:

The Shift key is always used together with a letter, a number or a punctuation mark.

This is how to type a capital letter:
- press the shift key and keep it pressed
- type the letter
- then release the Shift key

Type:
This line is about
Amsterdam, the
capital of
Holland.

Document - WordPad

File Edit View Insert Format Help

Arial   10   Western   B *I* U   ≡ ≡ ≡ ≣

this is a first lineThis line is about Amsterdam, the capital of Holland.|

For Help, press F1

Words on the Next Line

With word processing programs, the program itself spreads the text over the page. If you type multiple sentences in a row, the text will automatically continue on the next line. Take a look:

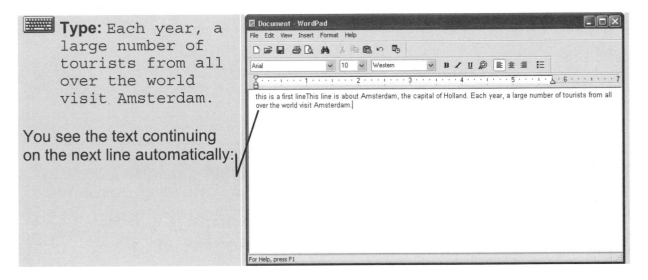

Type: Each year, a large number of tourists from all over the world visit Amsterdam.

You see the text continuing on the next line automatically:

The computer always makes sure that even long sentences will fit nicely on the page. This is done automatically.

A New Line

If you want to start a new sentence on the left, you'll have to start a new line yourself.

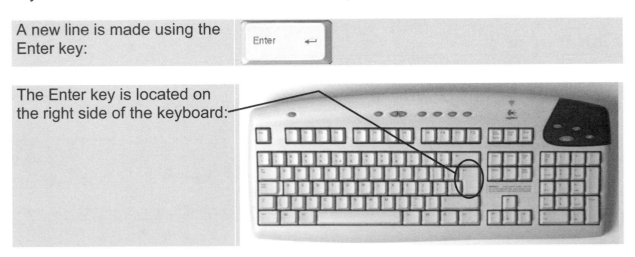

A new line is made using the Enter key:

The Enter key is located on the right side of the keyboard:

If you press the Enter key, the cursor (the little blinking line) will move down one line.

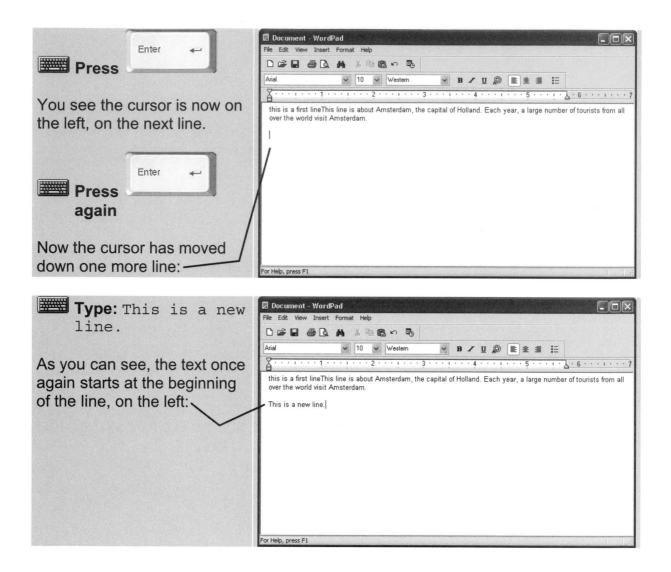

Press   Enter   ←

You see the cursor is now on the left, on the next line.

Press again   Enter   ←

Now the cursor has moved down one more line:

Type: This is a new line.

As you can see, the text once again starts at the beginning of the line, on the left:

Colon or @?

The Shift key is also used to type various other characters.

Examples are: : ? @ * % $ + | } < ! ~ & ^

Many of these characters are located at the top of a key:

The character at the top of these keys is typed using the Shift key, just as you do for capital letters.

Type: ! ? : @ +

The Cursor Keys

Everyone makes a typing error now and then. You often don't notice until later, after you've typed more text. To remove the error with the Backspace key, you'd have to remove all of the other text as well. Naturally, that's not very handy. It's better to move the cursor to the place where the error is.

You can move the cursor using the four special cursor keys. These are the keys with the arrows. They're grouped together:

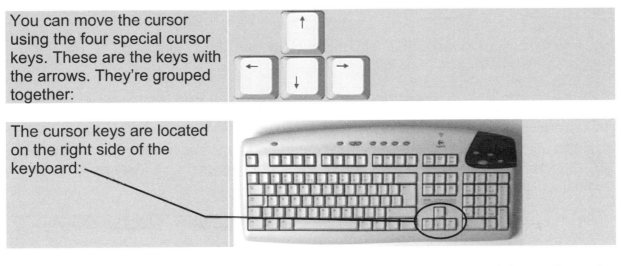

The cursor keys are located on the right side of the keyboard:

You can use these keys to move the cursor to the left or right, up and down, through the text.

The cursor is blinking after the +:

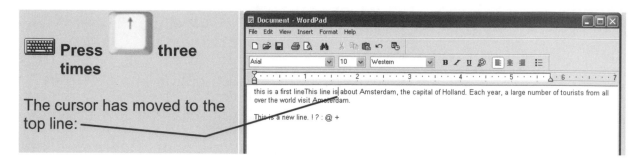

Press [↑] **three times**

The cursor has moved to the top line:

If you move to the left or right, the cursor follows through the text:

Press [→] **until the cursor moves to the second line**

You see the cursor move to the right, through the text, until it jumps to the next line.

The Beginning and End of the Text

You can use the cursor keys to move the cursor to anywhere you want in the text. But you can't move the cursor over the entire sheet of paper. The text has a beginning and an end. Try it:

Press [←] **until the cursor is at the beginning of the top line**

The cursor will not move any further than the beginning of the text. On some computers, the program may even sound a warning signal.

Press ↓ **until the cursor is at the beginning of the bottom line**

The cursor won't go any further.

You cannot move the cursor any further than the last letter or punctuation mark:

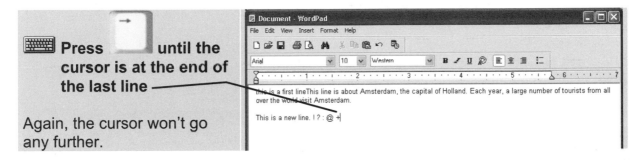

Press → **until the cursor is at the end of the last line**

Again, the cursor won't go any further.

As you've seen, the cursor can't be moved further than the beginning or the end of the text you've typed. You can, of course, type more text there.

Type a space

Type: `are special characters`

The text appears at the end:

Of course, you can always add empty lines to the text. The end of the text is then the last (empty) line:

Press Enter **twice**

You see empty lines at the bottom of the text:

Now you know how to move the cursor through the text. That's handy when you want to correct errors or change the text.

Correcting Mistakes

You can move the cursor to the spot in the text where you want to make a change. For example:

Now you can also change the first letter of the text into a capital:

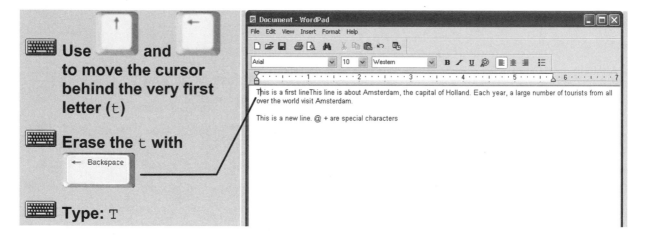

Removing Empty Lines

You can remove empty lines the same way. Move the cursor to an empty line and press the Backspace key:

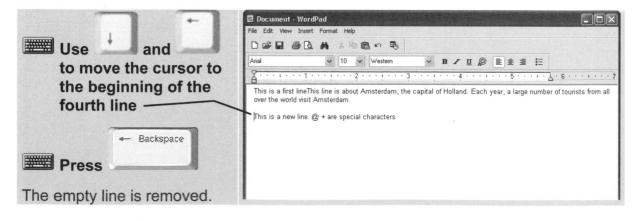

Making Jumps

You have now used the most important keys for word processing. However, there are some more handy keys on your keyboard. There are two special keys that will move the cursor through the text even faster.

These are the Home and End keys:

You'll find these keys in a separate group above the cursor keys:

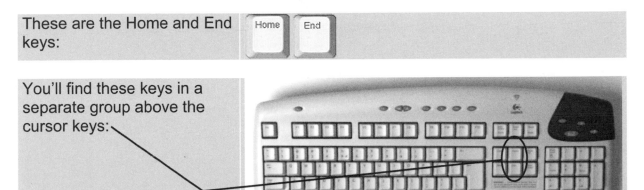

The Home key is used to move the cursor to the beginning of a line, and the End key is used to move it to the end of a line. In other words: to jump from here to there. Try it:

Press End

As you can see, the cursor has jumped to the end of the line.

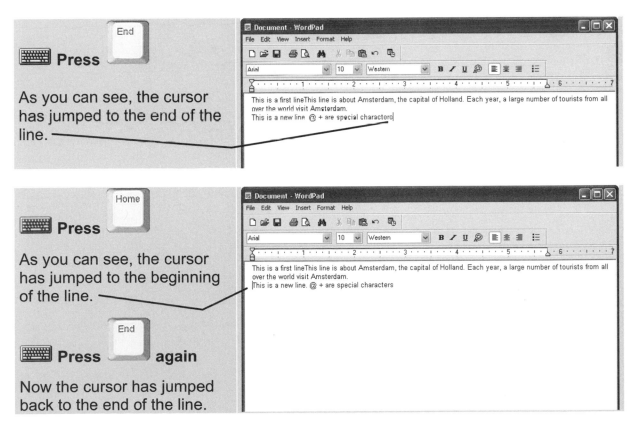

Press Home

As you can see, the cursor has jumped to the beginning of the line.

Press End **again**

Now the cursor has jumped back to the end of the line.

Starting a New Text

You've now practiced enough with the keyboard. It's time to start with a new, empty text. This is how:

🖱️ **Click on** File

🖱️ **Click on** New...

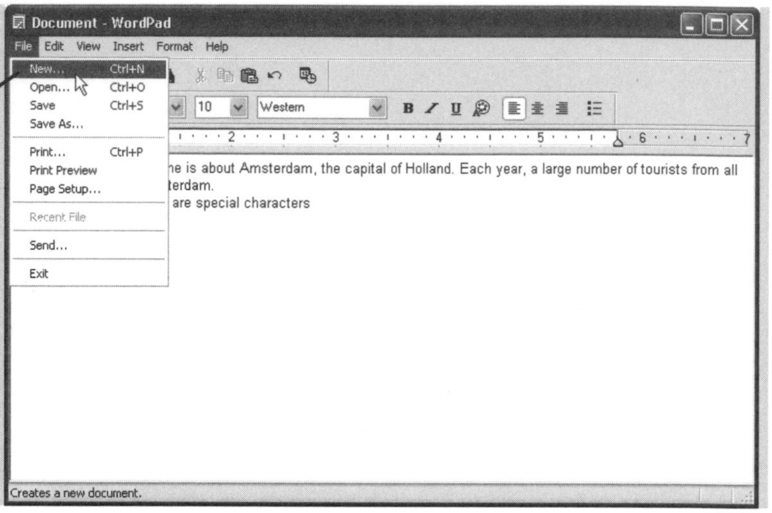

WordPad asks you what kind of file you want.
The standard option *Rich Text Document* is what you want this time.

🖱️ **Click on** OK

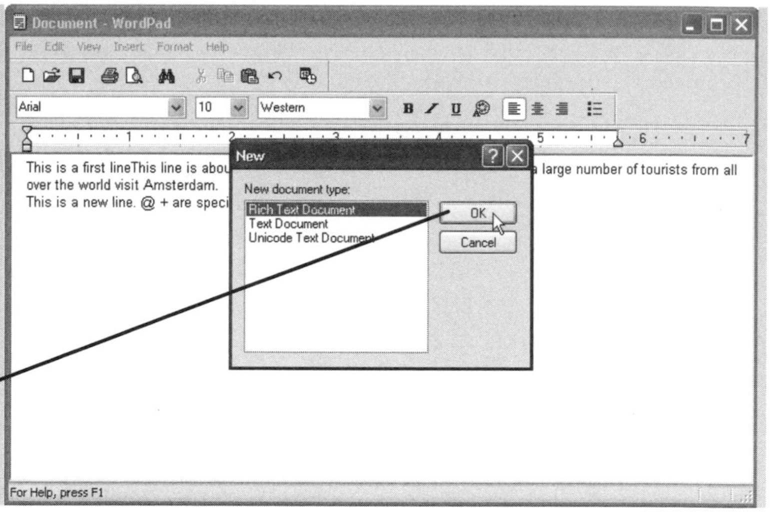

WordPad now asks you whether you want to save the changes to your practice text. You don't need to, so:

☞ **Click on** No

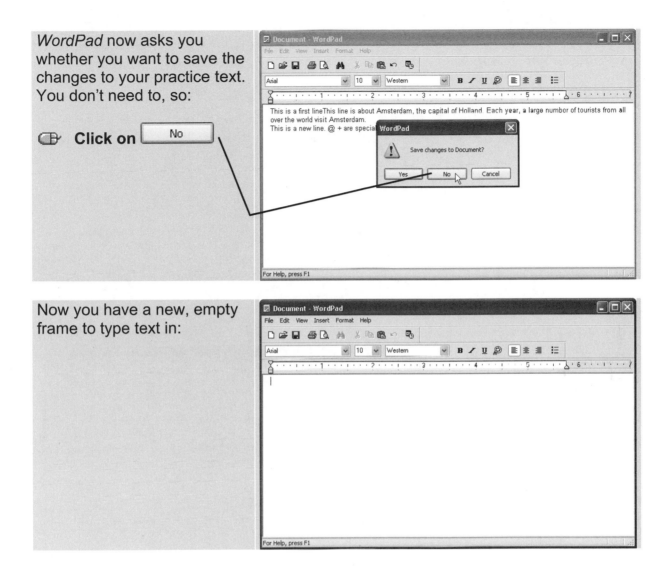

Now you have a new, empty frame to type text in:

Accents and Other Special Punctuation

When you look at the keyboard, you won't see any letter keys with accents or other special punctuation such as ç, ñ or é.
But these letters aren't difficult to type. This is done using what are called the "dead" keys.

Those are these two keys:

These keys are used in combination with the letter to which the special punctuation is to be added. For example:

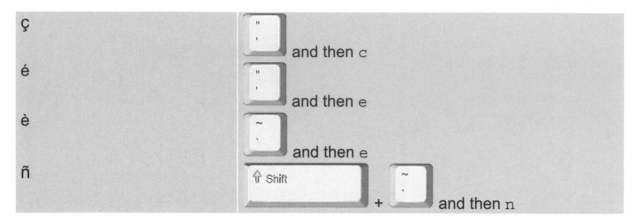

ç   and then c

é   and then e

è   and then e

ñ   ⇧ Shift + ~ and then n

Try it:

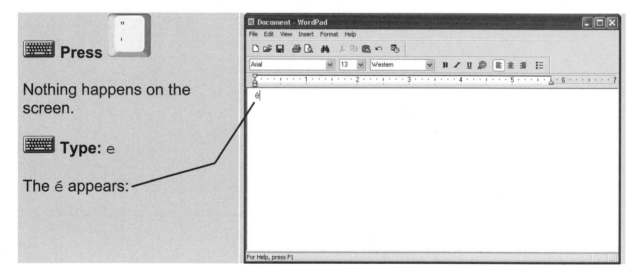

Press [key]

Nothing happens on the screen.

Type: e

The é appears:

The keys are called "dead" because nothing happens when you press them. A character does not appear until after you press another key.

Try now to make another letter, such as the ñ. It's a bit more complicated because you have to use the Shift key in order to type the ~.

HELP! It isn't working.

If you aren't able to type accents, take a look at **Appendix C, Changing Your Keyboard Settings**, on page 337.

Press ⇧ Shift
and keep pressing

Press ~

Now release ⇧ Shift

Nothing happens on the screen.

Type: n

The ñ appears:

This is how you can type any special letters, such as é, è, ç or ñ.

Typing Apostrophes

If the key for an apostrophe is dead, how can you type an apostrophe?
This is done using the key together with the space bar. Try it:

Press "

Nothing happens on the screen.

Type a space

The apostrophe appears:

Stopping WordPad

Now you can close the *WordPad* program. This is how:

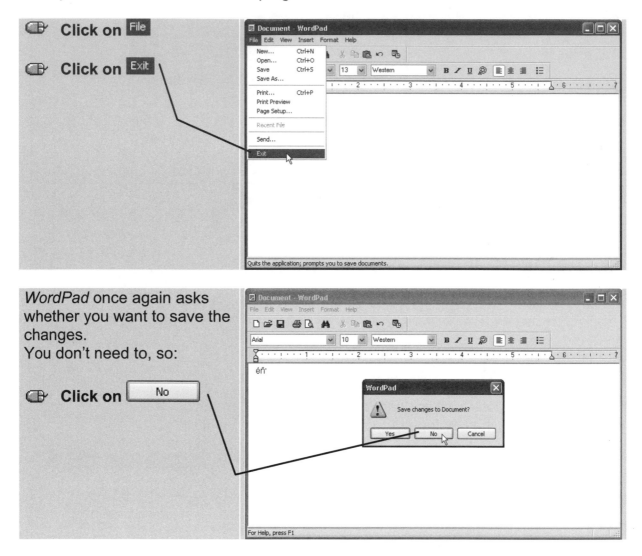

In the next chapter you'll read how to save a text, such as a letter. For the time being, you don't need to save the practice texts.

Exercises

The following exercises will help you master what you've just learned. Have you forgotten how to do something? Use the number beside the footsteps to look it up in the appendix *How Do I Do That Again?*

Exercise: Typing a Text

✓ Start *WordPad*. 👣 **1.14**

✓ Type the following text:
Canberra is the capital of Australia.
Canberra is exactly halfway between Sydney and Melbourne,
two other large cities.

✓ Move the cursor to the end of the first line. 👣 **4.1**

✓ Now make a new, empty line. 👣 **4.4**

✓ Type the following text:
Most people think that Sydney is the capital.

✓ Move the cursor to the end of the last line of the text. 👣 **4.1** Type a space.

✓ Type the following text:
For a long time, people argued about whether Sydney or
Melbourne should be the capital.
They finally decided to pick the city in between the two.

✓ In the last sentence, erase the word **the** and type **a** in the same place. 👣 **4.5**
They finally decided to pick ~~the~~ city in between the two.

✓ This is what the practice text looks like now:

✓ Move the cursor to the beginning of the line. ℓℓ 4.2

✓ Move the cursor to the end of the line. ℓℓ 4.3

✓ Start a new text and don't save the changes. ℓℓ 1.18

✓ Close *WordPad*. ℓℓ 1.15

Exercise: Corrections

With this exercise, you can practice correcting typing errors.

✓ Start *WordPad*. ℓℓ 1.14

✓ Maximize the *WordPad* window. ℓℓ 1.2

✓ Type the following text:
Many people drink tea in the us. It is not as important hear as in other contries where a ceremony is made of drinkingtee, like in japan. They pay much closer attention to the qality of the te. Other exampels of these countries are china and Ingland.

✓ Correct the following mistakes:
Many people drink tea in the **US**. It is not as important **he**re as in other co**u**ntries where a ceremony is made of drinking te**a**, like in **J**apan. They pay much closer attention to the q**u**ality of the te**a**. Other examp**l**es of these countries are **C**hina and **E**ngland.

✓ Start a new text and don't save the changes. ℓℓ 1.18

✓ Close *WordPad*. ℓℓ 1.15

Background Information

Typing Skills

It is certainly not necessary to learn to type like a professional typist in order to work with the computer. Most people have never learned to type, but learn as they go along, with two or sometimes four fingers. A time comes when you can quickly find any key and then increase your typing speed.

It's striking that, despite all of the innovations of the computer era, the arrangement of the keyboard is still virtually the same as that of the typewriter. The normal arrangement used in the United States is still QWERTY. Look at the letters at the top left of the keyboard. A long time ago, the letters were placed in this order to make sure that the typewriter keys wouldn't get stuck even when typing very rapidly. Apparently, people have become so familiar with this arrangement that they don't want any of it changed.

The keyboard has a separate section for typing numbers. This was designed especially for people who have to enter many numbers and amounts. This section is called the *numeric keypad*.

More and more keys are being added. Many of today's keyboards also have special keys used for the Internet. By pressing a single key, for example, you can collect your e-mail.

The Proper Working Posture

It's important to arrange your computer properly. This not only makes it more pleasant to work with the computer, but also minimizes the risk of various complaints. You'll be surprised at the number of hours you'll spend working with your PC.
A proper working posture is therefore essential. Attention should be devoted to the following:

- You need a table that is sufficiently deep and has the proper height. Your wrists should lie level with the table top when typing and using the mouse.

- An adjustable desk chair with arm rests is ideal because you can adjust it to achieve proper support for your back and legs. If your feet don't touch the ground, put something under them to support them - a few thick books, for example.

- The keyboard should be directly in front of you. The mouse should be next to the keyboard on the correct side: on the right if you are right-handed and on the left if you are left-handed.

- Place the monitor straight in front of you, at about the same level as your eyes. Do not place the monitor to the left or right because this would force you to constantly strain your neck to turn your head.

- The monitor should be about one arm's length (24 to 27 inches) from your eyes.

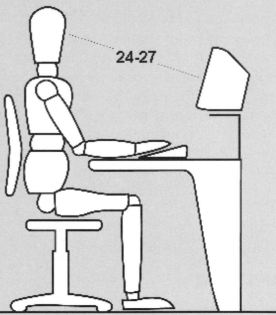

- The monitor should not be too low or too high, forcing you to look up or down all the time. If you wear glasses or lenses that are multi-focal (with a special section for reading), having the monitor at the wrong height could force you to use the reading section instead of the "far-off" section of the lenses. You can always raise the monitor by putting something under it (another thick book?).

- Make sure there's no direct or indirect light shining into the monitor that would make it hard to read.

More ways to customize your computer to make it more pleasant to work with are explained in Chapter 11.

Tips

💡 Tip

Capitals Only
The keyboard has a special key that's used to type capital letters.
This is the key that says *Caps Lock*:

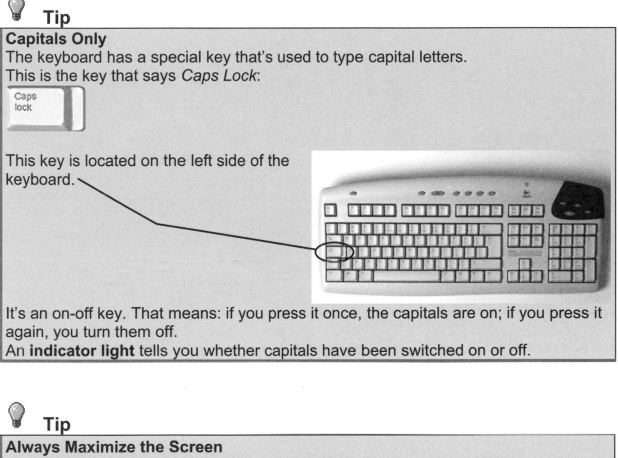

This key is located on the left side of the keyboard.

It's an on-off key. That means: if you press it once, the capitals are on; if you press it again, you turn them off.
An **indicator light** tells you whether capitals have been switched on or off.

💡 Tip

Always Maximize the Screen
WordPad doesn't always automatically start with a large screen. It will be much more pleasant to work with *WordPad* if the screen is maximized.

☞ **Always click on** ▣

4. Writing a Letter

It's hard to find an office anywhere that still uses a typewriter to type letters.
Without endless retyping and without correction fluid, it's easy these days to produce letters, reports and other texts without errors using the computer.
Texts or letters used before can be used again with a few changes, or can be used to send to a large number of readers or addressees.
Writing texts and letters with the computer is also handy for you because you can easily change them until they say exactly what you want them to. You can also save a text and work on it again later.
In this chapter, you'll start by writing a letter using the computer. This is also done with the program *WordPad*. Once you're familiar with this program, you'll also be able to use more detailed programs, such as *MS Word*.

In this chapter, you'll learn how to:

- write a letter
- enter the date
- save a letter
- open a letter
- see the print preview
- print the text
- save changes or not save changes

Starting a Letter

The easiest way to write a letter is to use the program *WordPad.* You start by starting this program:

☞ **Start *WordPad*** 🦶🦶1.14

Again you see the empty *WordPad* screen:

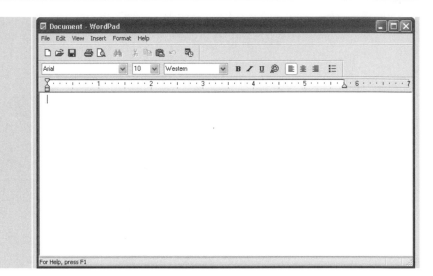

A Larger Font

The letters that *WordPad* automatically uses are a bit small, and may be unpleasant to work with. This can be easily changed, just like almost everything else in *Windows XP.* When typing a letter, it's handy to start by choosing a letter size that's a bit bigger. This is how:

🖰 **Click on** ⌄

🖰 **Click on** 12

You won't see anything happen on the screen. But when you start typing, you'll see that the letters are somewhat larger.

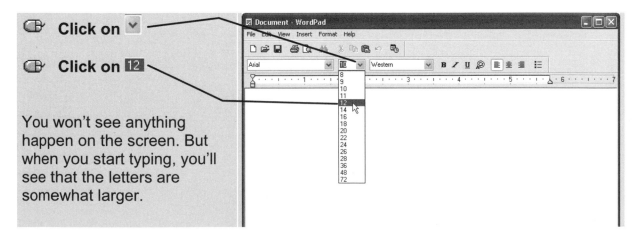

Elsewhere in this book, more information is given about types of fonts and font sizes.

Today's Date

Let's start an informal letter to someone you know. Naturally, a letter starts with the date. You don't have to type the date yourself. *WordPad* has a command that does it for you.

Click on `Insert`

Click on `Date and Time...`

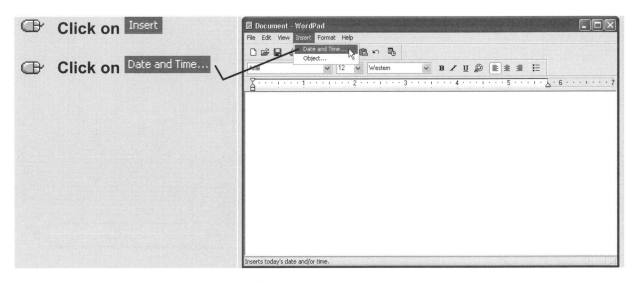

Now you can choose the way you want the date to be written.

Click on the long date notation

Click on `OK`

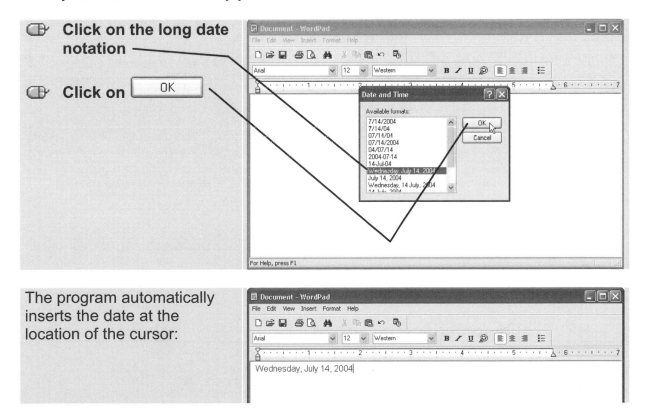

The program automatically inserts the date at the location of the cursor:

Naturally, the date on your letter will not be the same as in the illustration. The program inserts today's actual date.

Undoing

If something goes wrong while you're writing, or if you accidentally press the wrong key, nearly every *Windows* program has a command that will undo it. Try it:

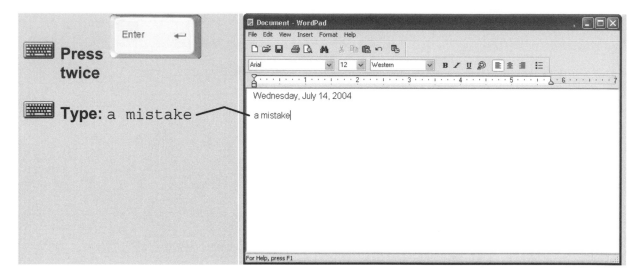

Press twice

Type: a mistake

The program always remembers the last thing you did. So you can always remove it:

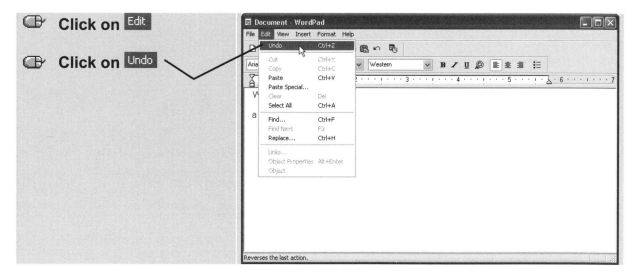

Click on Edit

Click on Undo

The last line you typed has been removed.

HELP! Did something go wrong?

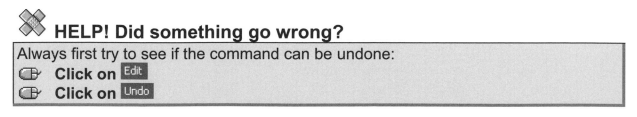

Always first try to see if the command can be undone:

Click on Edit

Click on Undo

Now you can type the rest of the letter.

Typing a Letter

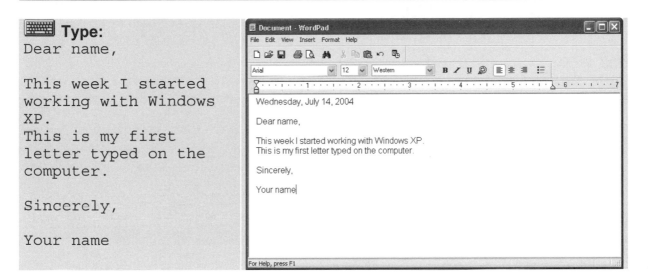

You'll save this practice letter on your computer so that you can work on it again later. In daily life, however, you don't necessarily have to save every letter you type. You can also immediately print it and send it.

If you want to save your letter on the computer, you must always tell the computer to do so. If you don't, your letter may be lost. A text is not automatically saved. The text stays in the computer's memory until you stop the program or switch off the computer. The memory that the computer works with is temporary. The text will not be permanently stored until you save it.

Saving a Text

This first practice letter will be stored on the computer. Storing a text is called **save** in *Windows*. This is how:

👆 **Click on** File

👆 **Click on** Save

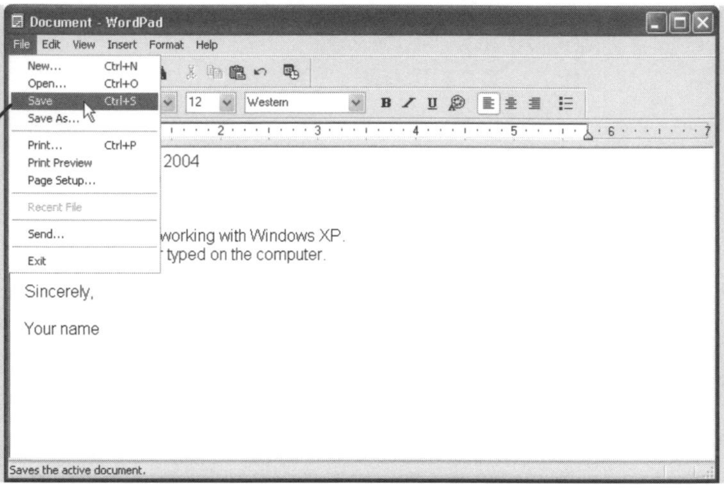

You now see this window:

The practice letter needs to have a name.
This is done in the box next to
File name: :

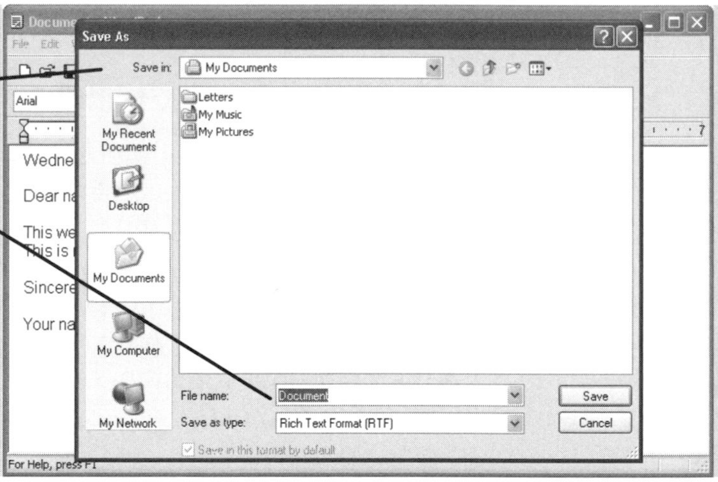

⌨ **Type:** first letter

👆 **Click on** Save

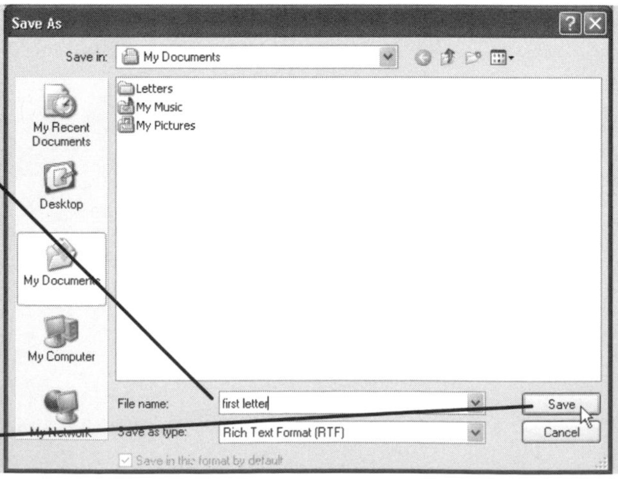

Now the letter is being saved on your computer's hard disk. How this is done is explained a bit further.

Now the name of your letter appears at the top of the screen:	

HELP! The file already exists.

Did this window appear?

> **Save As**
>
> ⚠ C:\Documents and Settings\Addo\My Documents\first letter.rtf already exists. Do you want to replace it?
>
> [Yes]   [No]

If so, you (or someone else) already saved a text with the name *first letter*. You can replace it with your own letter.

👉 **Click on** [Yes]

Closing WordPad

Now you must stop *WordPad* for a bit. This is done so that you can see how to bring your practice letter back again later:

👉 **Close *WordPad*** 🦶1.15

Now you can start *WordPad* again:

👉 **Start *WordPad* again** 🦶1.14

You see an empty screen, without your practice letter. The name *Document* is shown at the top:	*Document - WordPad* File Edit View Insert Format Help

Document is the default name for a new text. In order to get your practice letter to appear on the screen, you need to "open" it first.

Opening a Text

If you want to use a letter that's been saved on the computer, you must "open" it first. This is how:

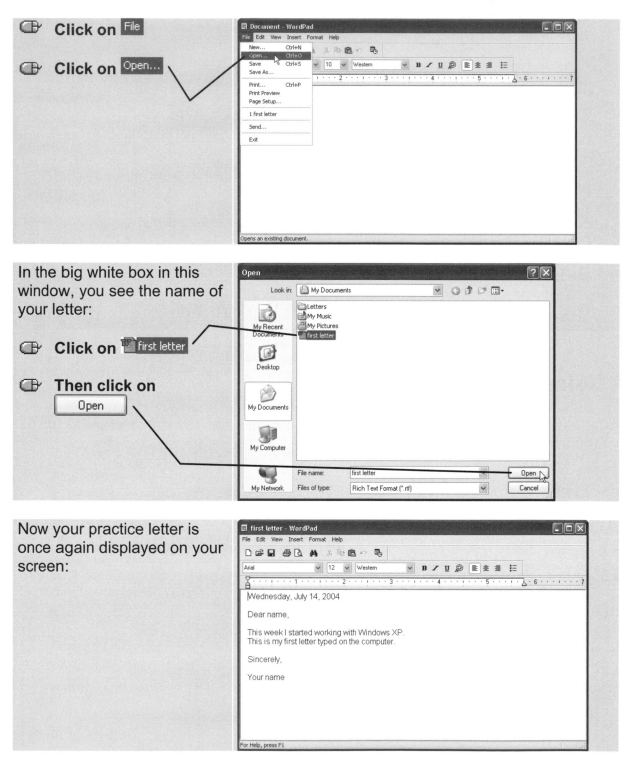

Click on File

Click on Open...

In the big white box in this window, you see the name of your letter:

Click on first letter

Then click on Open

Now your practice letter is once again displayed on your screen:

You can continue to work on it now and print it.

⇨ **Please note:**

If you have the program *Microsoft Word* on your computer, you will see this icon 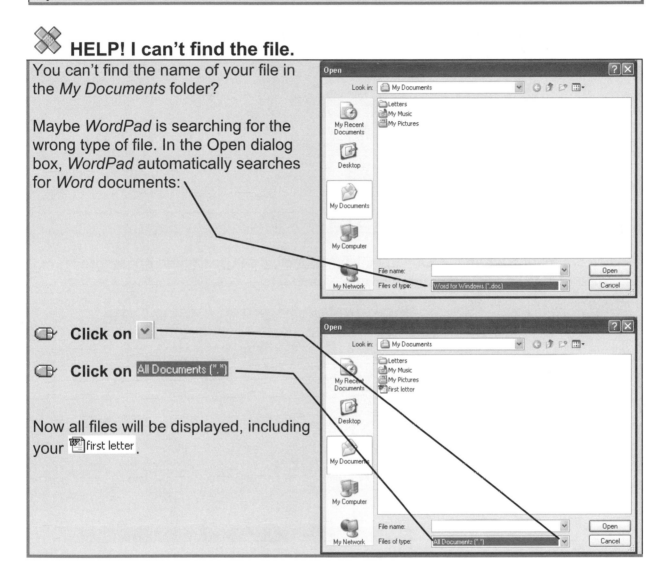.
If you don't have *Word*, the icon will look like this: .

HELP! I can't find the file.

You can't find the name of your file in the *My Documents* folder?

Maybe *WordPad* is searching for the wrong type of file. In the Open dialog box, *WordPad* automatically searches for *Word* documents:

Click on

Click on All Documents (*.*)

Now all files will be displayed, including your first letter.

Printing the Letter

When you write a letter, you'll want it printed on paper unless you'll be sending it via the Internet, not with the mail.

Printing is done with a printer:

HELP! No printer?

If you don't have a printer, you can skip this section.

Before you print a letter, it's wise to look first at how it will be printed on paper. *WordPad* has a special command for this:

☞ **Click on** File

☞ **Click on** Print Preview

Now this screen appears, with a miniature of the page as it will be printed in the middle:

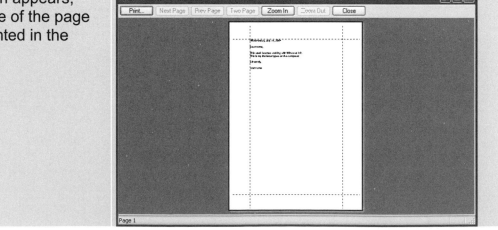

The way the letter is positioned on the page, with the text at the very top left, isn't very appealing. You can easily change this by adding some empty lines at the top.

Click on `Close`

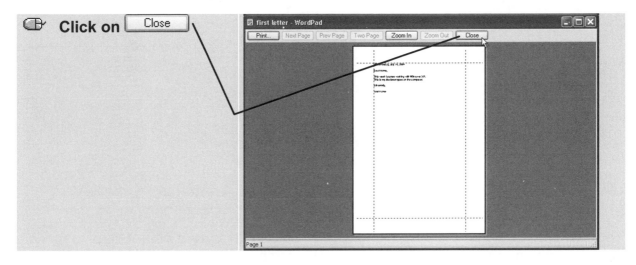

Now you can add the empty lines.

Type 10 empty lines at the top of the letter

𝄞4.4

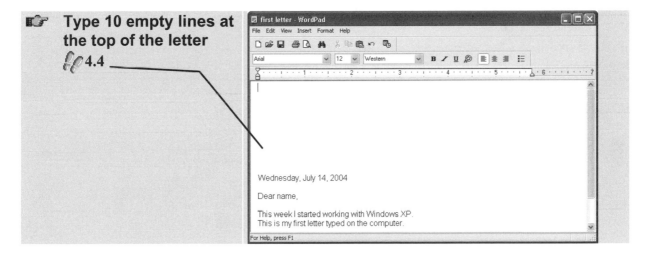

You can see the results using the *Print Preview:*

Click on File

Click on Print Preview

Now the letter has moved down the page a bit:

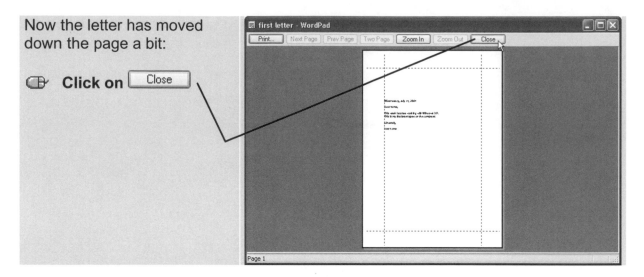

☞ **Click on** [Close]

You can print the letter the way it is for now. You can do a lot of other things to make the letter look more appealing, for example by using a different type of font and text effects, but this will all be explained a bit further along in the book.

⇨ **Please note:**

It's important to always check to make sure your printer is ready to use before you tell the computer to print anything.

☞ **Make sure the printer is on**

☞ **Make sure there is paper in the printer**

Is everything ready? Then you can tell the computer to print the letter:

Your letter will be printed.

Save Changes?

You can never accidentally lose something you've saved. *Windows XP* always checks to see if something is about to be lost. You should give it a try. Since the last time you saved your practice letter, you've made some changes. You added empty lines to the top of the letter. If you stop now, *WordPad* will warn you:

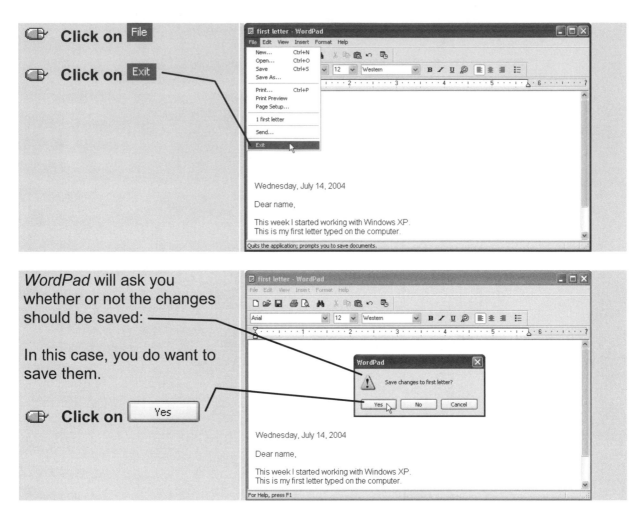

Click on File

Click on Exit

WordPad will ask you whether or not the changes should be saved:

In this case, you do want to save them.

Click on Yes

The changes will be saved and *WordPad* will be closed.

Tip

To many people, this screen is confusing:

WordPad	✕
⚠ Save changes to first letter?	
Yes	No	Cancel

If you unexpectedly see this screen, you apparently made at least one change. No matter how small, even if the change is simply one space, it's still a change to *WordPad*.

● **If you click on** Yes **, the changes will be saved.**

● **If you click on** No **, the changes will not be saved.**

● **If you click on** Cancel **, nothing happens and you will return to *WordPad*.**
  This button is for when you made a mistake.

Now you can open your practice letter again to see what happens when you save the changes first yourself.

☞ **Start *WordPad* again** 🖐1.14

☞ **Open the practice letter again** 📑first letter 🖐3.1

Now you'll first make a change to the letter:

⌨ **At the top of the letter, type** test

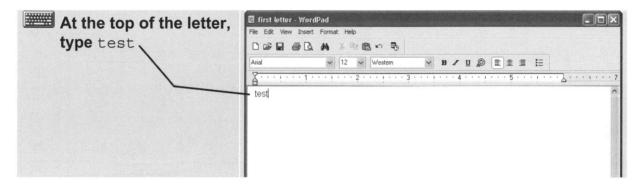

Now you can save this small text change:

🖱 **Click on** File

🖱 **Click on** Save

Have you noticed you haven't been asked to select a name? The text already has a name, after all: 📑first letter .

☞ **Close *WordPad*** 🖐1.15

Did you notice that the screen asking whether to *save changes* hasn't appeared? That's because you saved the last changes yourself.

With the next exercise, you can practice saving texts.

Exercises

Exercise: Saving Changes

The following exercises will help you master what you've just learned. Have you forgotten how to do something? Use the number beside the footsteps to look it up in the appendix *How Do I Do That Again?*

✔ Start *WordPad.* 🦶**1.14**

✔ Type the following short letter:

Date

Dear Sirs,

With this letter I want to thank you for your excellent service.

Sincerely,

Your name

✔ Save this letter and name it *exercise 1.* 🦶**2.1**

✔ Start a new text. 🦶**1.16**

✔ Open the letter 📄 *exercise 1* again. 🦶**3.1**

✔ Add the line printed in bold letters below:

Date

Dear Sirs,

With this letter I want to thank you for your excellent service.
I would also like to inform you that the appliance works perfectly.

Sincerely,

Your name

✔ Print the letter. 🦶**1.19**

✔ Start a new text, and while doing so have the changes saved. 🦶**1.17**

Background Information

Printers
The printer most commonly used in the home is called an **inkjet** printer.
This type of printer prints characters by squirting minute drops of ink onto the paper. Many of these printers can also make color prints. These printers have not only a cartridge with black ink, but also another cartridge with at least three colors. Any color imaginable can be copied by mixing the various colored inks. Each type of printer has different cartridges.

Inkjet printer

Inkjet printers can print on regular paper as well as on special types of paper, depending on the quality of print you want. You can get special photo paper to print photos, for example.

Laser printers are often used in the office sector. These printers are based on an entirely different principle, much like regular copiers.
A laser printer uses an extremely fine-grained powder called *toner*. Using this powder, the shape of the characters is melted into the paper at an extremely high temperature. Laser printers often give high-quality prints. Usually, however, they can only print in black and white. Color laser printers exist, but they are extremely expensive. Laser printers print on regular paper.

Laser printer

A recent development is the **photo printer**, which uses special photo paper to print digital photographs. You can connect this kind of printer to the computer, but there are also models that can print directly from a digital camera's memory card. In this case, the camera's memory card fits into a card reader that's built into the printer.

Photo printer

Saving on the Computer

The computer has a certain amount of *working memory*. This working memory consists of chips in which the information is temporarily saved. When you turn the computer off, however, the memory is emptied. This is why you also need to be able to save information more permanently. This type of memory exists in various types: the computer's *hard disk* or an external hard disk, but also *diskettes, CD-ROM disks, DVD disks, and USB memory sticks.*

Hard disk   *Diskette*   *CD-ROM*

External hard disk   *USB memory stick*

The most important saving method uses the hard disk on your computer. The hard disk is a small, sealed box that has been built into your computer.

Hard disk   *Inside the system cabinet*   *System cabinet*

In this box, a small disk rotates. The disk is magnetic, making it possible to save information on it.
You can determine what goes on the hard disk. You can save texts on it, or drawings, or computer programs. You can copy files onto it, and remove or *delete* them again.

Where to Save?

A computer always contains a **hard disk**. Almost all computers also have a **CD drive** and/or a **DVD drive** that can read and write (if the drive is a "burner") CDs and/or DVDs. There's also usually a **floppy drive**. If you don't have a floppy drive, you can save your work to a **USB memory stick**, the replacement for the floppy. USB sticks connect to the PC's USB ports.

In the *My Computer* window, you can see which items your PC contains. In this example, it contains the following items:

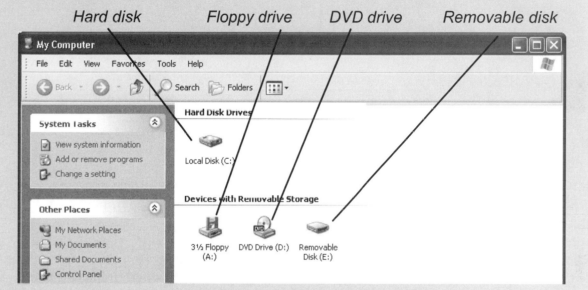

Windows gives every memory device a letter for a name.

- The floppy drive is always named **A**. The letter B is no longer used. It used to be the second floppy drive. If the computer doesn't have a floppy drive, the letter A isn't used either.
- The hard disk always gets the letter **C**. (If there's a second hard disk, it will get the letter D.)
- The CD or DVD drive gets the next letter of the alphabet. In the example above, that's **D**. If there are two such drives, the next one will be named **E**.
- The next device gets the letter **F**, and so forth.

In the window above, you see that the letter E has been given to a *Removable disk*. In this example, that's a USB memory stick inserted into the computer. But it could also be an external hard disk connected to the PC, or a digital camera's memory card sitting in a card reader connected to the computer. **Please note: Other items or devices may be present on your computer. The letters you see on your screen will belong to different devices.**

You usually save your work on your computer's hard disk. If you want to take your work with you to another computer, or if you want to make a backup copy of a file, then you can save your work onto a floppy disk or a USB memory stick. Another option for saving your work is to burn it onto a CD or DVD.

CD-ROM and DVD

These days, computers come standard with a CD-ROM player or DVD player, which you can use to read CD-ROMs or DVDs.

CD-ROMs and DVDs are *the* media for distributing computer programs. A CD-ROM can hold a large number of files, and a DVD can contain even more.

You can even put files on a CD or DVD yourself. You do need a different type of player for this, however: a *CD writer* or *DVD writer*. This kind of device can "write" onto a special kind of disk. These blank disks are called *CD-Recordables* or *DVD-Recordables* and can be bought in your local electronics, office supply, and discount department stores. This kind of disk isn't intended for temporarily saving a letter draft, but rather for storing large numbers of files. For example, you can make a back-up copy of your hard drive. These disks can only be written once.

The *CD rewriter* and *DVD rewriter* are two other devices for reading from and writing to CDs or DVDs. With these devices, you can write onto a disk multiple times, meaning you can erase or replace information on the disk.

You can't play DVDs in a CD-ROM player, but the other way around works just fine. If you have a DVD rewriter, for example, you can play and write (multiple times) to both CDs and DVDs.

Tips

Tip

Regularly Save Your Work

If you work for a lengthy period of time, you should regularly save your work. It's also wise to save your work first before making large changes. If anything goes wrong, you then have a spare copy that's been saved.

Tip

When Not to Save Changes?

When you close a program window, the computer shows you this question:

WordPad ✕

⚠ Save changes to Document?

[Yes] [No] [Cancel]

You can click on [No] if:
- you don't want to save the text
- the version of the text that you saved earlier is better than the current version. In that case, it would be a waste to replace it.

Tip

Rules for File Names

What rules apply to naming a text?

File name: [   ] ⌄

A file name may not:
- be longer than 255 letters or numbers, including spaces
- contain one of the following characters: \ / : * ? " < > . |

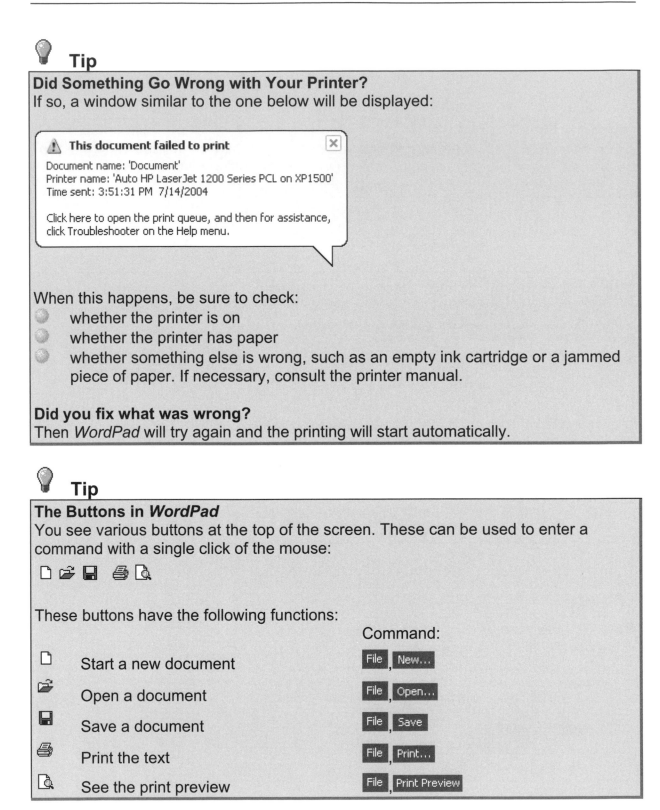

💡 Tip

Did Something Go Wrong with Your Printer?
If so, a window similar to the one below will be displayed:

⚠ **This document failed to print**   ☒

Document name: 'Document'
Printer name: 'Auto HP LaserJet 1200 Series PCL on XP1500'
Time sent: 3:51:31 PM 7/14/2004

Click here to open the print queue, and then for assistance,
click Troubleshooter on the Help menu.

When this happens, be sure to check:
- whether the printer is on
- whether the printer has paper
- whether something else is wrong, such as an empty ink cartridge or a jammed piece of paper. If necessary, consult the printer manual.

Did you fix what was wrong?
Then *WordPad* will try again and the printing will start automatically.

💡 Tip

The Buttons in *WordPad*
You see various buttons at the top of the screen. These can be used to enter a command with a single click of the mouse:

These buttons have the following functions:

		Command:
▯	Start a new document	File , New...
📂	Open a document	File , Open...
💾	Save a document	File , Save
🖨	Print the text	File , Print...
🔍	See the print preview	File , Print Preview

5. Word Processing

It's very easy to change a text using your computer. You can select a word that you want to move somewhere else, for example, or move paragraphs or sentences, or copy a piece of text to use it again somewhere else.

Because so many people use word- processing programs, many standard letters exist. One type of letter is made about a certain subject. Then bits are added or changed to make the letter more personal. The recipient's name is inserted and the letter is printed properly. That makes it seem like all the recipients have received a personal letter, even though the letter was typed only once.

This chapter primarily focuses on word processing. You'll discover how easy it is to change sentences: sometimes all you have to do is click and drag with your mouse.

In this chapter, you'll learn how to:

- move the cursor with the mouse
- select a single word or paragraph
- delete a word
- move a word or paragraph
- split a paragraph and paste it back together

The Cursor and the Mouse

☞ **Start** *WordPad* 🐾 **1.14**

You can move the cursor not only with the keyboard, but also with the mouse. In order to practice this, type the following words to a popular nursery rhyme.

⌨ **Type:**
```
mary had a little lamb
its fleece was white
as snow
and everywhere that
mary went
```

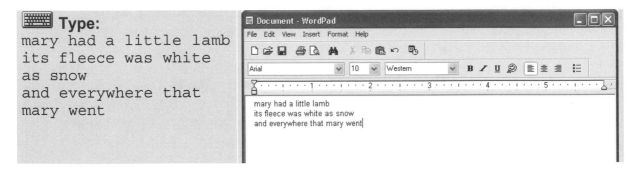

The regular mouse pointer ⌖ always turns into a different mouse pointer I when you hold it over the text. If you click the mouse somewhere in the text, the cursor will move to that spot.

🖱 **Move the mouse pointer I after the word** little

🖱 **Click with the mouse**

Now you see that the cursor appears after the word little:

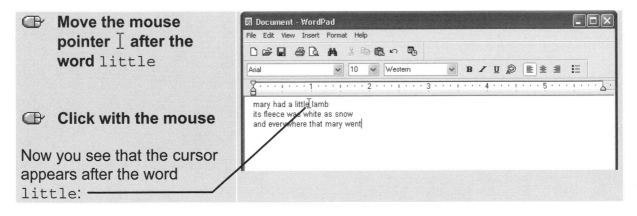

Now you can delete the word *little* using the Backspace key:

☞ **Delete the word**
little 🐾 **4.5**

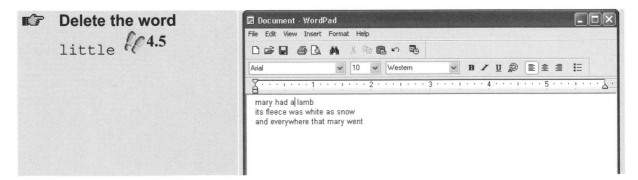

Selecting a Word

It isn't really handy to delete words using the Backspace key. There are faster ways to delete a whole word or even an entire paragraph all at once.
In order to do so, you must first *select* the part that you want to delete. Selecting is done with the mouse.

Move the mouse pointer ⌶ **to the word** `fleece`

Double click with the mouse

You see the word `fleece` turn blue:———

This means that the word has been selected.

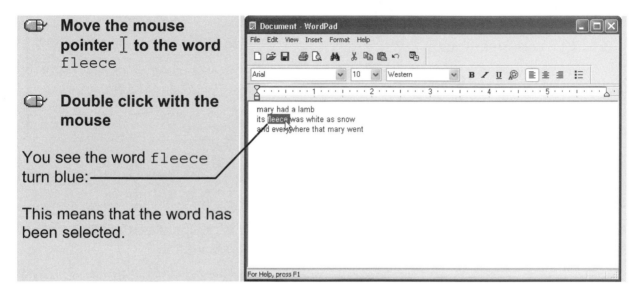

You can also select a different word the same way.

Move the mouse pointer ⌶ **to the word** `everywhere`

Double click with the mouse

You see that the word `everywhere` has now been selected:———

As you can see, you can only select a single word this way. The word `fleece` is no longer selected after you select `everywhere`.

Undoing a Selection

It's very easy to undo a selection. Simply click somewhere else in the window:

☞ **Move the mouse pointer ⊥ somewhere in the window**

☞ **Click with the mouse**

You see that the word is no longer selected:

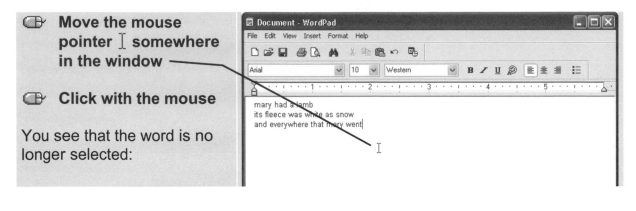

Deleting a Word

Once you've selected a word, you can do many things with it. You can delete it, for example. Later, you'll see that you can also do other things with it.

Deleting is done with the Delete key:
(Sometimes it only says *Del*.)

The Delete key is in the group of keys above the cursor keys:

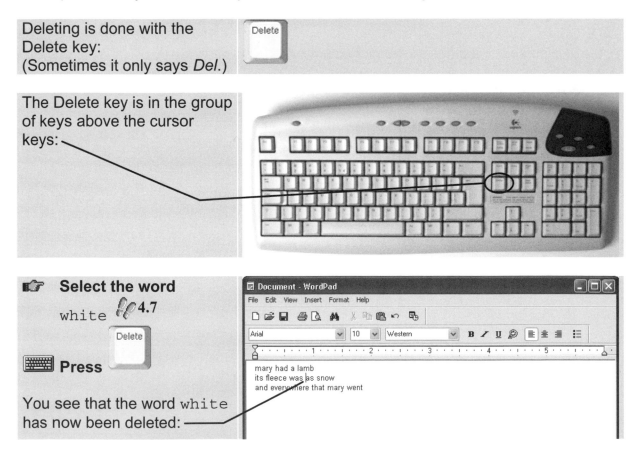

☞ **Select the word** white ✐4.7

⌨ **Press** Delete

You see that the word white has now been deleted:

Dragging a Word

You can drag a selected word to another place in the text. To practice this, first type the last line of the nursery rhyme. They're in the right order now, but won't be after this exercise.

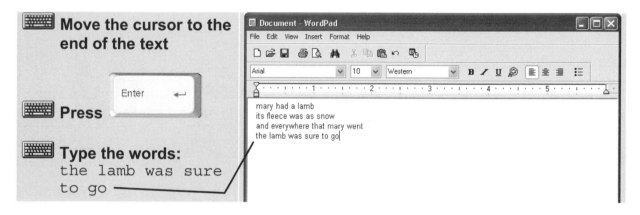

Move the cursor to the end of the text

Press Enter

Type the words: the lamb was sure to go

Before you can drag a word, you must select it:

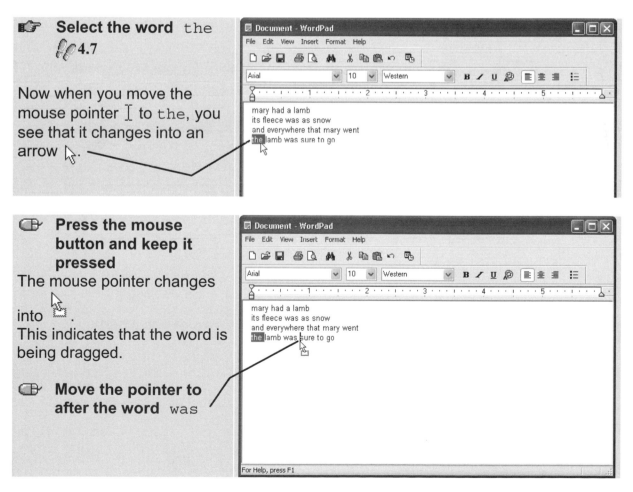

☞ **Select the word** the
🐾 4.7

Now when you move the mouse pointer I to the, you see that it changes into an arrow ▷.

Press the mouse button and keep it pressed
The mouse pointer changes into ▷.
This indicates that the word is being dragged.

Move the pointer to after the word was

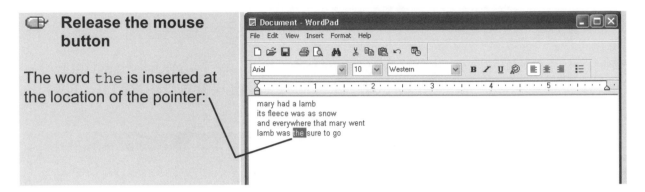

Release the mouse button

The word the is inserted at the location of the pointer:

Learning to drag words will take some time. At the end of this chapter, you'll find an exercise with which you can keep practicing. You need to save the text for this:

☞ **Undo the last change** 🐾**4.17**

☞ **Save the text** 🐾**2.1 and name it:** little lamb

Typing Over a Word

If you want to replace one word with another, it isn't always necessary to delete the word first. You can also type over a word that has been selected. Try it:

☞ **Select the word** go 🐾**4.7**

⌨ **Type:** walk

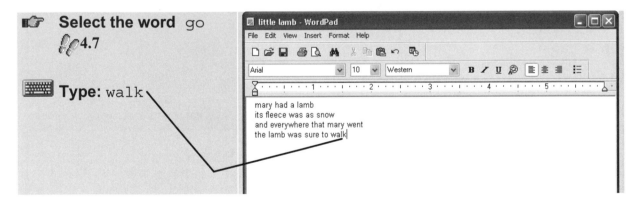

As you can see, the selected word is replaced by the new word you typed.

☞ **Start a new text; do not save the changes** 🐾**1.18**

Now you have an empty screen again, without text.

Selecting a Paragraph

You can also select a paragraph and delete or drag it. You can easily practice by placing the words of the national anthem in the right order. Type the first four lines. They've been put in the wrong order on purpose:

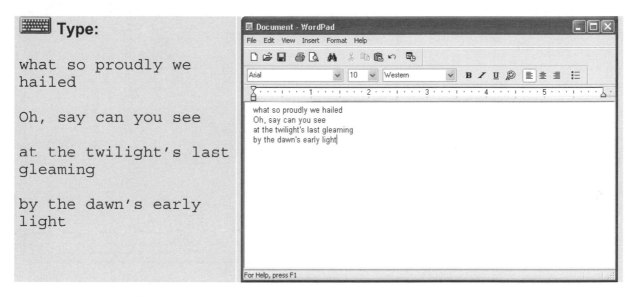

Type:

what so proudly we hailed

Oh, say can you see

at the twilight's last gleaming

by the dawn's early light

The start of a paragraph is indicated by beginning on a new line (using the Enter-key). The paragraph ends by using the Enter-key. A paragraph can be a group of sentences, one sentence alone or even just one line of text. In the text above every line is a paragraph.

It's easy to select a paragraph: double-clicking with the mouse selects a word. Triple-clicking selects the paragraph:

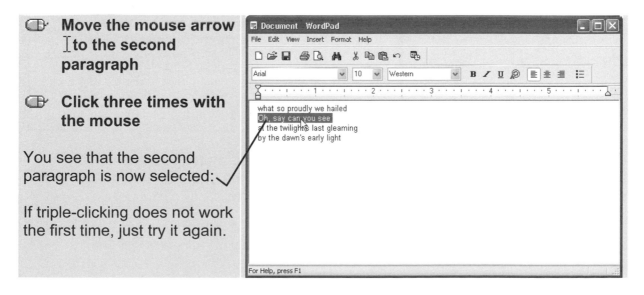

Move the mouse arrow Ι**to the second paragraph**

Click three times with the mouse

You see that the second paragraph is now selected:

If triple-clicking does not work the first time, just try it again.

Dragging a Paragraph

Dragging a paragraph is done the same way as dragging a word.
You can point to the selected paragraph and drag it to the place where it should be:

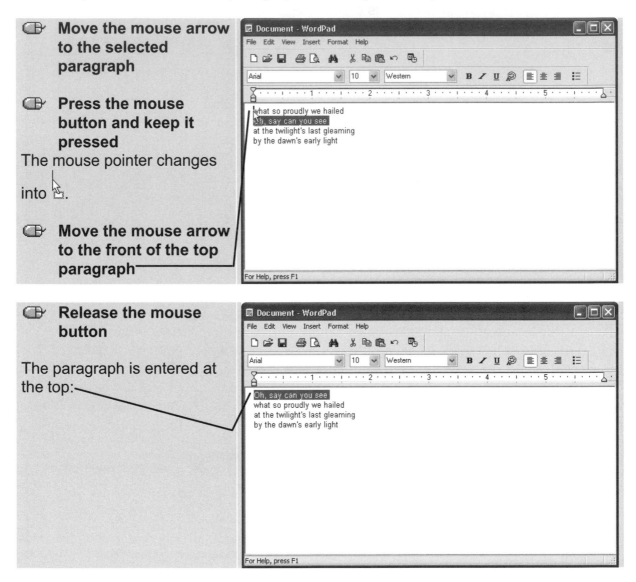

- **Move the mouse arrow to the selected paragraph**

- **Press the mouse button and keep it pressed**
The mouse pointer changes

into ▧.

- **Move the mouse arrow to the front of the top paragraph**

- **Release the mouse button**

The paragraph is entered at the top:

Dragging paragraphs will be easy once you've practiced more. See the relevant exercise at the end of this chapter. There you can put the entire anthem in the right order. You will be saving the text for this purpose shortly.

Mini Word Processing

Now you've learned the most important actions in word processing. Actually, you won't only be using these in the *WordPad* program to make changes in a text. These actions can also be handy in various other situations in *Windows XP*, for example when you're saving a text. Take a look:

Click on File

Click on Save

You now see this window:

In the box next to File name:, a tentative name is already shown, namely: Document.

This box acts like a kind of mini word processor. You can use all of the actions that you learned in *WordPad* in these boxes as well. Examples are:

- if the word is selected, you can delete it using the Delete key
- if you press the cursor keys, the cursor will move through the word
- if the word isn't selected, you can add letters or delete them

Go ahead and try:

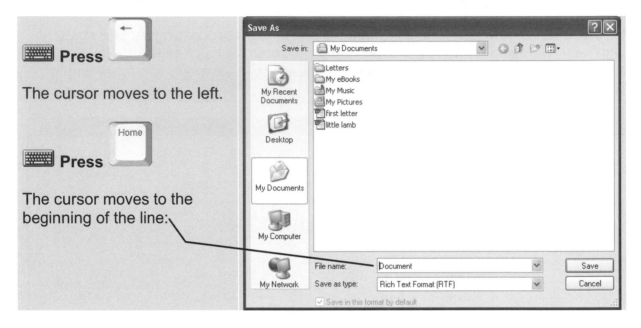

Press [←]

The cursor moves to the left.

Press [Home]

The cursor moves to the beginning of the line:

As you can see, the cursor acts the same way it does in *WordPad*. Selecting is also done the same way:

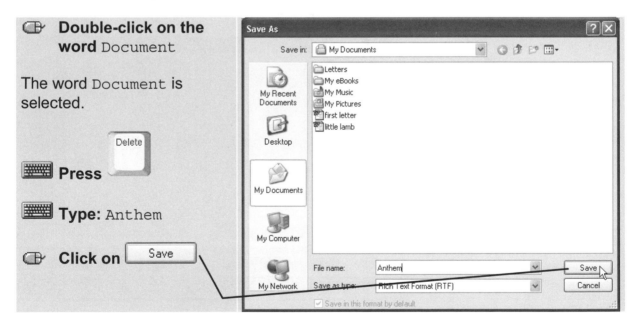

Double-click on the word Document

The word Document is selected.

Press [Delete]

Type: Anthem

Click on Save

The text is saved as *Anthem.rtf*.

☞ **Start a new text** ⫘ 1.16

Now you have an empty screen again, without text.

Splitting and Pasting Paragraphs

You've already seen that you can make empty lines (in fact empty paragraphs) by pressing the Enter key. You can also split a paragraph the same way. Sometimes this will happen accidentally when you press the Enter key. It's handy to know that you can **undo** this.

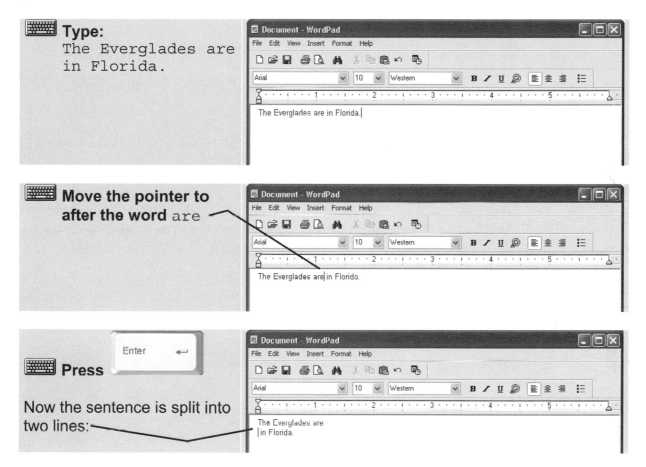

Type:
    The Everglades are in Florida.

Move the pointer to after the word are

Press Enter

Now the sentence is split into two lines:

Both lines are in fact seperate paragraphs. The bottom paragraph can easily be pasted back to the top paragraph using the Backspace key. In this instance, the cursor is still in the right place, at the beginning of the line.

Press ← Backspace

Now the sentence is pasted back together:

☞ **Start a new text; do not save the changes** 📖1.18

Copying, Cutting and Pasting

Windows has three commands that are really very similar: *copying, cutting* and *pasting.* Once you've copied or cut something, you can paste it somewhere else. You can do this in the same program, but you can also do it in two different programs: by copying a drawing from a drawing program and pasting it into a letter in *WordPad*, for example.

This can be practiced in *WordPad*. Type the following three lines:

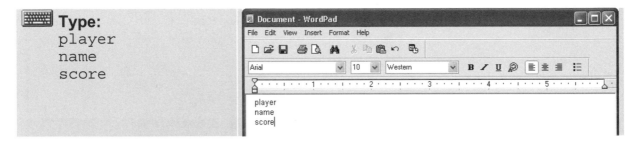

Type:
player
name
score

A piece of text, such as a word, is easy to copy and paste in somewhere else in the text. But before you can copy something, you must select it. Remember this rule:

➡ **Please note:**

Select first ... then act.

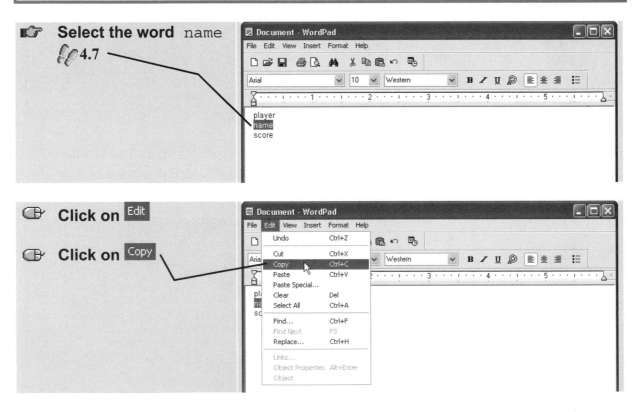

☞ **Select the word** name
 ✍ 4.7

☞ **Click on** Edit

☞ **Click on** Copy

You can not see anything happening, but the word `name` has now been copied to the *Clipboard*. *Windows Clipboard* is a temporary storage area.

You can paste the word `name` somewhere else. The cursor is used to indicate where to paste.

☞ **Make an empty line at the bottom**
✍ 4.4

⌨ **Move the cursor to that line**

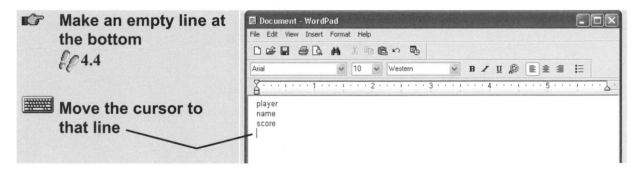

Now you can paste in the word*:*

🖱 **Click on** Edit

🖱 **Click on** Paste

The word `name` appears at the bottom:

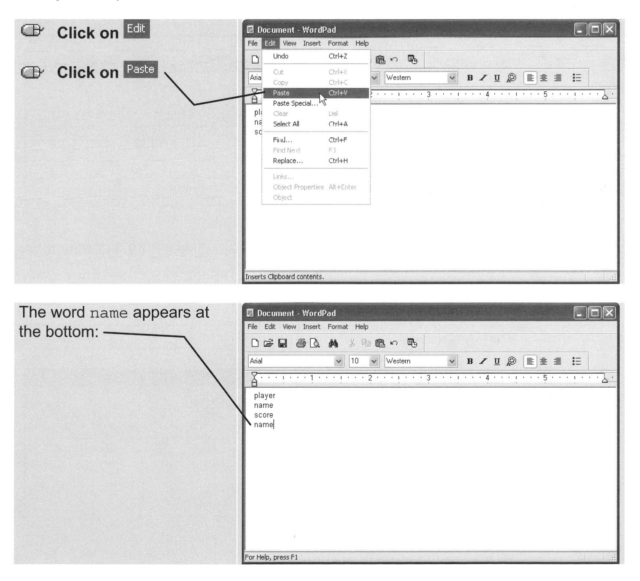

A word that you *select* and *copy* can be pasted as many times as you want. Take a look:

☞ **Click on** Edit **again**

☞ **Click on** Paste **again**

The word `name` appears again:

You can also cut out a word and paste it somewhere else. Give it a try, but remember the rule:

⇨ **Please note:**

Select first ... then act.

☞ **Select the word**

`player` 4.7

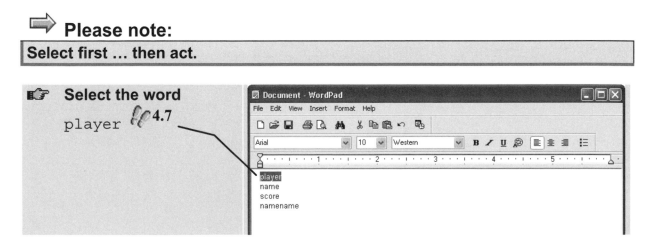

Now you can cut the word out:

Click on Edit

Click on Cut

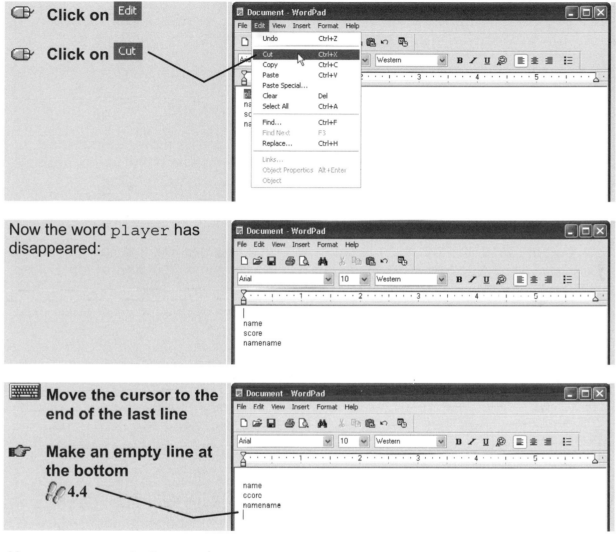

Now the word `player` has disappeared:

Move the cursor to the end of the last line

Make an empty line at the bottom
4.4

Now you can paste the word `player`:

Click on Edit

Click on Paste

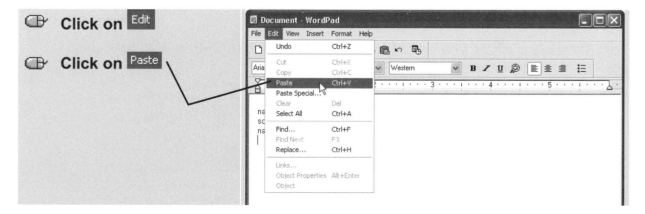

The word `player` appears at the bottom:

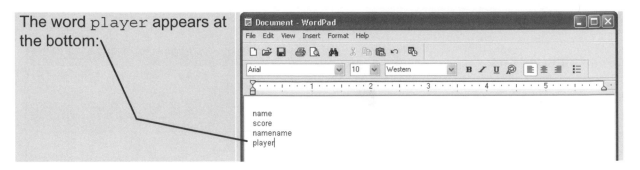

In this the way you see how easily words or sentences can be moved. First select, then cut, then paste your selection somewhere else. Please note that in this example, you'd have to type a space in the middle of the pasted word "namename".

 Please note:

You can only paste the last text you cut. If you cut a new text, the text you cut previously will be lost. You can always **undo** your last step, if you do not want to lose that portion of text.

☞ **Start a new text; do not save the changes** 🐾**1.18**

With the next exercises you can practice what you have learned in this chapter.

Exercises

🐾

The following exercises will help you master what you've just learned. Have you forgotten how to do something? Use the number beside the footsteps to look it up in the appendix *How Do I Do That Again?*

Exercise: The Song

This exercise will help you practice deleting and dragging words and attaching portions of text to one another.

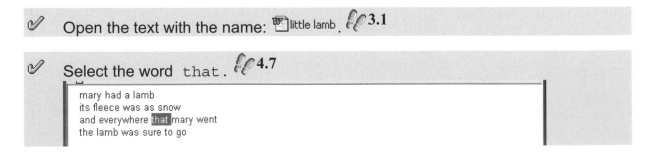

✓ Open the text with the name: 📄little lamb . 🐾**3.1**

✓ Select the word `that`. 🐾**4.7**

mary had a lamb
its fleece was as snow
and everywhere **that** mary went
the lamb was sure to go

✔ Delete the word `that`. 🐾 **4.6**

✔ Select the word `sure`. 🐾 **4.7**

✔ Drag the word `sure` and position it after the word `lamb`:

Now you can put the song on a single line:

✔ Attach the four paragraphs to make a single line. 🐾 **4.8** Add a space and a comma in the correct places.

✔ Save this document. 🐾 **2.2**

Exercise: The National Anthem

This exercise lets you practice dragging lines of text (paragraphs).

✔ Open the text with the name: 📄Anthem. 👣3.1

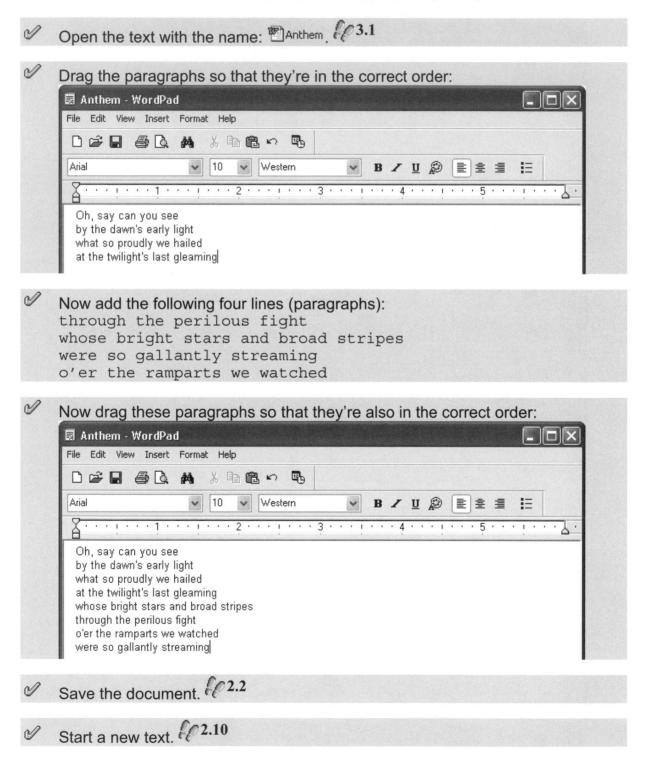

✔ Drag the paragraphs so that they're in the correct order:

✔ Now add the following four lines (paragraphs):
```
through the perilous fight
whose bright stars and broad stripes
were so gallantly streaming
o'er the ramparts we watched
```

✔ Now drag these paragraphs so that they're also in the correct order:

✔ Save the document. 👣2.2

✔ Start a new text. 👣2.10

Exercise: Copying and Pasting

✓ Type the following three lines (paragraphs):
```
two
three
points
```

✓ Select `points`. 👣**4.7**

✓ Copy `points`. 👣**1.25**

✓ Move the cursor after `two` 👣**4.1** and type a space.

✓ Paste here: `points`. 👣**1.26**

✓ Move the cursor after `three` 👣**4.1** and type a space.

✓ Now paste the word `points` here. 👣**1.26**

✓ At the bottom, select the word `points`. 👣**4.7**

✓ Cut the word `points`. 👣**1.27**

✓ Close *WordPad*; you do not need to save the changes from above. 👣**1.18**

Background Information

Word Processing Programs

Until now, you've worked with *WordPad*. It's a simple program that is more than sufficient for learning the basic principles. Its older brother is called *Microsoft Word*. This is a highly-detailed program that offers numerous functions.

You can make virtually anything you want with *Microsoft Word*: letters, minutes of meetings, folders, posters, flyers, cards, and other types of printed matter. The program has many functions for designing the layout of these items. It's very easy to make tables, for example. Last but certainly not least, the program has an excellent spelling checker. While you're typing, it identifies spelling errors and will even automatically correct them if you want it to.

Microsoft Word is available as a separate program, but is usually sold as part of the *Microsoft Office* package. This package has a number of programs, including the spreadsheet *Excel* (a program for making calculations).

Tips

Tip

Correcting On-Screen?
Many people find it difficult to correct texts on their screens. It's easy to miss typing errors. They often print their work out first so that they can correct it on paper. That's often a lot easier.
Nearly every word processing program, such as *Microsoft Word*, has an excellent spelling checker that can find most of the typing errors for you and correct them.

Tip

The Buttons in *WordPad*
You can see various buttons on the *WordPad* taskbar. These can be used to perform the commands *copy*, *cut*, *paste* and *undo* with a single click of the mouse:

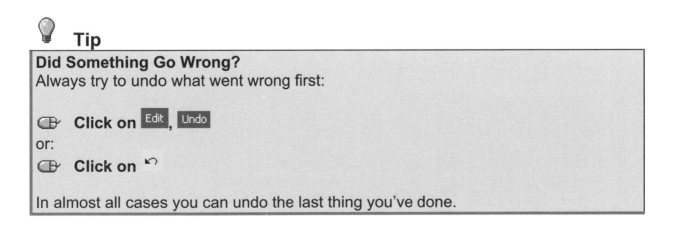

These buttons have the following functions:

		Command:
✂	Cut a selection	Edit , Cut
📋	Copy a selection	Edit , Copy
📋	Paste a selection	Edit , Paste
↶	Undo the last thing done	Edit , Undo

Tip

Did Something Go Wrong?
Always try to undo what went wrong first:

☞ **Click on** Edit , Undo

or:

☞ **Click on** ↶

In almost all cases you can undo the last thing you've done.

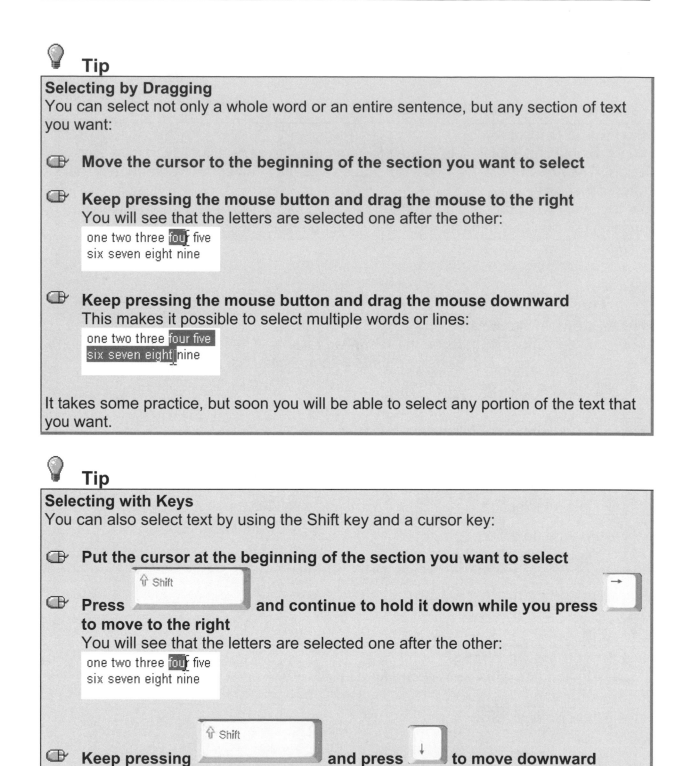

Tip

Selecting by Dragging
You can select not only a whole word or an entire sentence, but any section of text you want:

☞ **Move the cursor to the beginning of the section you want to select**

☞ **Keep pressing the mouse button and drag the mouse to the right**
You will see that the letters are selected one after the other:

one two three four five
six seven eight nine

☞ **Keep pressing the mouse button and drag the mouse downward**
This makes it possible to select multiple words or lines:

one two three four five
six seven eight nine

It takes some practice, but soon you will be able to select any portion of the text that you want.

Tip

Selecting with Keys
You can also select text by using the Shift key and a cursor key:

☞ **Put the cursor at the beginning of the section you want to select**

☞ **Press** ⇧ Shift **and continue to hold it down while you press** → **to move to the right**
You will see that the letters are selected one after the other:

one two three four five
six seven eight nine

☞ **Keep pressing** ⇧ Shift **and press** ↓ **to move downward**
This makes it possible to select multiple words or lines:

one two three four five
six seven eight nine

6. Folders, Documents and Files

In this chapter you'll learn to work with *folders, documents* and *files*. A *file* is the generic name for everything saved on the computer. A file can be a program, a data file with names, text you've written, or even a photo. Actually, everything that's on the hard disk of your computer is a *file*.

Because a hard disk can have thousands of files, they're neatly organized in *folders*. This keeps the contents of your hard disk manageable.

Windows XP has a special folder that you can save all of your work in. This folder is named *My Documents*. You've already saved some of your work in the *My Documents* folder. This keeps all of your work neatly together.

The word *document* refers to a file that you've made yourself with a program, such as a text using *WordPad* or a drawing using *Paint*.

Using the *My Documents* window, you can work with files that are on the hard disk, a CD-ROM, a diskette or USB memory stick. You can delete, copy or move files there. Perhaps at one time you'll want to put a text or a photo on a diskette or USB memory stick and send it to someone. You can do that in this window too. In *My Documents* you can also make your own folders, to keep all of your letters together, for example.

In this chapter, you'll learn how to:

- use *My Documents*
- make a new folder
- save something in a folder
- copy and delete files
- change the name of a file
- empty the *Recycle Bin*
- copy a file to a diskette or USB memory stick

The Folder My Documents

Windows XP has a special folder that you can save all of your documents in. This folder is named *My Documents*. You can open the folder *My Documents* by clicking on the icon:

Double-click on

You now see this window:

The contents of the *My Documents* folder is different on every computer: the window on your computer will not be exactly the same as this one.

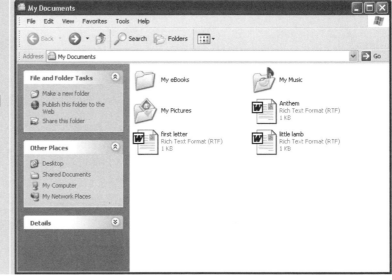

The Files

There are at least three files in the folder *My Documents:* the practice texts that you have made and saved while working with this book. But there may be more files in your folder. Various programs use the folder *My Documents* as the standard folder for saving files. You may see one or more of the following icons for files:

A folder. A folder may contain other folders.

A text made with *WordPad* or with *Microsoft Word.*

A text file that can be used with the program *Notepad.*

A drawing or photo, which can be edited using the program *Paint.*

These are only a few examples. There are many, many more icons because every program has its own icon for files.

Making a New Folder

You can make new files yourself. This can be handy, for example, to keep your letters separate from all of your other documents. That makes it easier to find them if you need to see them again. In this exercise, you'll make a new folder in the folder My Documents.

Click on

Make a new folder

You see a new folder, and you can enter a name:

⌨ **Type:** letters

⌨ **Press** Enter ↵

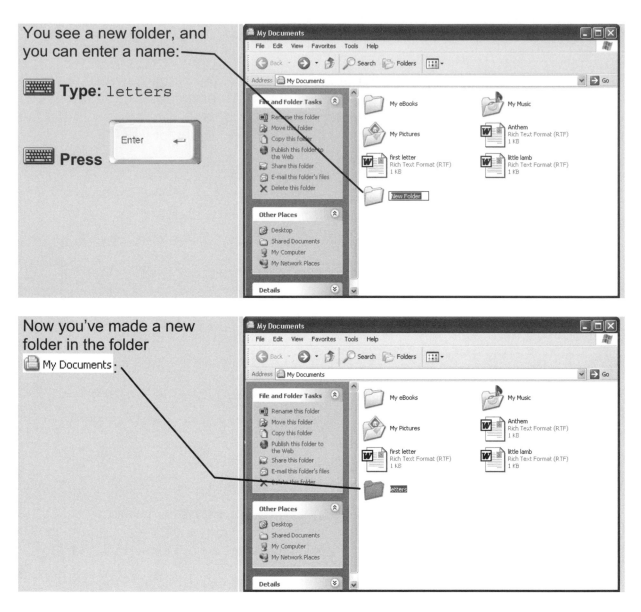

Now you've made a new folder in the folder
📁 My Documents.

You can use this folder *letters* to save a letter that you've written in *WordPad*, for example.

To do so, you can minimize the window *My Documents* and then start the program *WordPad*.

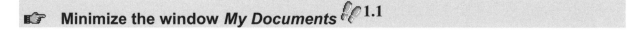

☞ **Minimize the window *My Documents*** 👣 1.1

Saving in a Folder

As an exercise, you'll first write a letter in *WordPad* and then you'll save it in the folder you made, 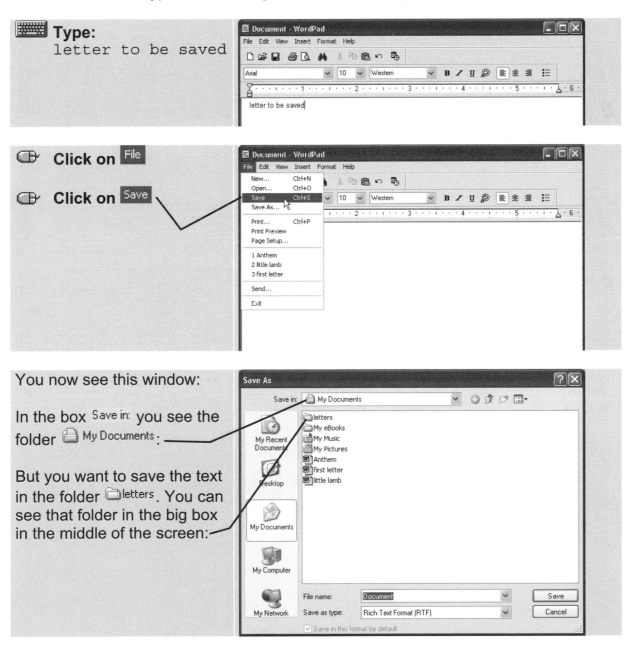 .

☞ **Start *WordPad*** 🐾1.14

As the "contents", type the following short sentence fragment:

⌨ **Type:**
   letter to be saved

🖱 **Click on** File

🖱 **Click on** Save

You now see this window:

In the box Save in: you see the folder 🗎 My Documents:

But you want to save the text in the folder 🗀 letters. You can see that folder in the big box in the middle of the screen:

You must open the folder 📁letters first. This is how:

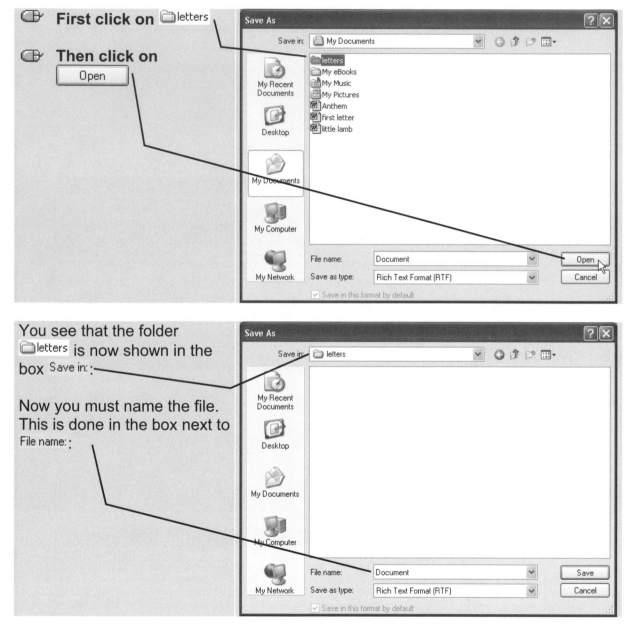

☞ **First click on** 📁letters

☞ **Then click on**

[Open]

You see that the folder 📁letters is now shown in the box Save in: :

Now you must name the file. This is done in the box next to File name: :

But a name is already shown there: *Document*. That's the name the program always shows. You can change the name, using the word processing skills you've already learned:

👆 **Click after** Document

👉 **Delete the name**
Document 🐾4.5

⌨ **Now type the name
you want, for example:**
note

👆 **Then click on**
[Save]

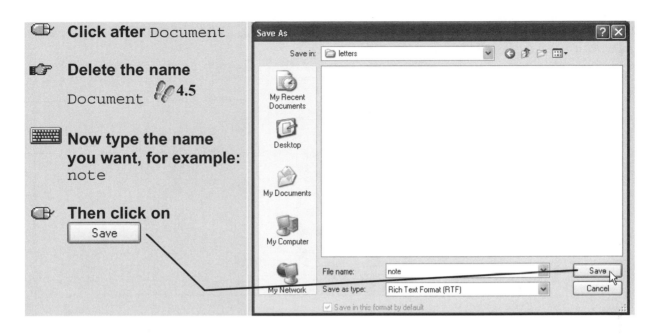

You'll see an hourglass ⏳ while the text is being saved. Now you can start with a new file in *WordPad:*

👉 **Close the window *WordPad*** 🐾1.4

Now you can reopen the window *My Documents*, where you can see that your file is in the folder *letters*.

👉 **Open *My Documents* on the taskbar** 🐾1.29

👆 **Double-click on**
📁 letters

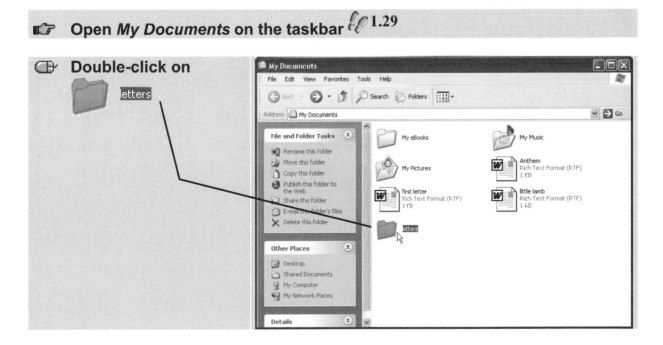

In the window you do indeed see your saved *WordPad* file:

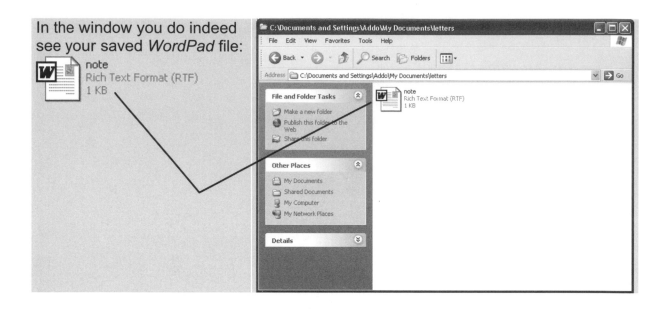

Copying Files

You can also copy files and paste them into a different file. For example, you can make a second copy of a letter that you want to change slightly. To practice, you can copy your practice texts.

First go back to the folder 📁 *My Documents*.

☞ **Click on** ⬅ Back ▾

Now you see the documents in this folder:

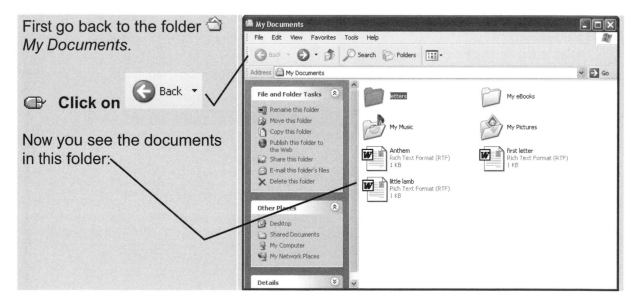

HELP! There's no *Back* button.

You don't see the *Back* button?

If this is the case, click on View, Toolbars, Standard Buttons

You can now copy one of the practice texts, but remember the rule:

Please note:

Select first ... then act.

Selecting a file is easy: simply click on it.

Click on

Anthem
Rich Text Format (RTF)
1 KB

The name turns blue to indicate that it's been selected:

HELP!

Do you see a frame around the name as well?
Has the mouse pointer changed into ⟂?

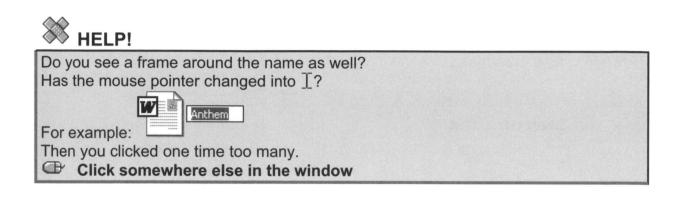

For example:
Then you clicked one time too many.
👆 **Click somewhere else in the window**

Selecting Multiple Files

In actual practice, you may want to copy more than one file at a time. If so, you must select them first. Go ahead and try:

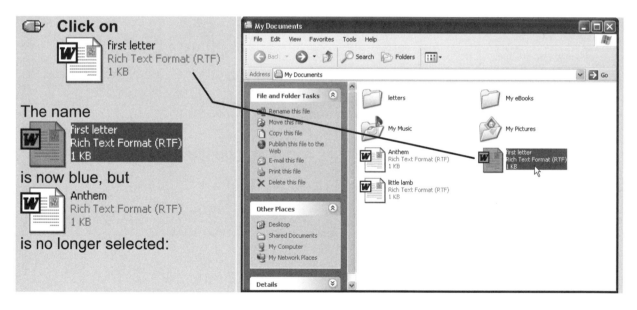

You can select only one file at a time by clicking. But you can select more than one file if you use a special key on your keyboard:

| the *Control* key. It always shows the abbreviation Ctrl: | Ctrl |

The Ctrl key is located at the bottom left of the keyboard:

The Ctrl key is used together with the mouse.

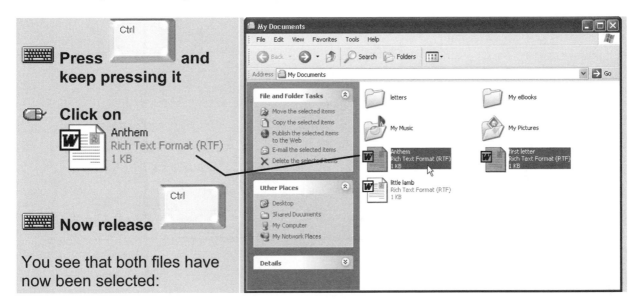

Now you can copy these two files.

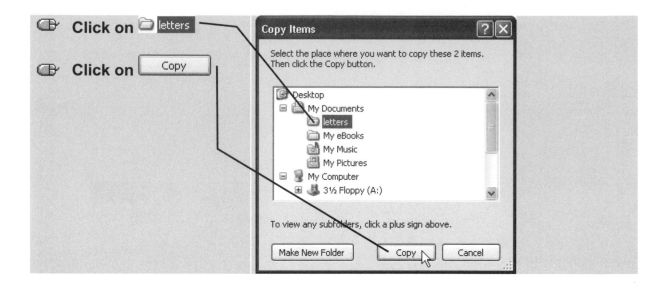

HELP! No letters folder?

You don't see the folder 📂 letters ?

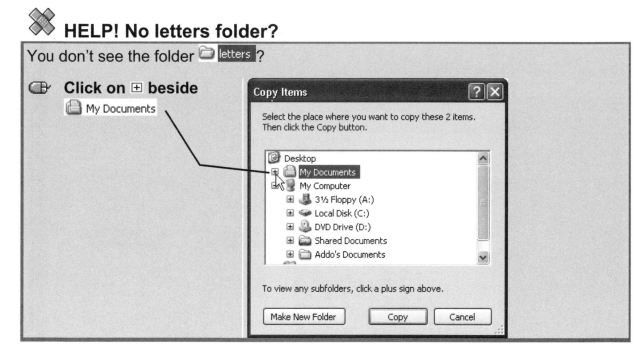

Now you can check to make sure the two documents have really been copied to the folder *letters*:

This is the quickest way to do that:

☞ **Click on**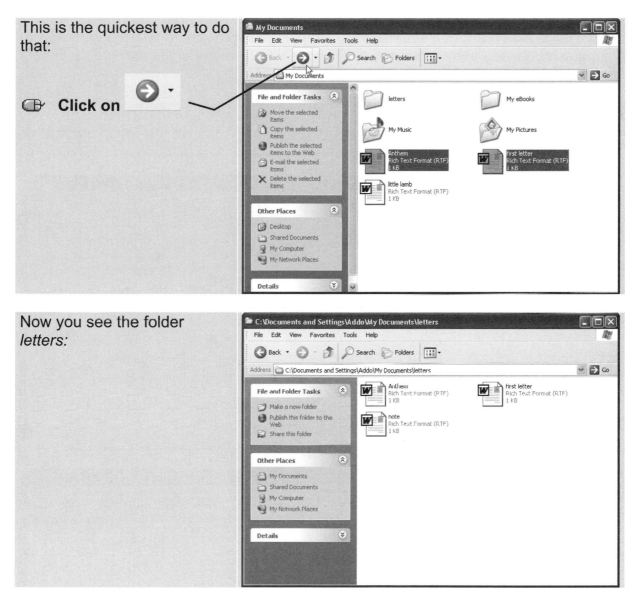

Now you see the folder *letters:*

The two files are indeed in this folder.

Changing the File Name

Sometimes you may want to give a file a different name, because you've written more than one text about a subject, for example, and you want to be able to distinguish between them more clearly. You want to give one of the two practice letters a different name.

⇨ **Please note:**

Select first ... then act.

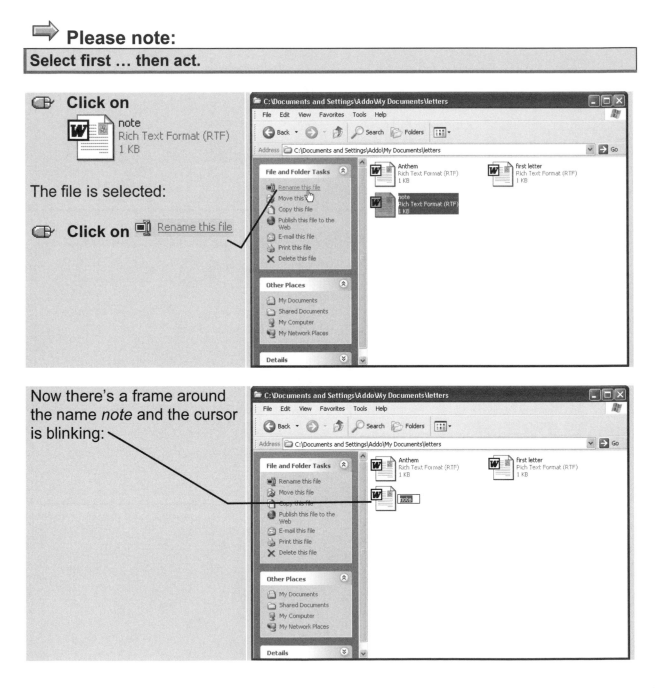

☞ **Click on**

  note
  Rich Text Format (RTF)
  1 KB

The file is selected:

☞ **Click on** 🗐 Rename this file

Now there's a frame around the name *note* and the cursor is blinking:

HELP!

Do you unexpectedly see the window for *WordPad* or *Microsoft Word?*
If so, you double-clicked on the file name, and opened the program.

☞ **In that case, close the window for *WordPad* or *Microsoft Word* using** ☒

Now you can type a different name, for example:

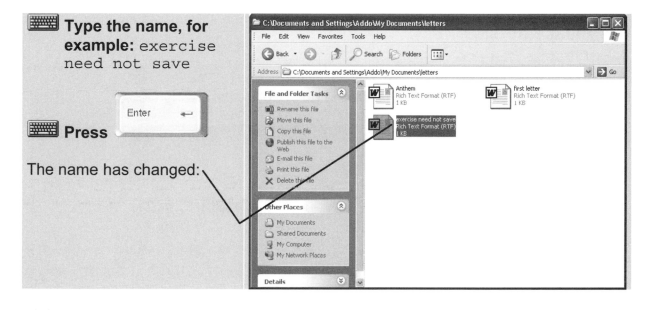

Type the name, for example: exercise need not save

Press Enter

The name has changed:

HELP!

You can't put more than one file with the same name in a folder.
If you try to give a file a name that already exists, you'll see:

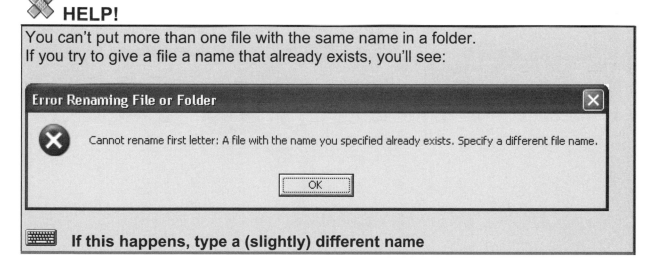

Error Renaming File or Folder ☒

Cannot rename first letter: A file with the name you specified already exists. Specify a different file name.

OK

If this happens, type a (slightly) different name

Deleting Files

It's wise to regularly "spring clean" your hard disk. You can delete files you no longer need to keep your hard disk manageable. It's a good idea to regularly delete files you no longer want.

To practice, you can delete the document *Anthem* in the folder 🗀 *letters*, because this is a copy that you don't really need.

⇨ **Please note:**

Select first ... then act.

It's important to select carefully, so that you don't delete the wrong files.

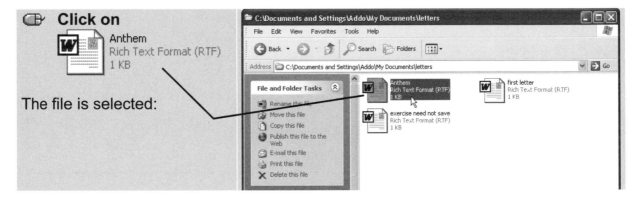

Now you can delete the file. It will be "tossed" in the *Recycle Bin*.

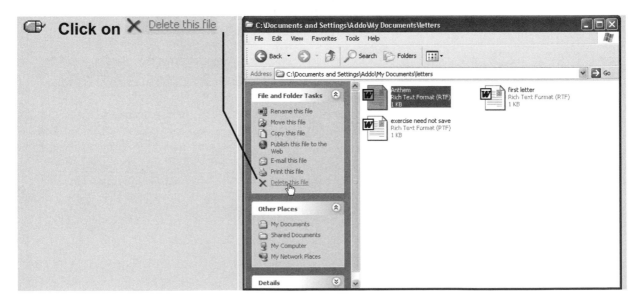

Windows XP will ask whether the file should be put in the *Recycle Bin*:

 Click on

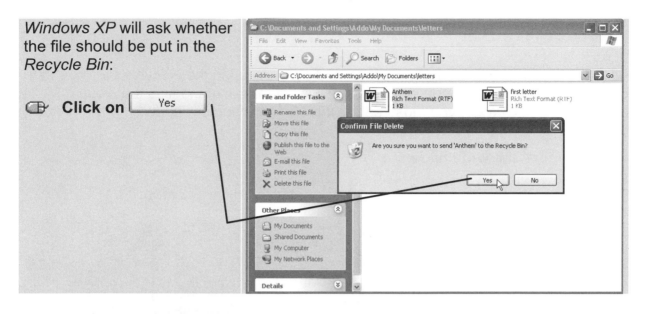

The file has now disappeared from the window *letters*. Files that have been deleted aren't gone forever. As a kind of safety catch, they're put into the *Recycle Bin* first. They aren't really gone forever until you empty the *Recycle Bin*. As long as a file is in the *Recycle Bin*, you can get it back if you need it.

💡 Tip

Selecting Multiple Files
You can also delete multiple files at one time. You must select them first by clicking on them while pressing the Ctrl key. Then you can delete them.

💡 Tip

Selecting an Entire Folder
You can also select an entire folder 🗀 to delete it. You can select a folder by clicking on it; then you can delete it.

💡 Tip

Only Your Files
Be careful when deleting files. Only delete files that you yourself have made. Never delete files or folders for programs that you don't use. Program files must be deleted in a different way.

The Recycle Bin

All of the files that you delete from your hard disk end up in the *Recycle Bin*. You can open the *Recycle Bin* to see what's in it. It will contain all of the files that you've deleted. First, however, you must reduce the *My Documents* window:

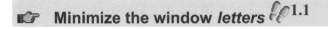 **Minimize the window** *letters* $\ell\ell$1.1

The *Recycle Bin* has its own icon, which is displayed on the *Desktop*:

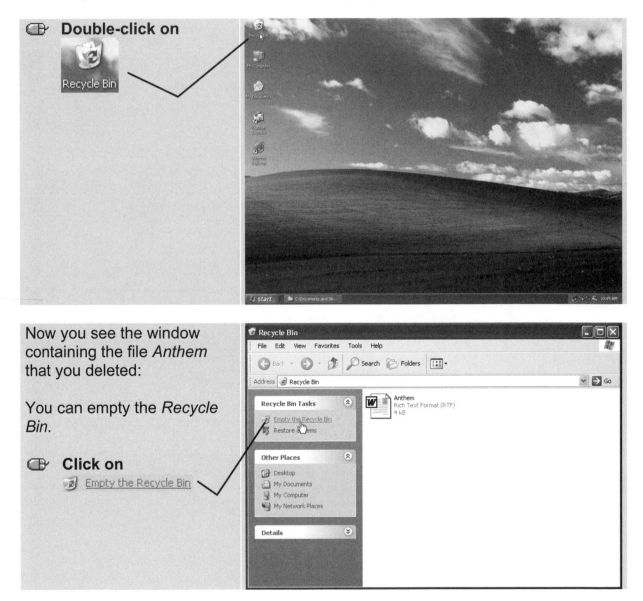

Double-click on

Recycle Bin

Now you see the window containing the file *Anthem* that you deleted:

You can empty the *Recycle Bin*.

Click on

Empty the Recycle Bin

To be certain, you'll be asked to confirm that you want to empty it.

☞ **Click on** [Yes]

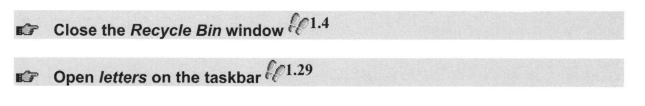

Now the file has been permanently deleted and cannot be retrieved. You can close the *Recycle Bin* window.

☞ **Close the *Recycle Bin* window** 🦶1.4

☞ **Open *letters* on the taskbar** 🦶1.29

 Tip

When to empty the Recycle Bin?
You don't have to empty the *Recycle Bin* every time you delete a file. You only need to empty it when you want to permanently delete a file. It's better to collect your deleted files in the *Recycle Bin* and to wait to empty it until you do your "spring cleaning".

Tip

Is there anything in the Recycle Bin?
You can tell by the icon for the *Recycle Bin* whether there's anything in it. You don't have to open the window to see:

Recycle Bin not empty   Recycle Bin empty

Copying to a Diskette or USB Stick

You may sometimes need to copy something to a diskette ("floppy") or USB stick. For example, you might want to transfer a file to another PC or store a backup copy of the file away from the computer. This section covers copying files to both a floppy and a USB stick. You can decide which of the two you'd like to do.

⇨ **Please note:**

In order to work through this section, you need an empty diskette or USB stick:

If you don't have a diskette or USB stick, you can skip this section.

Let's try copying the Anthem to a diskette or USB memory stick. You have a copy of it in the folder 🗀 *My Documents*:

Click on ← Back ▾

Diskette into the floppy drive

Are you using a diskette? Insert it into the computer now. Here's how you do that:

☞ **Put the diskette in the computer**

Connecting the USB stick

Are you using a USB stick? Insert it into the computer now.

☞ **Locate the USB port on your computer**

A USB port can be on the front or the back of the computer, or both.

☞ **Insert the USB stick into the USB port and gently press it in**

Having trouble?
☞ **Then turn the stick over and try again**

☞ **Wait a moment until *Windows XP* recognizes the USB stick**

ⓘ **Found New Hardware** ☒

Your new hardware is installed and ready to use.

You see this text balloon appear:

Now you can select the document.

🖰 **Click on**

Anthem
Rich Text Format (RTF)
1 KB

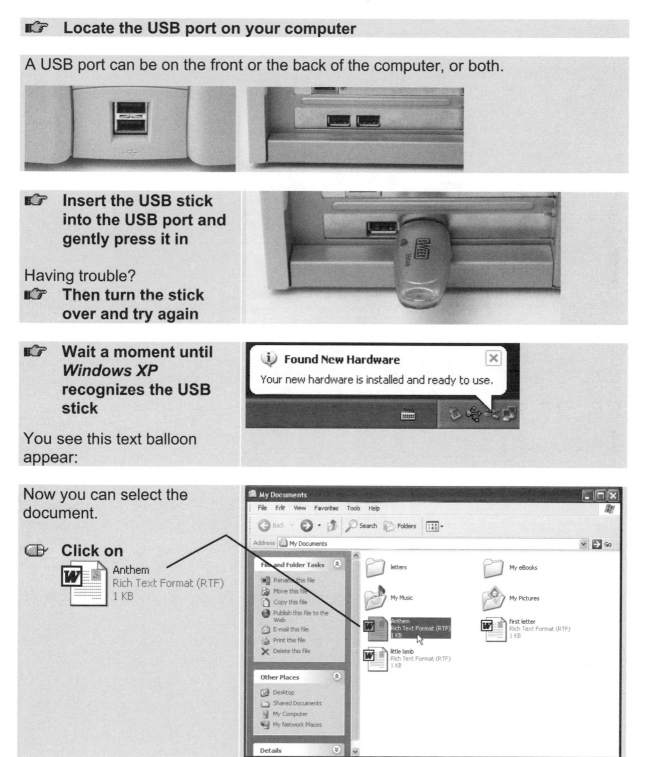

Now you can copy the file to the diskette or USB stick:

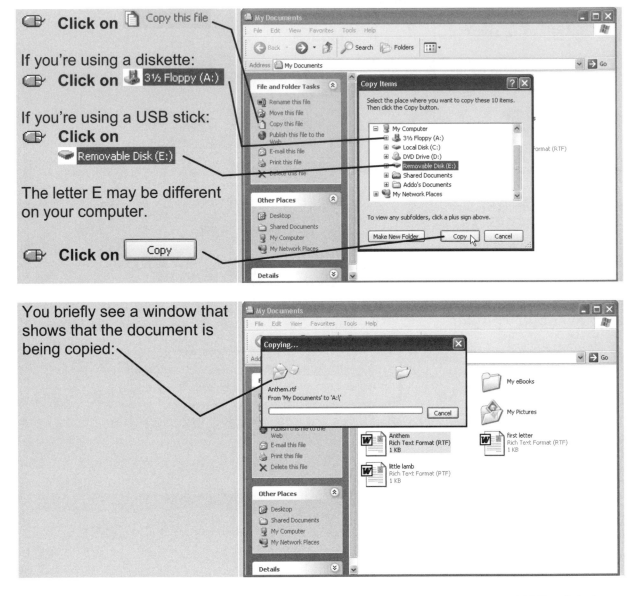

📠 **Click on** 🗋 Copy this file

If you're using a diskette:
📠 **Click on** 💾 3½ Floppy (A:)

If you're using a USB stick:
📠 **Click on**
  💾 Removable Disk (E:)

The letter E may be different on your computer.

📠 **Click on** [Copy]

You briefly see a window that shows that the document is being copied:

After *Windows XP* is finished copying, you can remove the diskette or USB stick from the PC.

If you're using a diskette:

👉 **Press the button on the floppy drive**

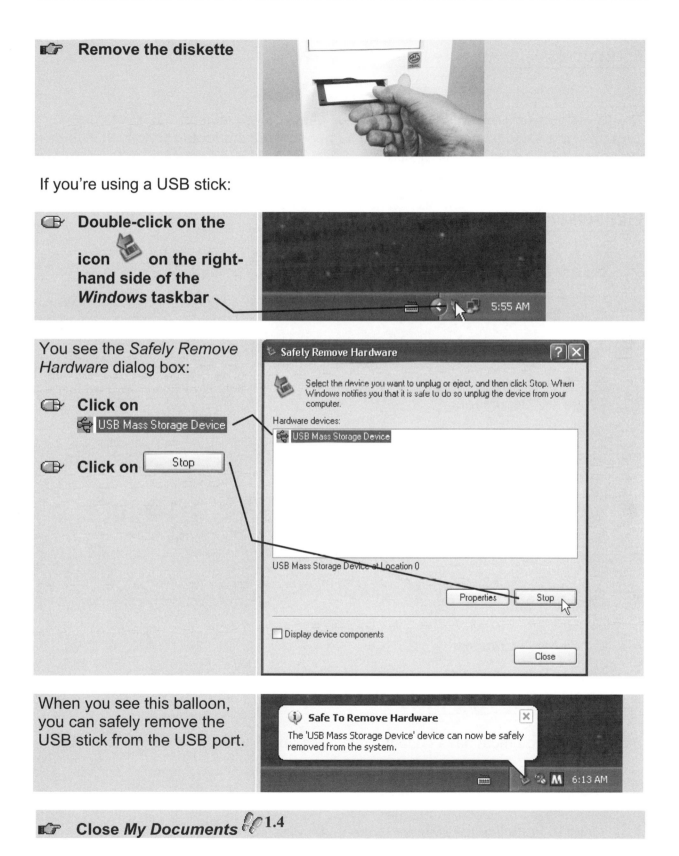

Remove the diskette

If you're using a USB stick:

Double-click on the icon on the right-hand side of the *Windows* taskbar

You see the *Safely Remove Hardware* dialog box:

Click on 🖧 USB Mass Storage Device

Click on Stop

When you see this balloon, you can safely remove the USB stick from the USB port.

Close *My Documents* 1.4

Now you can try the exercises for this chapter. You can also stop and close *Windows XP*.

Exercises

The following exercises will help you master what you've just learned. Have you forgotten how to do something? Use the number beside the footsteps to look it up in the appendix *How Do I Do That Again?*

Exercise: My Documents

✔ Start *My Documents*. 5.1

✔ Open the folder *letters*. 5.2

✔ Open the folder *My Documents* again. 5.3

✔ Close *My Documents*. 1.4

Exercise: Making a New Folder

✔ Start *My Documents*. 5.1

✔ Create a new folder with the name *practice*. 5.4

✔ Open the new folder *practice*. 5.5

✔ Close *My Documents*. 1.4

Exercise: Copying Files

Please note: you must have done the exercises above in order to do this exercise.

✔ Start *My Documents*. 5.1

✔ Copy the practice file *Anthem* to the folder *practice*. 5.6

✔ Close *My Documents*. 1.4

Exercise: Renaming a File

Please note: you must have done the exercises above in order to do this exercise.

✅ Start *My Documents.* 🐾 **5.1**

✅ Open the new folder *practice.* 🐾 **5.5**

✅ Change the name of the practice file *Anthem* to *song.* 🐾 **5.7**

✅ Close *My Documents.* 🐾 **1.4**

Exercise: Deleting Files

Please note: you must have done the exercises above in order to do this exercise.

✅ Start *My Documents.* 🐾 **5.1**

✅ Open the new folder *practice.* 🐾 **5.5**

✅ Delete the practice file *song* in this folder. 🐾 **5.8**

✅ Close *My Documents.* 🐾 **1.4**

Exercise: Copying a File to a Diskette or USB Stick

✅ Start *My Documents.* 🐾 **5.1**

✅ Copy the practice file *Anthem* to a diskette or USB stick. 🐾 **5.9**

✅ Close *My Documents.* 🐾 **1.4**

Background Information

Diskettes, USB Sticks, CD-ROMs, DVDs

Diskettes (floppy disks), USB sticks, CD-ROMs, and DVDs are storage media often used to store files outside the computer. For example, you can use them to transfer files to another computer or to save a *backup* copy. Software manufacturers often provide their products on CD-ROM or DVD.

Diskette

The current generation of diskettes are 3.5 inches in size. They can store up to 1.44 MB. You can write files directly to a diskette in *Windows XP*. The memory can be reused. To use a diskette, you need to have a floppy drive in your PC.

USB Stick

A USB stick is a small storage medium with a large storage capacity. You can insert it directly into your PC's USB port. The storage capacity can vary from 16 MB to 4 GB or more. The price depends on the capacity. You can write files directly to a USB stick in *Windows XP*. The memory can be reused.

CD-ROM

Many software manufacturers deliver their software on CD-ROMs. You can play these CDs, but you can't write to them. There are also two kinds of writable CD-ROMs: CD-Recordable (CD-R) and CD-Rewritable (CD-RW). You can write your own files to these two kinds of CDs, if you have a CD burner (CD writer) in your computer. You can only burn files to a CD-R once; you can reuse a CD-RW. The storage capacity is 640 to 700 MB. A CD drive in your PC can only play CD-ROMs. A CD burner can both play and write them. You can burn files directly to a CD-ROM in *Windows XP*.

DVD

These days, software manufacturers deliver very large programs on DVDs. Large files like movies are also released on DVD. You can play these in your DVD player. Now there are also writable DVDs: DVD-Recordable (DVD-R; can be burned once) and DVD-Rewritable (DVD-RW; can be reused), which you can write to using a DVD burner (DVD writer). Unfortunately there are no accepted standards, so there are two kinds: DVD-**R(W)** and DVD+**R(W)**. Not all DVD players or burners can play and/or write to both variants. To burn a DVD-R(W), you need a DVD- burner in your computer, as well as separate burning software. The storage capacity is at least 4 GB and sometimes more (this also depends on the type of burner). A DVD burner can also write and play CD-ROMs.

The Parts of the *Open* Window

This is the window that you use in *WordPad* or *Paint*, for example, to open a file from your hard disk. See 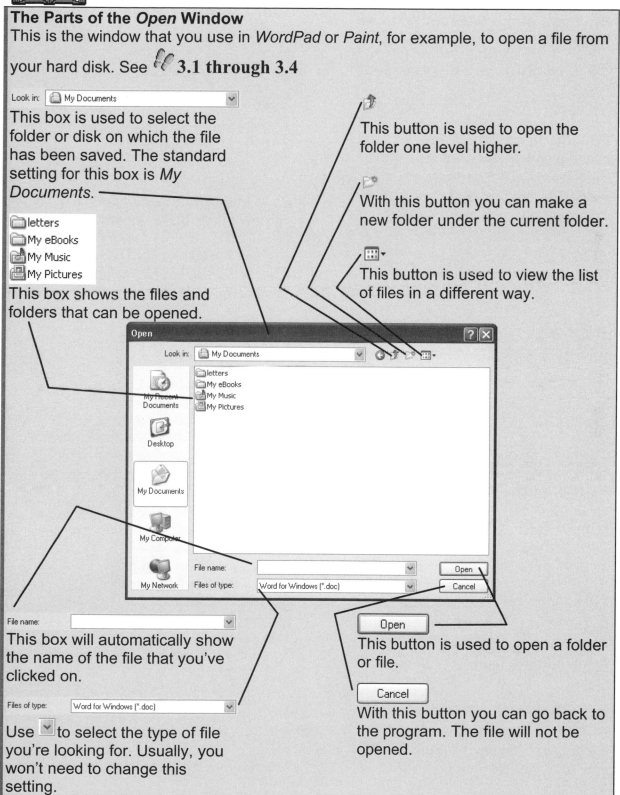 **3.1 through 3.4**

Look in: 📁 My Documents ▾

This box is used to select the folder or disk on which the file has been saved. The standard setting for this box is *My Documents*.

📁 letters
📁 My eBooks
📷 My Music
📷 My Pictures

This box shows the files and folders that can be opened.

This button is used to open the folder one level higher.

With this button you can make a new folder under the current folder.

This button is used to view the list of files in a different way.

File name: ▾

This box will automatically show the name of the file that you've clicked on.

Files of type: Word for Windows (*.doc) ▾

Use ▾ to select the type of file you're looking for. Usually, you won't need to change this setting.

This button is used to open a folder or file.

With this button you can go back to the program. The file will not be opened.

The Parts of the *Save As* Window

This is the window that you use in *WordPad* or *Paint*, for example, to save a file to your hard disk or to a diskette. See **2.1 through 2.4**

Save in: 🗀 My Documents ▾

With ▾ you can select the folder in which you want to save the file. The standard setting for this box is *My Documents*.

This button is used to open the folder one level higher.

With this button you can make a new folder under the current folder.

This button is used to view the list of files in a different way.

Save As ? ✕

Save in: 🗀 My Documents ▾ ⬅ 📁 📁 ▦▾

🗀 letters
🗀 My eBooks
🗀 My Music
🗀 My Pictures
📄 Anthem
📄 first letter
📄 little lamb

My Recent Documents
Desktop
My Documents
My Computer
My Network

File name: Document ▾ Save
Save as type: Rich Text Format (RTF) ▾ Cancel
☑ Save in this format by default

File name: Document ▾

In this box you can type the name that you want to give the file.

Save as type: Rich Text Format (RTF) ▾

Here you can select the type of file you want to save. Usually, you won't need to change this setting.

Save

This button is used to save the file.

Cancel

With this button you can go back to the program. The file will not be saved.

Tips

💡 Tip

Lost Document?

It will probably happen to you at least once: you've forgotten the name of a document. A quick way to find out the name is to start the program with which you saved the file. Suppose that you recently composed a letter in *WordPad* but you can't find it on the hard disk.

☞ **If that happens, start *WordPad***

🖱️ **Click on** File

In the menu *File* you can always see the last four texts that you saved:

| File | Edit | View | Insert | Fo |

New...	Ctrl+N
Open...	Ctrl+O
Save	Ctrl+S
Save As...	
Print...	Ctrl+P
Print Preview	
Page Setup...	
1 note	
2 Anthem	
3 little lamb	
4 first letter	
Send...	
Exit	

To open the file, simply click on the name in this list. This is also a quick way to open a text on which you want to keep working.

💡 Tip

Finding a File

Are you not able to find a file on the hard disk? When that happens, you can use the *Windows XP* Search function:

🖱️ **Click on** 🏁 start

🖱️ **Click on** 🔍 Search

🖱️ **Click on** → All files and folders

You now see this window:

Here you can type (part of) the name of the file or folder you want.

🖱️ **Click on** Search

Windows XP will search through your hard disk to find names that are the same.

7. Text Layout

Since the arrival of word-processing programs, much has changed in the way that people work with text when making books and magazines. Before word processing was used, a text was written by hand by the author, or typed, and submitted to the publishing house. The typesetter or layout staff took responsibility for the layout of the text. The printing company took care of the printing. Nowadays, word-processing programs and printers are so well developed that the average computer user can take responsibility for the layout of texts and print them on his or her own printer.
A text can be laid out in various ways. By experimenting with types of letters (fonts), letter sizes and a variety of graphic options, including bold and italicized, you can make a text look entirely different.
You can determine the layout of the text after you've typed it, but you can also choose the layout you want before you start typing the text.

In this chapter, you'll learn:

- what laying out a text is
- how to make words bold, italicized, or underlined or give them a different color
- how to apply various types of layout
- how to select a different font
- how to make letters larger or smaller
- how to apply layout options in advance or after the text has been typed

Text Layout

You can layout a text in order to make it clearer or more appealing. When displayed as a simple text, driving directions might look like this:

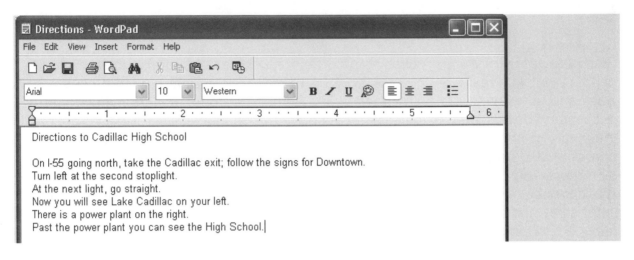

Below, a variety of layout effects have been used, including bold, italics and underlining. An illustration has also been added. Now the same driving directions can look like this:

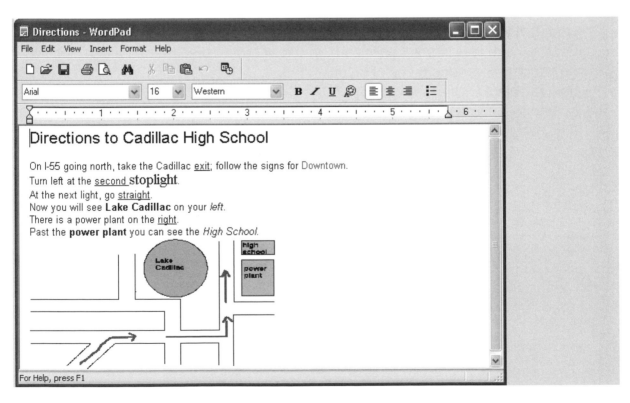

In this chapter, you'll learn how to apply the text layout shown above. In the next chapter, you'll learn how to make a drawing and insert it into a text.

Text Layout in WordPad

☞ **Start** *WordPad* 📖 1.14

In order to practice with text layout, type the following directions:

⌨ **Type:**
Directions to Cadillac High School

On I-55 going north, take the Cadillac exit; follow the signs for Downtown. Turn left at the second stoplight. At the next light, go straight. Now you will see Lake Cadillac on your left. There is a power plant on the right. Past the power plant you can see the High School.

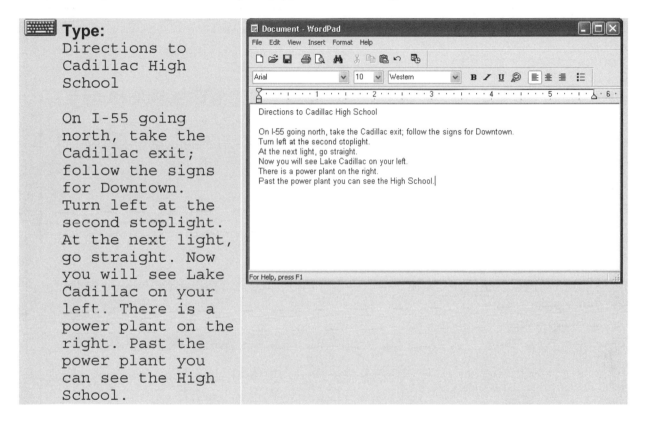

It's a good habit to save a text before you start to change it.

☞ **Save the text and name it** *Directions* 📖 2.1

Now you can change the text. You can start by changing the way the words are displayed. You can underline them, make them bold or italicized, or give them a color.

Selecting Text

You must always select the text before you can change the layout. Certainly you remember the rule:

Select first ... then act.

You learned how to select text in Chapter 5.

Underlining Words

You can start, for example, by <u>underlining</u> words. Nowadays people don't underline words very often, but it's still a way to make a word stand out. First you must select the word.

Select first ... then act.

You can select a word by double-clicking on it.

☞ **Select the word** exit
🖐4.7

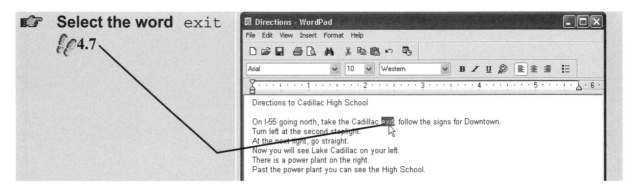

Now that you've selected the word, you can underline it. There are various buttons for text layout.

🖱 **Click on** <u>U</u>

The letter <u>U</u> on this button stands for *Underlined*.

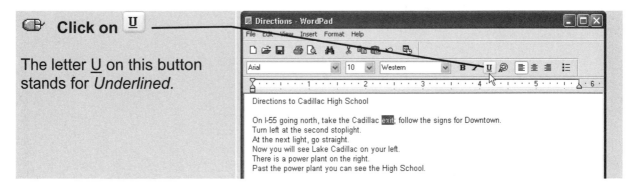

You won't be able to clearly see that the word is underlined until you remove the selection.

🖱 **Click somewhere in the text**

You see that the word exit is now underlined:

Bold Print

You can use the same method to print letters in **bold print**. Letters in bold print clearly stand out in a text. But first you must select the relevant word again:

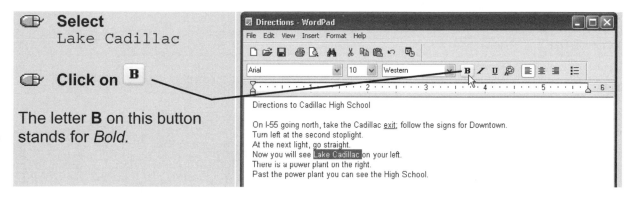

☞ **Select**
  Lake Cadillac

☞ **Click on** **B**

The letter **B** on this button stands for *Bold*.

Lake Cadillac is now displayed in bold print.

Italics

For text layout, *italics* are often used to distinguish names or phrases from the rest of the text. You can also do this in your text layout, but remember:

Select first ... then act.

☞ **Select the word** left
  4.7

☞ **Click on** *I*

The letter *I* on this button stands for *Italics*.

Colored Letters

You can also give letters a different color than black. You'll see the color on your screen, but you can only print it using a color printer. Adding a color is done the same way as the other layout effects.

Select first ... then act.

Select the word Downtown 4.7

Click on

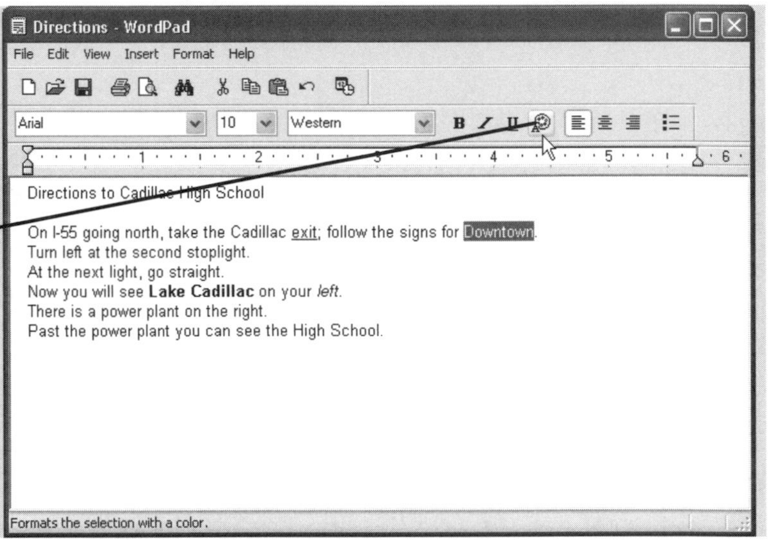

Traffic signs are often green, so you can make the letters green:

Click on Green

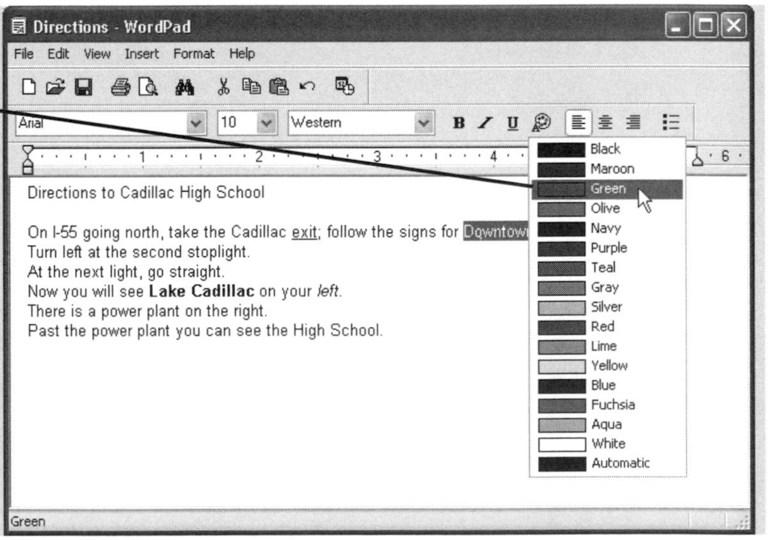

Now the word *Downtown* is green.

Other Types of Layout

You can change the text layout as many times as you want. You can even apply more than one type of layout to a single word: underlining, bold print and italics. Try it:

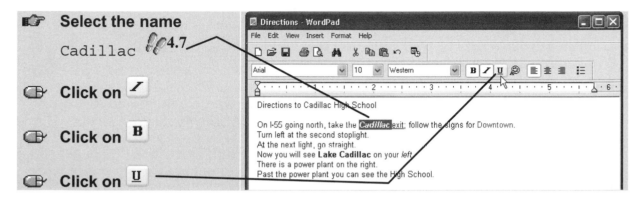

👈 **Select the name**

Cadillac 🐾4.7

🖱 **Click on** *I*

🖱 **Click on** **B**

🖱 **Click on** U̲

Now you can see that Cadillac is underlined and displayed in bold print italics.

Undoing Layout

You can also remove the layout. The layout buttons are like on-and-off buttons. Italics are on or off, for example.

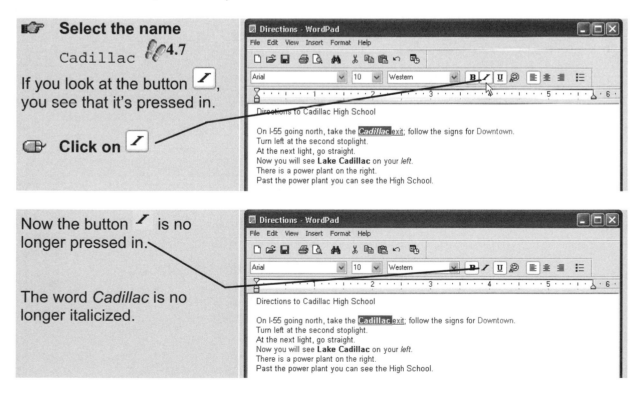

👈 **Select the name**

Cadillac 🐾4.7

If you look at the button *I*, you see that it's pressed in.

🖱 **Click on** *I*

Now the button *I* is no longer pressed in.

The word *Cadillac* is no longer italicized.

You can use this method to change the layout whenever you want.

The Font

There are many, many types of letters. They vary from straight and modern to the classical newspaper print. In *Windows XP*, two types of letters - called fonts - are used as a kind of standard:

- Times New Roman. This is the font that's often used in newspapers.
- **Arial**. This is a *sans-serif* font. That means that there are no little lines or curls on the individual letters.

When you start *WordPad*, the font setting is *Arial*. You can give the entire text a different font. But first, you must select the entire text. *WordPad* has a special command for this.

☞ **Click on** Edit

☞ **Click on** Select All

Now the entire text is selected.

Now you can change the font. This is how:

☞ **Click on** ⌄

You see a list of the various fonts:

You can use the sliding bar to scroll through this list. If you want to see the bottom part of the list, use the button ❯ next to it:

Click on ❯ **at the bottom a few times**

The list will scroll up.

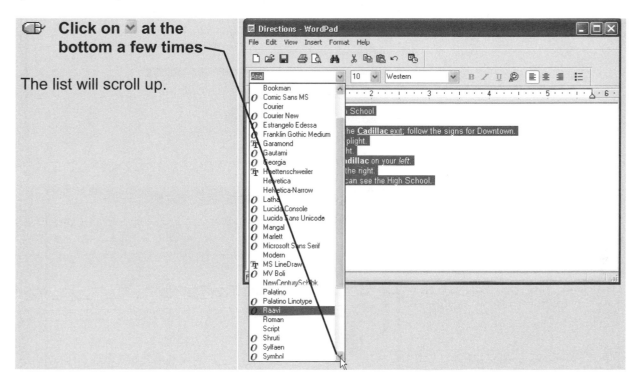

Continue through the list until you find the name *Times New Roman*:

Click on ❯ **as many times as necessary until you can see** Times New Roman

Now you can select this font:

Click on Times New Roman

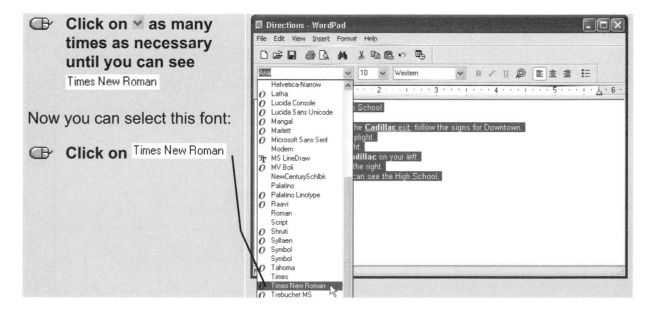

You can see that the font has changed.

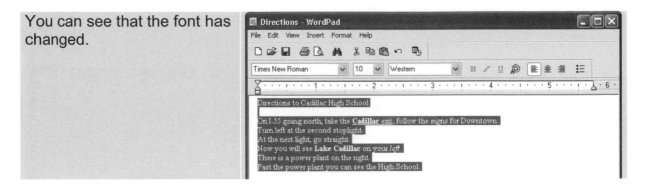

If you don't like this effect, you can always undo it:

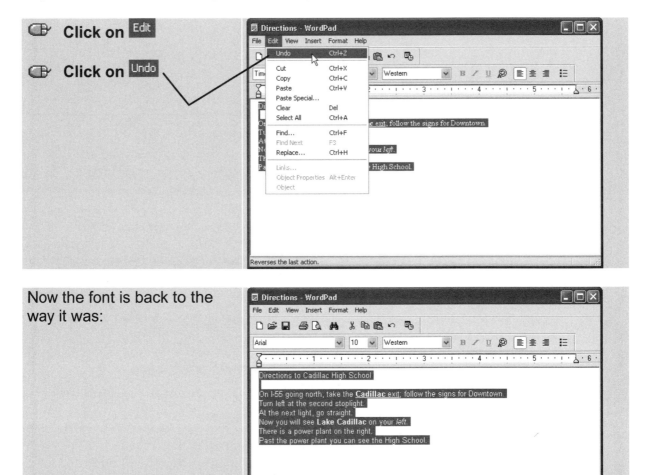

Now the font is back to the way it was:

Normally, the same font will be used for the layout of the entire text. You will only use a different font for a word than for the rest of the text in exceptional cases. But it is possible. You can also change the font for one or more words after you've selected them.

The Font Size

Fonts can be used in various sizes from extremely small to extremely large. You can give a title a larger font size, for example. First you must select the line. This is done by clicking on it three times.

☞ Select the top line
4.9

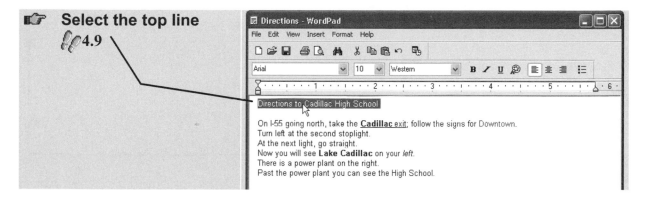

Now you can select the font size. The font size is expressed in a number. The number stands for the number of points used to construct the letters.

Click on ∨

You see a row of numbers.

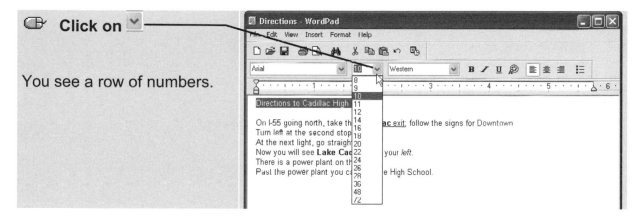

A small number means a small number of points, thus a small letter. The font size that *WordPad* normally uses is relatively small: 10 points. Now you can select a different font size from the list.

Click on 16

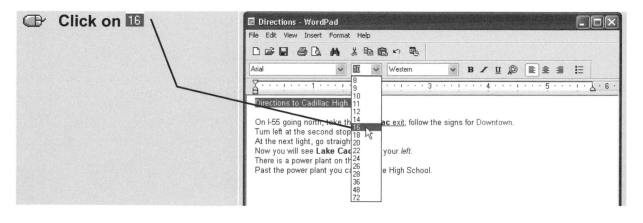

The selected letters are much larger now:

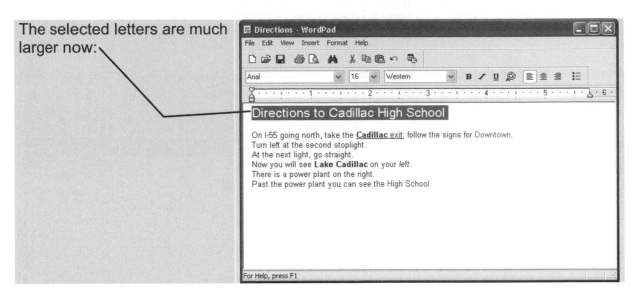

You can change the font size of the entire text, of whole lines, or of individual words this way. Now you need to save the text and start a new one.

☞ **Save the text** ⫽ℓ2.2

☞ **Start a new text** ⫽ℓ2.10

Determining Layout in Advance

Until now, you typed the text first and then changed the layout of some of the words and lines. When starting a new text, you can also choose a different layout before starting, such as a larger font size. That can make it more pleasant for you to work. The standard font size in *WordPad* is relatively small: only 10 points. A 12-point letter is much easier to read on the screen.
If you select a larger font before you start typing your text, it will automatically be used for the rest of the text.

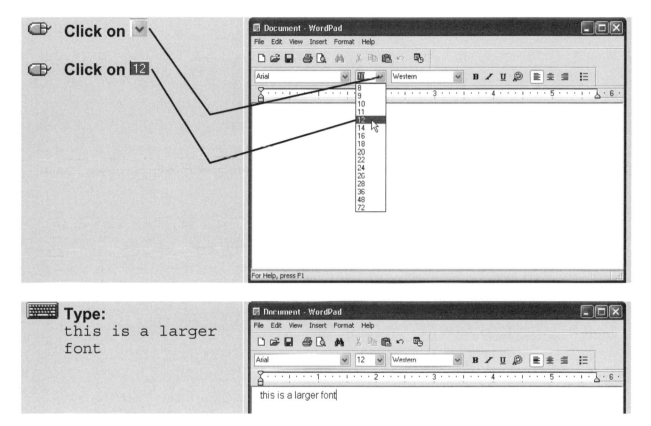

Click on ✓

Click on 12

Type:
this is a larger font

This is how to select a different letter size or font in advance so that you don't have to change them when you're done.

☞ **Start a new text; do not save the changes** 📎1.18

As an exercise, you can finish the layout of the directions.

Exercises

The following exercises will help you master what you've just learned. Have you forgotten how to do something? Use the number beside the footsteps to look it up in the appendix *How Do I Do That Again?*

Exercise: The Directions

✔ Open the text with the name: 📄Directions. 👣**3.1**

✔ Select the word `straight`. 👣**4.7**

✔ Underline the word `straight`. 👣**4.10**

✔ Select the word `second`. 👣**4.7**

✔ Underline the word `second`. 👣**4.10**

✔ Select the word `right`. 👣**4.7**

✔ Underline the word `right`. 👣**4.10**

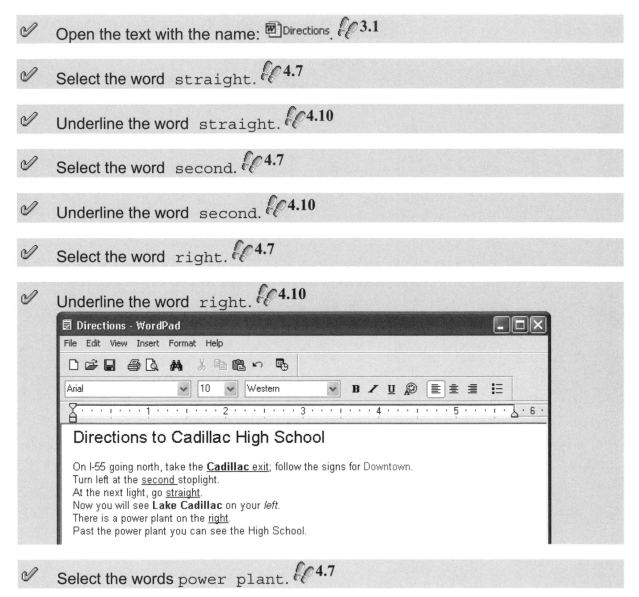

✔ Select the words `power plant`. 👣**4.7**

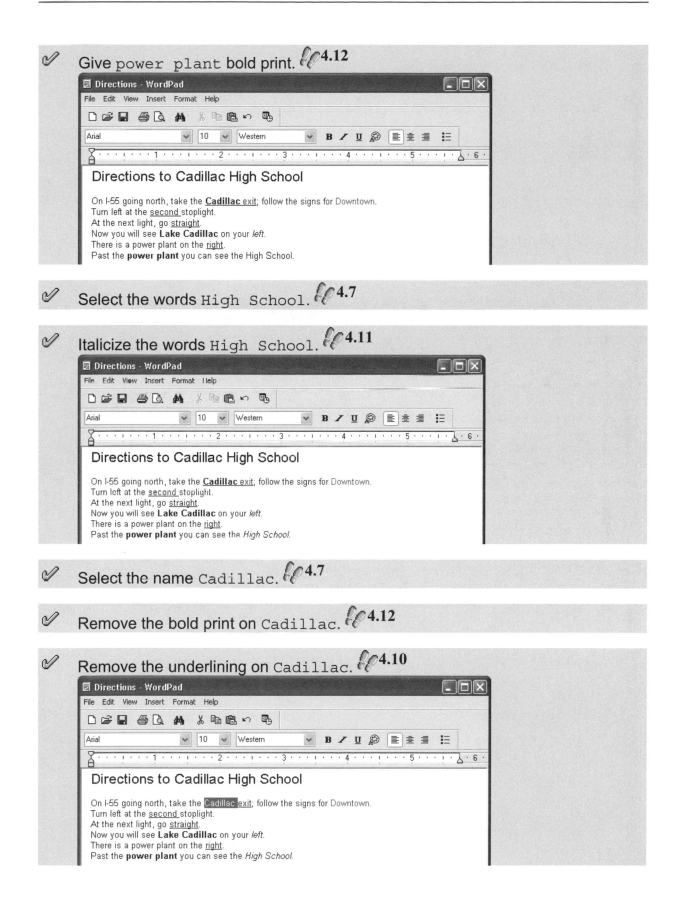

✓ Give power plant bold print. 🐾4.12

✓ Select the words High School. 🐾4.7

✓ Italicize the words High School. 🐾4.11

✓ Select the name Cadillac. 🐾4.7

✓ Remove the bold print on Cadillac. 🐾4.12

✓ Remove the underlining on Cadillac. 🐾4.10

✅ Select the word `stoplight`. 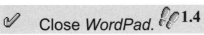4.7

✅ Change the color of the word `stoplight` to blue. 4.13

✅ Make sure that the word `stoplight` is still selected. 4.7

✅ Change the font to *Times New Roman.* 4.14

✅ Make sure that the word `stoplight` is still selected. 4.7

✅ Change the letter size to 14 points. 4.15

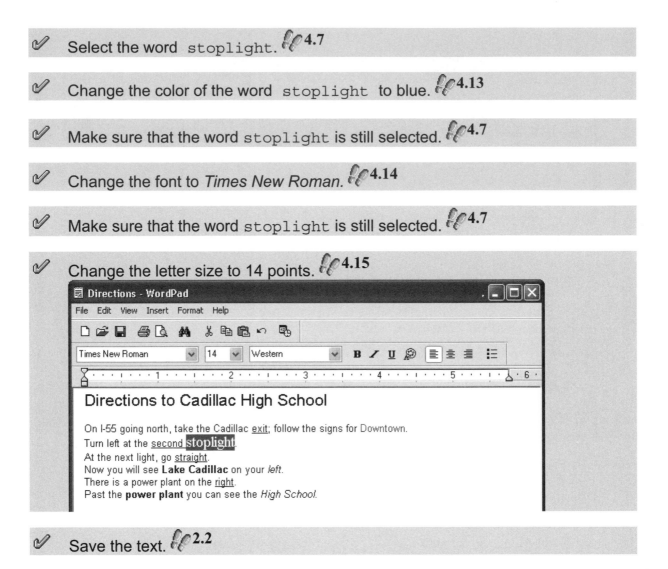

✅ Save the text. 2.2

✅ Close *WordPad.* 1.4

Background Information

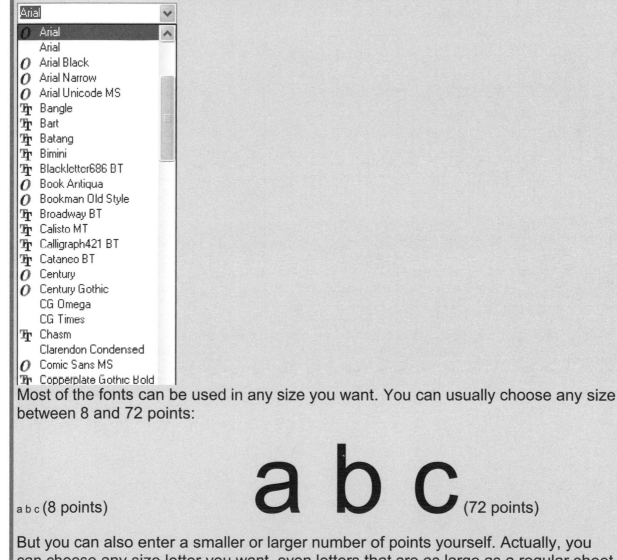

Fonts

A large number of fonts have been developed for the PC. You can see which fonts have been installed on your computer by viewing the list in *WordPad*:

Most of the fonts can be used in any size you want. You can usually choose any size between 8 and 72 points:

a b c (8 points)   a b c (72 points)

But you can also enter a smaller or larger number of points yourself. Actually, you can choose any size letter you want, even letters that are as large as a regular sheet of paper. You can use these large letters if you want to make a poster, for example.

Characters

In addition to the letters of the alphabet, numbers, and punctuation marks, every font also has some symbols that aren't included on the keyboard, for example: ®, ¼ or §:

Character Map		□ □ ⊠

Font : [Arial ▼]   [Help]

!	"	#	$	%	&	'	(	)	*	+	,	-	.	/	0	1	2	3	4
5	6	7	8	9	:	;	<	=	>	?	@	A	B	C	D	E	F	G	H
I	J	K	L	M	N	O	P	Q	R	S	T	U	V	W	X	Y	Z	[	\
]	^	_	`	a	b	c	d	e	f	g	h	i	j	k	l	m	n	o	p
q	r	s	t	u	v	w	x	y	z	{	|	}	~		¡	¢	£	¤	¥
¦	§	¨	©	ª	«	¬	-	®	¯	°	±	²	³	´	µ	¶	·	,	¹
º	»	¼	½	¾	¿	À	Á	Â	Ã	Ä	Å	Æ	Ç	È	É	Ê	Ë	Ì	Í
Î	Ï	Ð	Ñ	Ò	Ó	Ô	Õ	Ö	×	Ø	Ù	Ú	Û	Ü	Ý	Þ	ß	à	á
â	ã	ä	å	æ	ç	è	é	ê	ë	ì	í	î	ï	ð	ñ	ò	ó	ô	õ
ö	÷	ø	ù	ú	û	ü	ý	þ	ÿ	Ā	ā	Ă	ă	Ą	ą	Ć	ć	Ĉ	ĉ

Characters to copy : [   ]   [Select]   [Copy]

☐ Advanced view

U+0021: Exclamation Mark

Besides regular font types, *Windows XP* also has fonts that exist solely of symbols such as √, ©, ♣, ∑, or π.

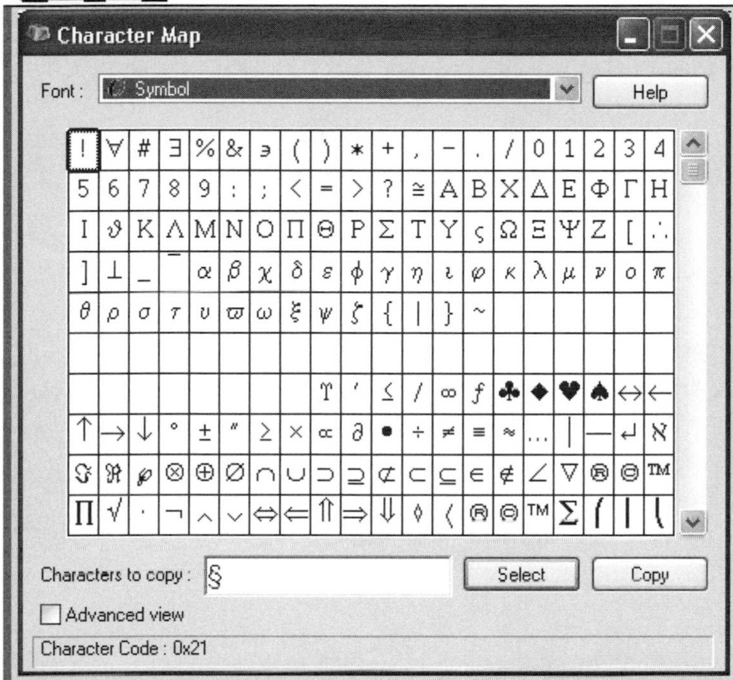

Using the program shown above, *Character Map*, you can insert these symbols into a text or drawing. This is how to start this program if it has been installed on your computer:

Click on 🏁 **start**  , **All Programs**  ▶ , 📁 **Accessories**

Click on 📁 **System Tools**

Click on 📄 **Character Map**

No Need to Type

There are various ways of putting a text into a computer without having to (re)type it yourself.

If a text is *digital*, meaning that it has already been made available for the computer, you can open it on your computer from a diskette or USB memory stick, or via e-mail.

If you have an existing text that's on paper, you can read the text into the computer using a **scanner.**

Many scanners are supplied with what is known as an *OCR program*. OCR is an abbreviation that stands for *Optical Character Recognition*. You lay the paper on the scanner and the OCR program scans it and translates it into text. The text can then be used in a word processing program such as *WordPad* or *Microsoft Word*.

Scanner

Do you not want to type a new text yourself? You can also choose to install a *voice recognition program.*

However, a microphone must be connected to your computer for this. You start the voice recognition program and then speak your text into another program, such as *Microsoft Word*. The program automatically translates your voice into words and sentences, as if you were typing it yourself. This technology is still in its infancy.

Microphone

Tips

💡 Tip

WordPad has three buttons that you can use to work with files.

Commands:

💾   Save a document   `File` , `Save`

📂   Open a document   `File` , `Open...`

🗋   Start a new text   `File` , `New...`

💡 Tip

Using the program *Character Map* you can insert these symbols into a *WordPad* text. This is how to start this program if it has been installed on your computer:

🖰 **Click on** `start` , `All Programs` , `Accessories`

🖰 **Click on** `System Tools` , `Character Map`

☞ **In the** Font: **list, select** `O Symbol`

🖰 **Click on** ♣

🖰 **Click on** `Select`

🖰 **Click on** `Copy`

☞ **Start a new text in *WordPad***

🖰 **Click on** 📋

8. Drawings and Illustrations

Because the speed and capacity of computers is constantly improving, the possibilities for working with graphic illustrations have increased. To an increasing degree, photos used in books and magazines are prepared on computers. You, too, can work with illustrations and photos on your computer. *Windows XP* has a simple drawing program that you can use to make small drawings. The fun thing about programs of this type is that you can change the drawing as many times as you want until you have exactly what you need. A drawing program also has a variety of tools that can help you make your drawing. Even if you couldn't draw a circle on paper with a pencil, you'll be surprised at what you can do with a drawing program. You'll also discover how easy it is to insert your drawing into a text.

In this chapter, you'll learn how to:

- start the program *Paint*
- draw by dragging the mouse
- draw figures
- color figures
- insert text into a drawing
- copy a drawing in *Paint*
- paste the drawing in *WordPad*

Starting Paint

Windows XP has the drawing program *Paint* that you can use to make simple drawings. To practice, you will be making a map to go with the directions. This is how to start the program *Paint:*

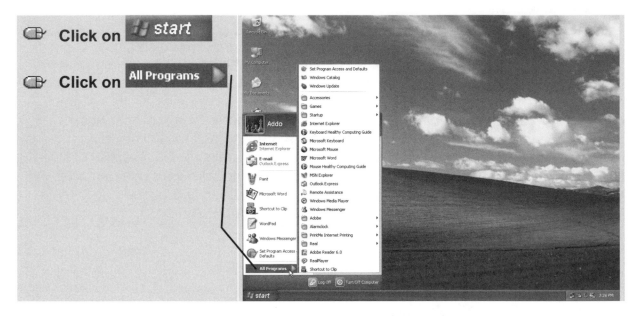

The *Paint* program is located in the folder 🗁 that is named *Accessories*.

Once the program has started, you see this window:

On the left there is a vertical bar with various tools:—

At the bottom you see a bar with colors:—

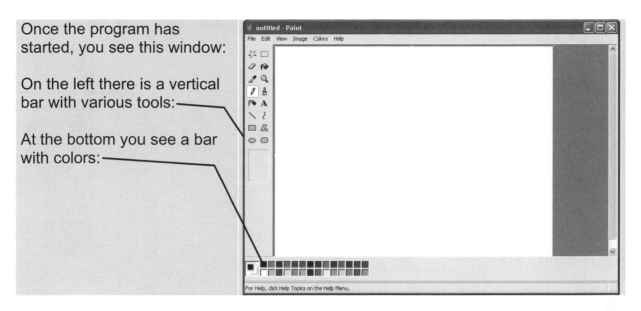

The big white box in the middle is where you'll be drawing.

Drawing by Dragging

Drawing in *Paint* is primarily done by dragging the mouse. Try it:

Move the mouse pointer ✐ **to the white box**—

Press the mouse button

Drag with the mouse

A line is drawn

Release the mouse button

The line is no longer drawn.

As you can see, drawing is relatively simple: if you press the mouse button, you draw. If you release the mouse button, you don't. The line you just drew is black, but you can also select a different color.

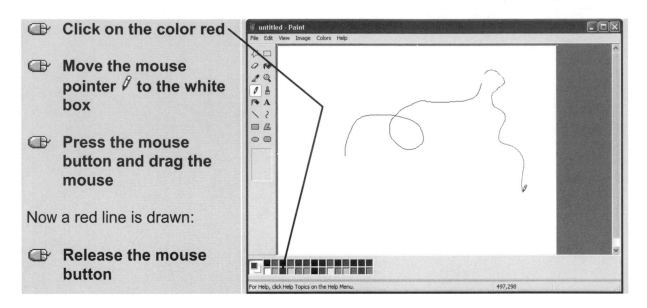

Click on the color red

Move the mouse pointer ℓ to the white box

Press the mouse button and drag the mouse

Now a red line is drawn:

Release the mouse button

Until now in this exercise, you have been drawing with a pencil ℓ, but the program offers many other possibilities.

Drawing Figures

It's not very easy to draw precisely with the mouse. That's why the program offers various tools with which you can draw figures, such as a line, a square or a circle. You can try to draw a square.

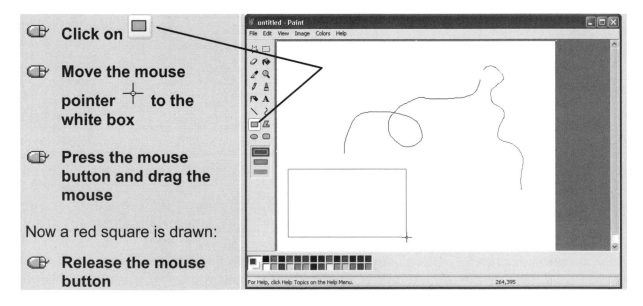

Click on ▣

Move the mouse pointer ┼ to the white box

Press the mouse button and drag the mouse

Now a red square is drawn:

Release the mouse button

It's virtually impossible to draw a straight line with your mouse, which is why the program also has a tool for that.

👆 **Click on**

👆 **Move the mouse**

  pointer ⊹ **to the white box**

👆 **Press the mouse button and drag the mouse**

Now a line is drawn:

👆 **Release the mouse button**

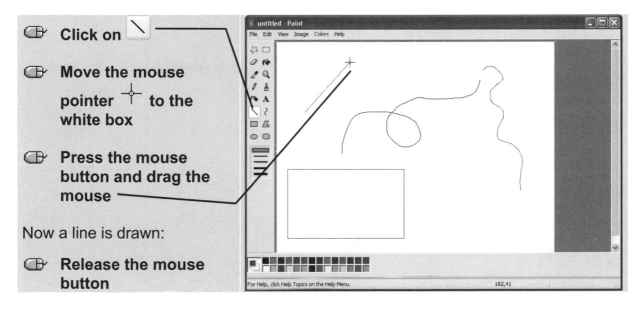

The last tool that you will be trying out is the oval.

👆 **Click on**

👆 **Move the mouse**

  pointer ⊹ **to the white box**

👆 **Press the mouse button and drag the mouse**

Now an oval is drawn:

👆 **Release the mouse button**

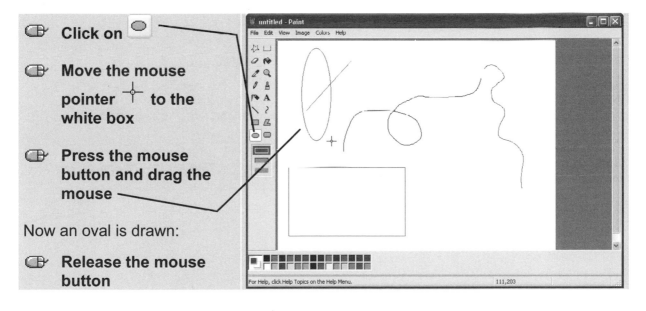

Coloring

Every closed figure can be colored in. *Paint* has yet another special tool for this: the paint can. You can color the square red, for example.

☞ **Click on** 🎨

☞ **Move the mouse to inside the square you've drawn**

☞ **Click with the mouse**

Now the square is colored with red paint:

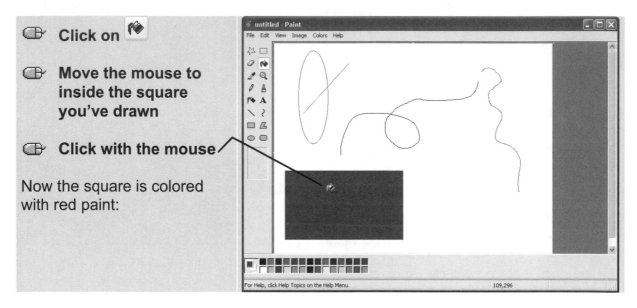

Undoing

Naturally, you might make mistakes in your drawing. Or you don't like the way a figure turned out. Like in the other programs you've worked with, it's easy to undo the last thing you did in *Paint.* Try it:

☞ **Click on** Edit

☞ **Click on** Undo

The red paint colored into the square has disappeared.

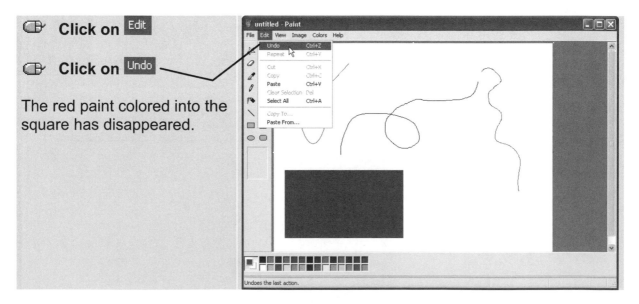

You can undo the last four things you've done this way.

Inserting Text into a Drawing

It's very easy to add a text to your drawing. This is how:

👉 **Click on** **A**

👉 **Move the mouse pointer ⌖ to the white box**

👉 **Press the mouse button and drag the mouse**

Now a rectangle with dotted lines is drawn:

👉 **Release the mouse button**

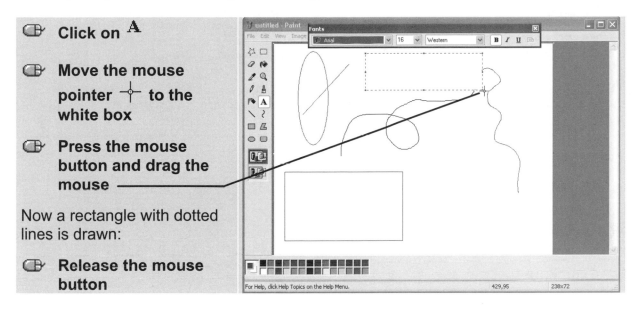

This dotted rectangle is the box in which you'll be typing. The larger you make this box, the more text or the larger the letters that will fit into it. A small box, however, can only contain a bit of text or extremely small letters.

⌨ **Type:** `letters`

The letters appear in the dotted rectangle.

👉 **Click somewhere outside of the rectangle**

The dotted rectangle disappears and the letters are displayed in the drawing.

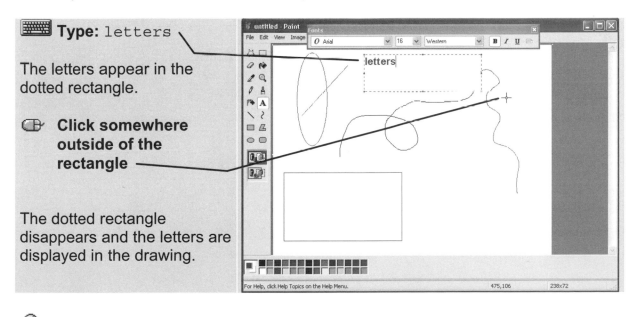

💡 **Tip**

The letters will have the same color as the one you've selected.

The selected color is shown at the bottom left:

Tip

The font, the letter size and the layout can be selected in a separate box:

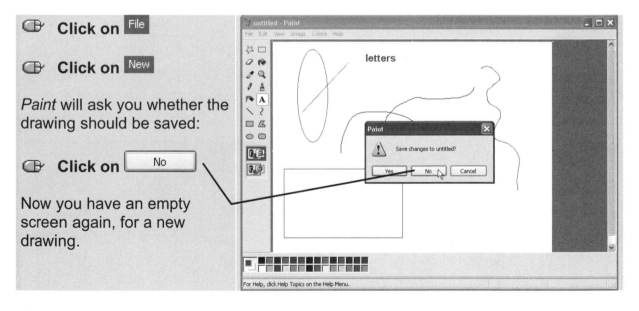

You can change these as long as the dotted rectangle is displayed in the drawing. Once you've clicked outside of the rectangle, the text cannot be changed. You can, of course, undo the typing and type a new text.

A New Drawing

You can start a new drawing in the usual manner:

Click on **File**

Click on **New**

Paint will ask you whether the drawing should be saved:

Click on **No**

Now you have an empty screen again, for a new drawing.

Tip

When you start *Paint*, the tool will always be a **pencil**.

The pencil can be used to draw a thin line with the mouse.
But there is another tool: the **paintbrush**.

You can make thicker lines using the paintbrush.

Exercises

The following exercises will help you master what you just learned. Have you forgotten how to do something? Use the number beside the footsteps to look it up in the appendix *How Do I Do That Again?*

Exercise: The Pencil

✓ Select the color blue. 6.5

✓ Try to draw a face like this one: 6.2

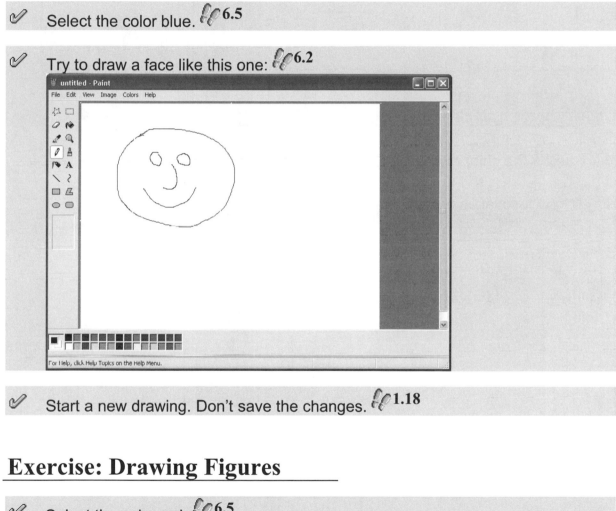

✓ Start a new drawing. Don't save the changes. 1.18

Exercise: Drawing Figures

✓ Select the color red. 6.5

✓ Draw a red rectangle. 6.3

✓ Select the color green. 6.5

✔ Draw straight green lines through the corners of the rectangle. ◀◀**6.4**

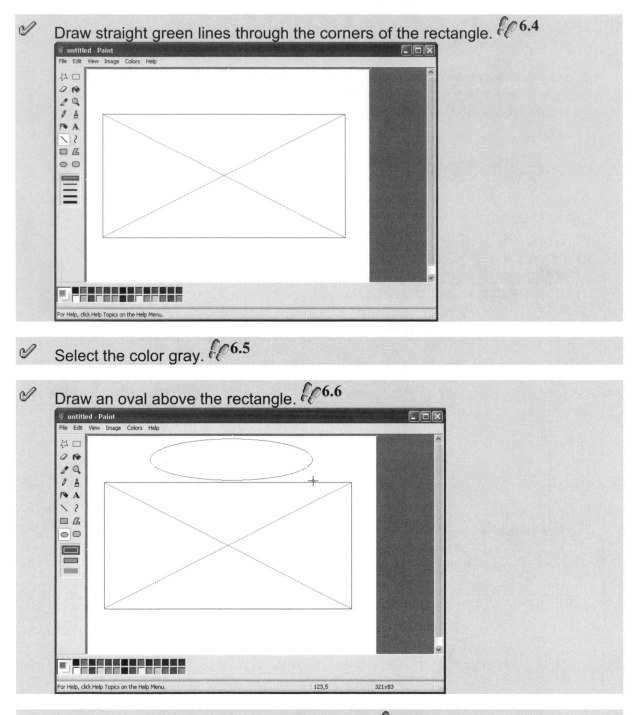

✔ Select the color gray. ◀◀**6.5**

✔ Draw an oval above the rectangle. ◀◀**6.6**

✔ Start a new drawing; don't save the changes. ◀◀**1.18**

Exercise: A Map

You've practiced drawing the various figures. Now you can try to draw a map. It doesn't have to be perfect; you need a drawing to use in the exercises elsewhere in this chapter with the directions you wrote in the previous chapter.

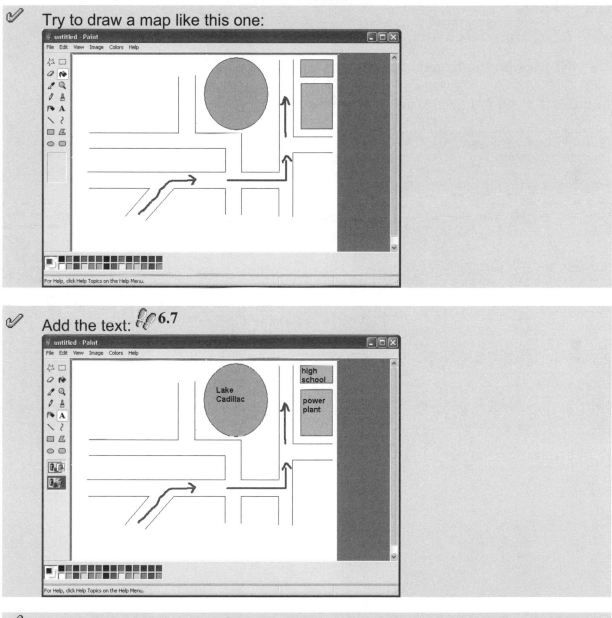

Try to draw a map like this one:

Add the text: 6.7

Save the drawing and name it *map*. *Paint* will automatically select the folder *My Pictures.* 2.1

You've saved the drawing, so you can stop now and continue with this chapter later. Or you can continue now.

Copying in Paint

It's relatively simple to copy a picture in *Paint* and paste it into a *WordPad* text. You can paste the map you drew in the directions that you typed in the previous chapter, for example.

Did you close *Paint*?

☞   **If so, start** 🖐 Paint   👣**6.1**

☞   **Now open the drawing named *map*** 👣**3.1**

In order to copy a drawing, you must select it first.

Select first ... then act.

Paint has another tool for selecting.

🖱 **Click on** ⬚

Now you can select part of the drawing.

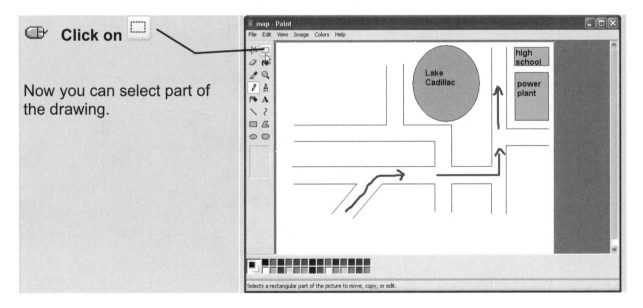

⏚▷ **Move the mouse pointer ⊹ to the top left of the drawing**

⏚▷ **Press the mouse button and drag the mouse to the bottom right** ──────

Now a rectangle with dotted lines is drawn:

⏚▷ **Release the mouse button**

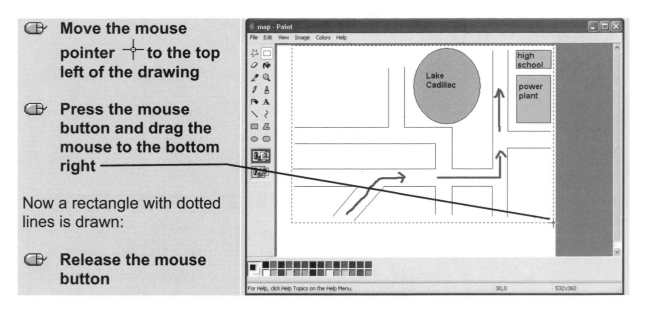

The section inside the dotted lines has now been selected. Now you can copy it.

⏚▷ **Click on** Edit

⏚▷ **Click on** Copy ──

You can't see anything happening, but the drawing has now been copied.

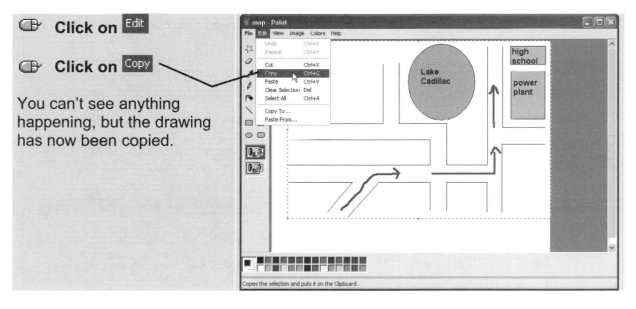

Now you can start *WordPad* and paste the drawing into a text.

Pasting in WordPad

First, start *WordPad*. Then open the directions you typed in the previous chapter.

☞ **Start *WordPad*** 📖 **1.14**

☞ **Open the text named *Directions*** 📖 **3.1**

Pasting is always done at the place where the cursor is. This is why you need to move the cursor to the right place. You see this text with the cursor at the beginning:

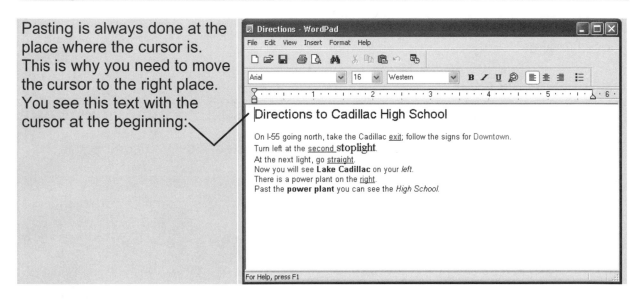

The drawing will come after the text, meaning that you must move the cursor to the bottom of the text.

⌨ **Move the cursor to the bottom of the text**

Now you can paste in the drawing.

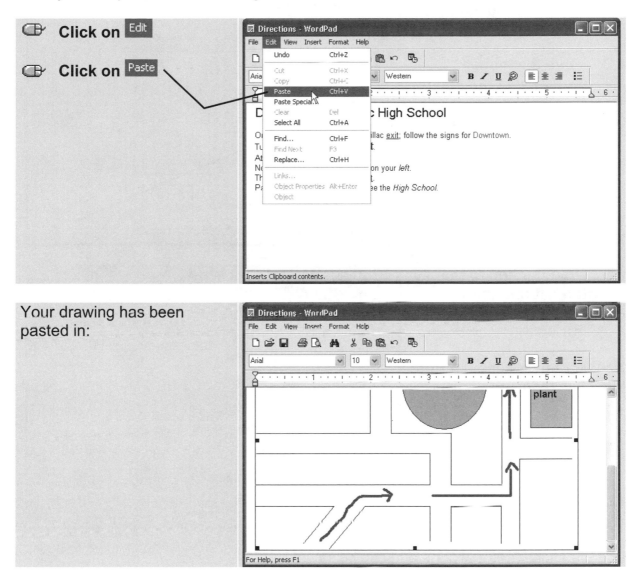

The drawing is a bit big, but it's easy to make it smaller.

Small squares are shown
around the edges of the
drawing:

☞ **Move the mouse
     pointer I to the small
     box at the bottom right**

The mouse arrow changes
into a double arrow ↙.

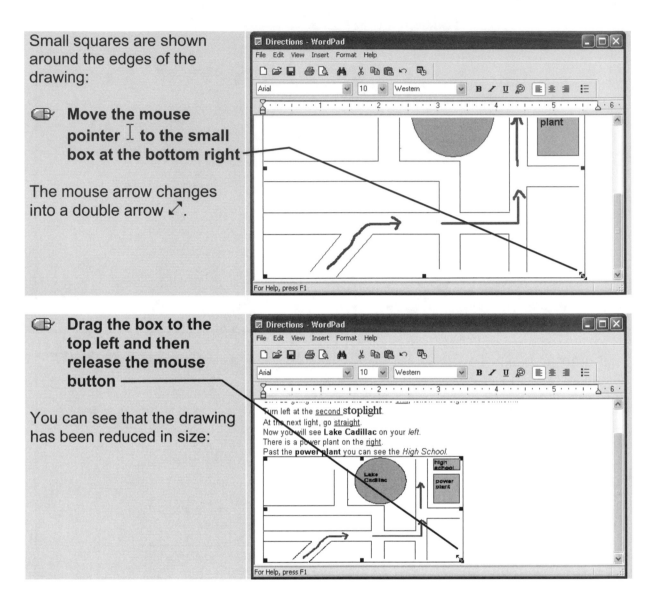

☞ **Drag the box to the
     top left and then
     release the mouse
     button**

You can see that the drawing
has been reduced in size:

The directions are now done and can be saved.

☞ **Save the text** ⅋ **2.2**

💡 **Tip**

In Chapter 10 you'll learn how to send these directions as an attachment to an e-mail.

Background Information

Pixels

Every kind of picture on the computer (drawings or photos) is composed of dots. These dots or points are called *pixels*. A **drawing** made in *Paint* is also composed of pixels. If you click on View , Zoom , Show Grid , you can see the colored dots:

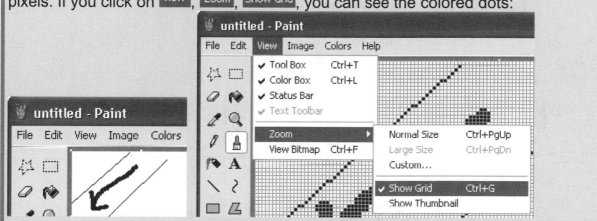

Actually, a drawing is a grid with many dots. A drawing is often referred to as a *bitmap* (a map made up of bits). You will sometimes come across this term in *Windows XP.*

Photos are composed in the same manner.

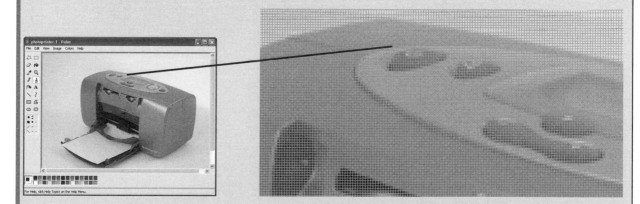

The quality of the photo depends on the number of dots used. If many bits are used for a photo, it will be highly accurate. If not, it will be fuzzier. The quality is also determined by the number of colors used. The more colors used, the more realistic the photo. The number of colors currently used on a regular PC is 16 million. Professional photos, however, use many, many more colors.

Photos

Perhaps you're wondering how you can put a photo on your computer. There are a variety of ways to do this.

A photo that has been printed can be copied using a **scanner**.

The photo is placed under the cover, it is closed and the photo is scanned into the computer. This is also called *digitizing*.

Film negatives can also be scanned, or when the film is developed you can ask to have the photos put on a CD-ROM.

Scanner

The newest way of taking photos, however, does not involve a roll of film or printed photos. The picture is saved digitally. This is done with a **digital camera**.

The camera is connected to the computer with a cable and the photos are transferred directly onto the computer.

The photos can also be saved on a small memory card or stick. The computer can "read" this memory.

Digital camera

Because the Internet is so popular, so are **web cameras** or **webcams**.

These are placed in a fixed position near the computer and a flow of moving video images or individual shots are sent to the computer via a cable. With a simple mouse click, these images can be sent to someone else via the Internet.

Webcam

The Clipboard

When copying and pasting a drawing, you use a clipboard. You can't see the clipboard because it works in the background.

But you should be familiar with the characteristics of the clipboard. You can "clip" a (piece of a) drawing, photo or text to the clipboard. This is done with these two commands:

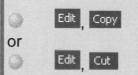

or

Edit , Cut

When you copy or cut something, it's attached to the clipboard:

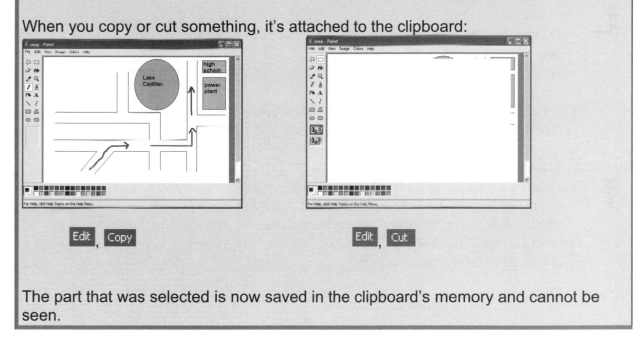

Edit , Copy   Edit , Cut

The part that was selected is now saved in the clipboard's memory and cannot be seen.

The Clipboard

Once a drawing or text has been attached to the clipboard, you can paste it into any other program:

Edit , Paste

When working with the clipboard, you should take notice of the following:

- You can copy or cut something and paste it into a different program, or in the same program.
- You can copy or cut something and paste it into the same drawing or text if you want.
- Once something is on the clipboard, you can paste it once, twice or even a thousand times.
- You can only put one thing at a time on the clipboard. If you cut or copy a second drawing or text, it will be placed on the clipboard.
- If nothing has been selected, the commands Copy and Cut in the menu are gray. You can't use them:

Edit	View	Insert	Format	Help
Undo			Ctrl+Z	
Cut			Ctrl+X	
Copy			Ctrl+C	
Paste			Ctrl+V	
Paste Special...				
Clear			Del	
Select All			Ctrl+A	

- If there's nothing on the clipboard, the command Paste in the menu is gray. You can't use it:

Edit	View	Insert	Format	Help
Undo			Ctrl+Z	
Cut			Ctrl+X	
Copy			Ctrl+C	
Paste			Ctrl+V	
Paste Special...				
Clear			Del	
Select All			Ctrl+A	

Tips

Tip

Using the Text Box A in Paint
The shape of the dotted rectangle determines how the text will fit into it:

If the dotted rectangle is long:

> This text fits this box.

If the dotted rectangle is narrow:

> This
> text fits
> this
> box.

Tip

Have you selected the line ╲ , the square ▢ or the oval ◯ tool?

Then at the bottom of the toolbar, you can select a thin or thick line:

Tip

Are you using the paintbrush 🖌 tool?
Then at the bottom of the toolbar, you can select the type of line that will be drawn:

Tip

Do you want to erase part of the drawing?
Paint has a special eraser for this:

☞ **Click on** ⬦ **and erase by dragging the mouse**

Tip

Do you want to select the entire drawing?
There is a special command for this:

☞ **Click on** Edit / Select All

💡 **Tip**

Internet Explorer 7
In the next chapter you will need to be running the program *Internet Explorer 7* on your computer. *Internet Explorer* version 7 was released in January 2007 by *Microsoft* via Automatic Update to all *Windows XP* Service Pack 2 users. If you do not have **Automatic Updates** (the latest security updates for the *Windows* operating system and other Microsoft products you have installed) turned on in your settings of *Control Panel* than it is possible that you have not yet received the new version of *Internet Explorer 7*. In that case you will first need to download and install version 7 on your computer.

This can be a rather daunting task for the beginning computer user. You may want to seek help by going to your computer dealer or by requesting assistance from someone you know who has experience with computers.
On the webpage **www.visualsteps.com/ie7install** you will find instructions for downloading and installing *Internet Explorer 7*. If you are not sure which version of *Internet Explorer* is running on your computer, you can find out by going through the following process. Check which version is installed:

👆 **Double-click on** [Internet Explorer icon] **on the** *Desktop*

You do not need an Internet connection.
If you see a dial-up Internet connection window such as this:

👆 **Click on** [Work Offline]

You will now see the *Internet Explorer* window.

If the top section of the window looks like this, you have *Internet Explorer* version 7:

In this case you can proceed with chapter 9.

If the top section of the window looks like this, you have *Internet Explorer* version 6:

In this case you will first need to install *Internet Explorer* version 7 on your computer.

9. Surfing the Internet

The Internet consists of millions of computers that are all interconnected. The *World Wide Web* is one of the most exciting parts of the Internet. *World Wide Web* means exactly what it says: a web of computers where an infinite amount of information is located regarding every imaginable topic. No matter where you are in the world, you can access that information with your computer.

On the Internet, a source of information is called a *website*. It is a site somewhere on the Web. Within the website, you can browse from one page to another by clicking with your mouse. You can even jump from one website to another. This is called *surfing*. The type of program you need to surf the Internet, is called a *browser*. You might browse through a printed catalog, but these days you can also *browse* just as easily through the company's online catalog.

In order to get on the Internet, you must initiate a connection with a computer that is permanently connected to the Internet. This is done by means of an *Internet Service Provider* (ISP). If you want to use the provider's services, you must subscribe to them or pay for them in another way. The provider then assigns you a *username* and a *password*. The username and password will give you access to the Internet.

If you are connected to the Internet, you are *online*. In this chapter, first you will learn to go *online* and then how to *surf*.

In this chapter, you'll learn how to:

- start *Internet Explorer*
- contact your Internet Service Provider
- use a web address
- browse forward and backward
- save a web address
- use a *favorite*
- stop using the Internet

➡ **Please note:**

For the exercises in this chapter, you must have an Internet connection that works. If necessary, contact your Internet Service Provider or your computer supplier.

Some Information First: The Modem

The Modem
Understandably, the telephone network is used to connect computers together that can be hundreds or thousands of miles apart. After all, nearly everyone has a telephone. It's also not uncommon for cable television providers to offer Internet services, using their cable network to connect to the Internet.
In order to connect to the Internet via the telephone line or cable, you need a special piece of equipment: the **modem.** A modem makes it possible for your computer to communicate with the Internet Service Provider. There are two different types of modems: internal and external.

An **external modem** is a separate box that is connected to your computer with a cable.
Another cable leads from the modem to the plug for the telephone line or the cable connection.

Nearly all new computers, however, have a modem that is built in. This is called an **internal modem**.
The only thing you see of the modem is a contact point for a telephone plug or the cable connection, located at the back of your computer.

Modems that are connected to the telephone line also have a cable that leads to the telephone's plug. Sometimes a double plug is used, so that your telephone can remain plugged into the same contact point.

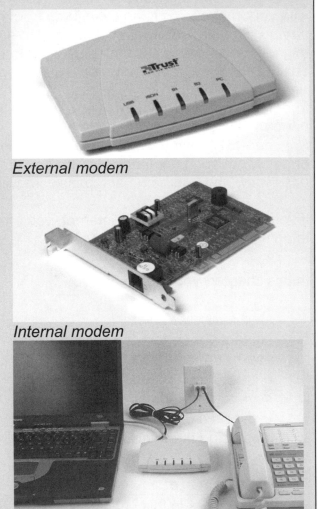

External modem

Internal modem

Laptop computer with external modem and double plug

Is Your Modem Ready?

It's important for you to make sure that your modem is ready before you continue with this chapter.

 Check to make sure your modem is connected to the telephone or cable network

Do you have an external modem?
 If so, turn the modem on

Do you have an internal modem?
 If so, you don't need to take any action

Starting Internet Explorer

The program that is used to connect to the Internet in *Windows XP* is called *Internet Explorer.*
This is how to start the program:

Double-click on

The program will start, after which an Internet connection can be established.

If you are using *dial-up networking* to connect to the Internet, you will see a *Dial-up Connection* window. If you have an Internet access subscription, your ISP has given you a **username** and a **password**. If everything's set up properly, both of these will already be displayed in the window.

Are your username and
password not displayed?

⌨ **In that case, type your
username and
password in the
appropriate boxes**

Are your username and
password displayed?

🖱 **Click on [Connect]**

> **Dial-up Connection**   ☒
>
> Select the service you want to connect
> to, and then enter your user name and
> password.
>
> Connect to: AOL ▾
>
> User name: XXXXXX
>
> Password: •••••
>
> ☐ Save password
>
> ☐ Connect automatically
>
> [Connect] [Settings...] [Work Offline]

Take note:
If you are connected to the internet by cable or DSL, then this Dial-Up Connection screen will **not** appear. Your computer is already connected to the internet. In this case, you can continue on page 226.

Contacting Your Internet Service Provider

Now your computer will contact your ISP using the modem. If your modem is connected to the telephone line, the modem goes through the following steps:

- the modem dials the number of the internet provider
- then it connects to your ISP's computer
- your computer sends your username and password to the ISP's computer
- the ISP's computer checks your username and password
- and then gives you access to the Internet

If your modem is connected to the telephone line, you'll usually hear quite a bit of beeping and humming while this is going on. If you have a cable, ISDN or DSL connection, the process doesn't make noise.

You can follow the computer
as it goes through the steps
in the window:

> Dialing...1-456-456-4556

Once you're connected to the Internet, a home page will be displayed in the *Internet Explorer* window.
This is usually a page of the company that made *Internet Explorer, Microsoft*.

At the right in the taskbar, you see an icon with two

computers , indicating that you are *online*:

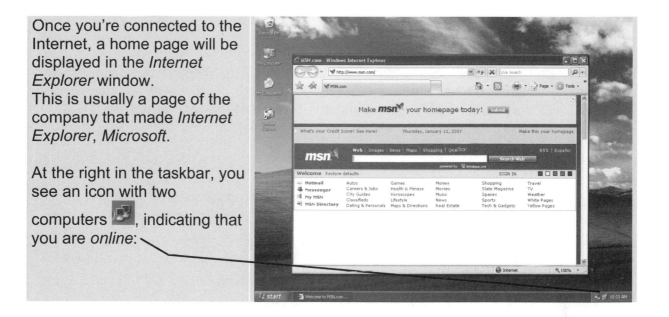

The modem is busy doing something if the computer displays in this icon  are blinking.

⇨ **Please note:**

The start page on your computer may not be the same as the one in the illustration. You might, for example, see a start page that someone else has specified in your settings.

✖ **HELP! No connection?**

Are you not connected to the Internet?
This could be because your ISP's number is "busy":

```
Dialing...
Dialing...
Dialing...
Unable to establish a connection.
```

When that happens, try again later.

✖ **HELP! Still no connection?**

After trying to connect to the Internet a number of times, you may still not be able to. When this happens, it's usually because the settings on your computer are not correct. Contact your ISP to fix the problem.

Typing an Address

Every website has its own web address on the *World Wide Web*. These are the addresses that start with www that you see everywhere.
You can use these addresses to find a website on one of the many Internet computers. The web address of the website for this book is:

www.visualsteps.com

☞ **Click in the address bar at the top left of the window**

Now you can type the web address in this box:

⌨ **Type:**
www.visualsteps.com

⌨ **Press** Enter

After a few moments, you see the opening page for this website:

This website is updated frequently. You may see other pictures in your window.

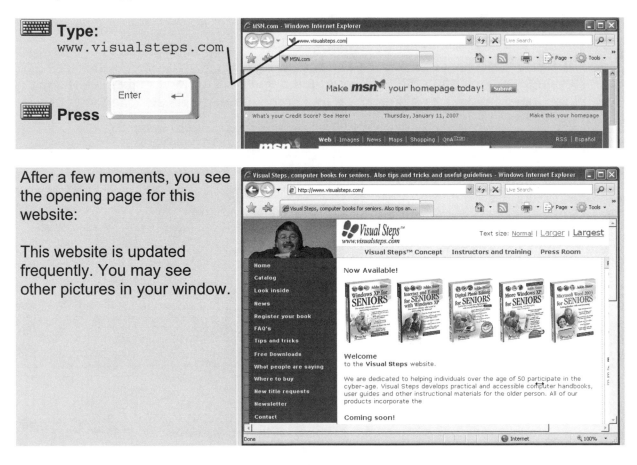

Wrong Address

It's only logical that typing errors can be made when typing an address, or that a certain address no longer exists. This is especially true because the Internet is highly dynamic, changing every day. Private individuals often regularly change their web addresses. Sometimes you'll see an address that starts with **http://**. That's additional information, indicating that the address is for a website. With *Internet Explorer*, you don't need to type in **http://**. The program automatically understands that you want a website and will add it to the address.

When typing a web address, you should take note of the following:

> Make sure that any dots (.) or forward slashes (/) are typed in the correct places. If they aren't, you'll receive an error message.
>
> Never type spaces in a web address.

If even one dot is missing, an error message will appear. Try it:

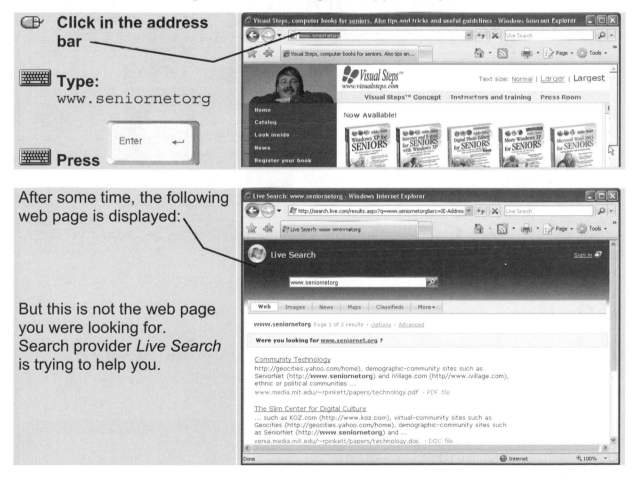

Click in the address bar

Type:
www.seniornetorg

Press Enter

After some time, the following web page is displayed:

But this is not the web page you were looking for.
Search provider *Live Search* is trying to help you.

Live Search asks: **Were you looking for www.seniornet.org ?** *Live Search* has made this assumption because the address you typed - **www.seniornetorg** - was wrong. The dot before **org** is missing.

The correct address for the *SeniorNet* website is: **www.seniornet.org**
Try the correct address:

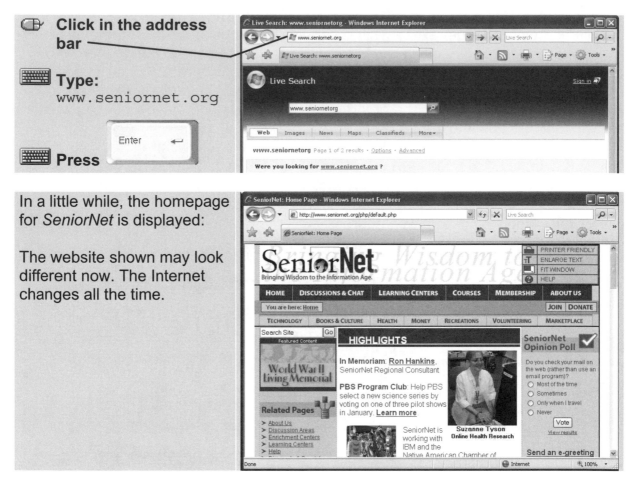

As you've discovered, forgetting even one dot can mean that the program can't find the website you want.

Refreshing a Page

Sometimes a page is not displayed on your screen as it should be. When that happens, you can tell *Internet Explorer* to get the page again: to *refresh* it. Just watch what happens:

Everything that's shown on your screen must be sent in through the telephone line or the cable. That takes time. Sometimes it will seem like nothing's happening. But there is a way to see that *Internet Explorer* is busy doing what you asked it to:

At the bottom of the screen, the green bar indicates that information is being received:

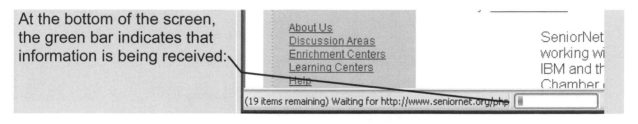

Not all information is immediately shown on your screen; it takes some time to show the entire page.

Forward and Backward

You don't need to retype the web address of a website if you want to go back to it. *Internet Explorer* has a number of buttons that help you to navigate over the Internet.

At the top left of the window, click on

The website you viewed before the current one will be opened.

What you see now is the web page where search provider *Live Search* was helping you:

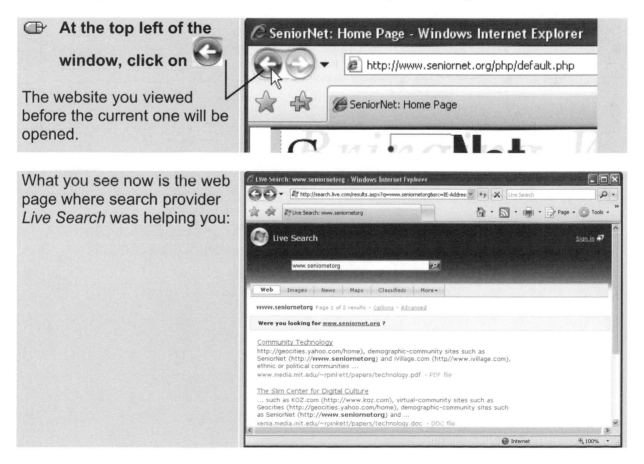

Perhaps you noticed how quickly this is done. *Internet Explorer* retains the websites you recently visited in its memory so that you can quickly look at them again without needing all of the information sent over the telephone line or cable.

Click two more times on

Now the website you first visited will be displayed.

Once again, the start page is displayed:

Now you can no longer browse back. That's because this was the first website you opened.

The button is gray and can no longer be used:

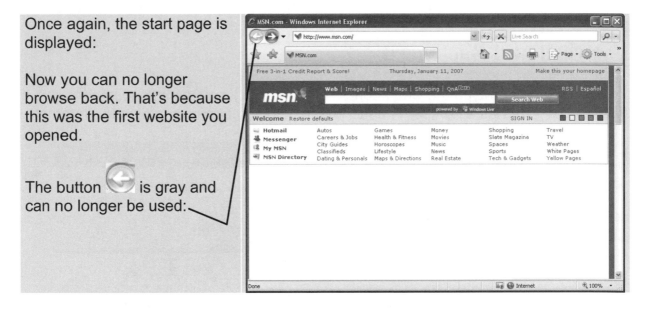

You can, however, browse the other way. There's a special button for this as well.

Click on

Now you see the same website on the screen as you did before:

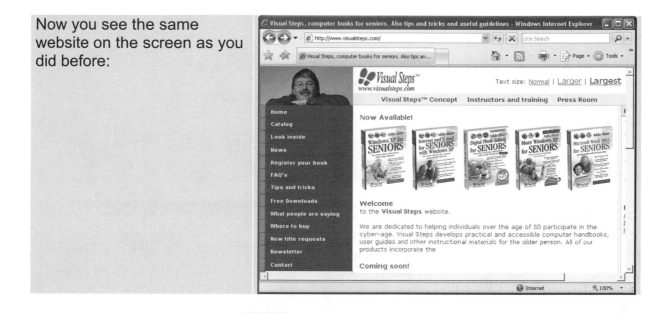

As you've seen, the buttons can easily be used to switch between the websites you've viewed. This is called "surfing" the Internet.
However, these websites will not remain in memory forever. When you close *Internet Explorer,* the websites will be removed from the browser's memory.

Clicking to Browse

Every website has a page with a table of contents of the topics you can find on the site. So does this website. You can see the list of topics on the left. By clicking on a topic, you can go to another page.

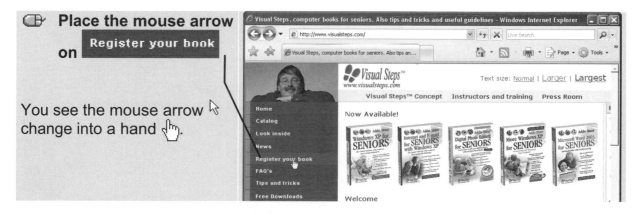

Whenever the mouse arrow changes into a hand, you can click. It may change on a button, but it can also change somewhere in the text or over a picture.
A word, button or picture on which you can click is called a **link**. Sometimes it's also called a **hyperlink**.

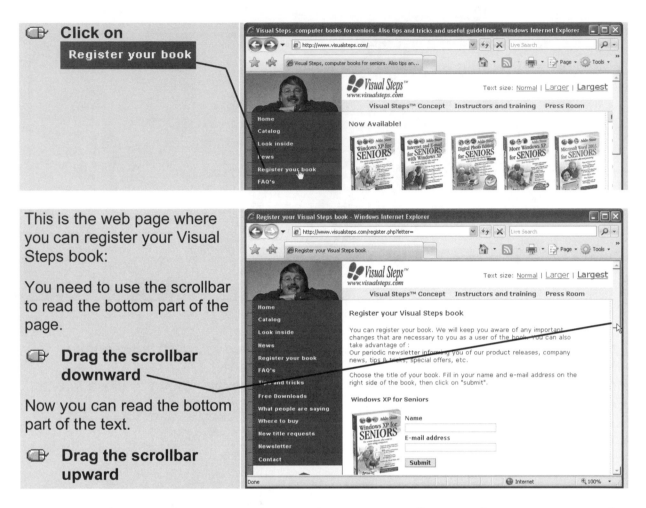

Click on **Register your book**

This is the web page where you can register your Visual Steps book:

You need to use the scrollbar to read the bottom part of the page.

Drag the scrollbar downward

Now you can read the bottom part of the text.

Drag the scrollbar upward

A good website is made in such a way that you can easily move from one page to the next without getting lost. Most websites, for example, have a button marked *Home* or *Start* that when clicked will return you to the website's home page.

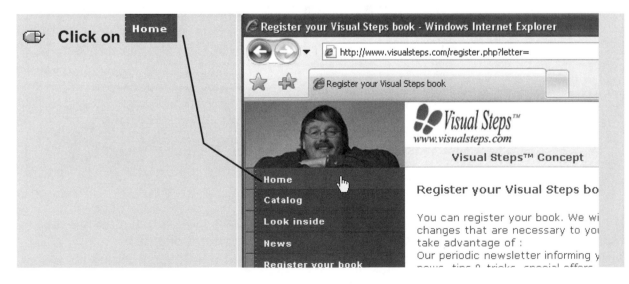

Click on **Home**

Once again, the homepage is displayed.

Printing a Web Page

It's not always easy to read a web page on your screen, especially if it contains a lot of text. You can always choose to print the page and read it later.

No printer?

If you don't have a printer, you can skip this section.

☞ **Make sure the printer is turned on**

At the top right of the window:

☞ **Click on** [printer icon]

Shortly thereafter, the page will be printed.

Saving a Web Address

If you find an interesting website, you can save its address. Then you'll always be able to quickly open the site without having to type the address.
Websites for which you have saved the address are called **Favorites** in *Internet Explorer.*
You can only save an address of a website while it is being displayed. In this example, this is the *Visual Steps* website.

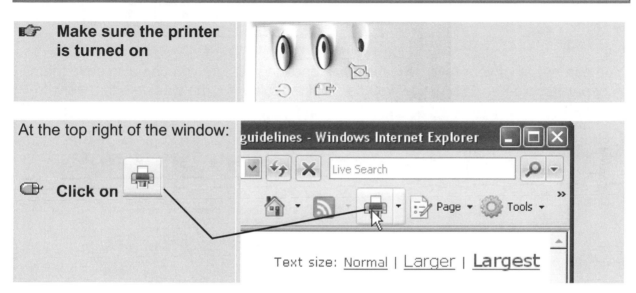

At the top left of the window:

☞ **Click on** [star icon]

A menu appears:

☞ **Click on** Add to Favorites...

Now you see a small window on the top of the web page in which the name has already been inserted:

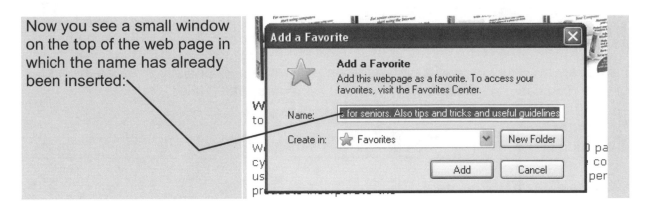

You can put all of your favorite websites in one long list, but you can also save them in separate folders. To practice, you can make a folder for the websites that go with this book.

☞ **Click on** New Folder

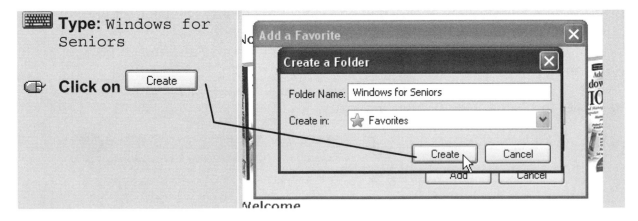

A new window appears on top of the others. Now you can type in the name you want to give the new folder.

⌨ **Type:** Windows for Seniors

☞ **Click on** Create

Now your new folder has been given a name.

You see the new folder. It's already been opened for you:

☞ **Click on** Add

The Favorite will be saved in your new folder.

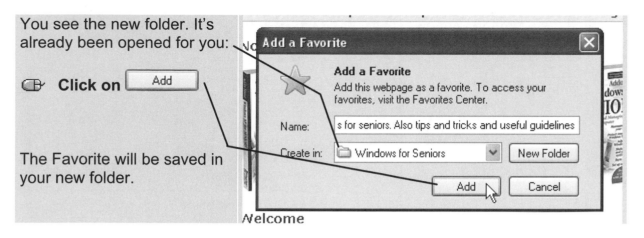

Now you can check to make sure that you can quickly open this favorite website.

The Home Button

To see how a Favorite works, start by going to a different website. You can go to your homepage, for example. This is the page that's automatically opens when you start *Internet Explorer*. There's a special *Home* button for this.

In the top right area of the window:

☞ **Click on**

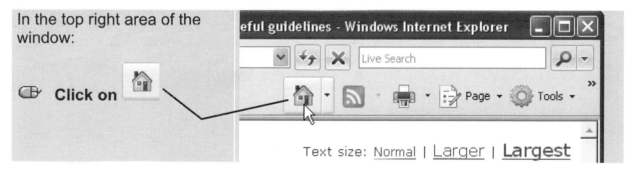

Your homepage is displayed. Now you can open your Favorite.

Opening a Favorite

This is how to quickly open one of your favorite websites:

At the top left of the window:

☞ **Click on**

On the left side of the window a white pane is opened:

👆 **Click on** ⭐ Favorites

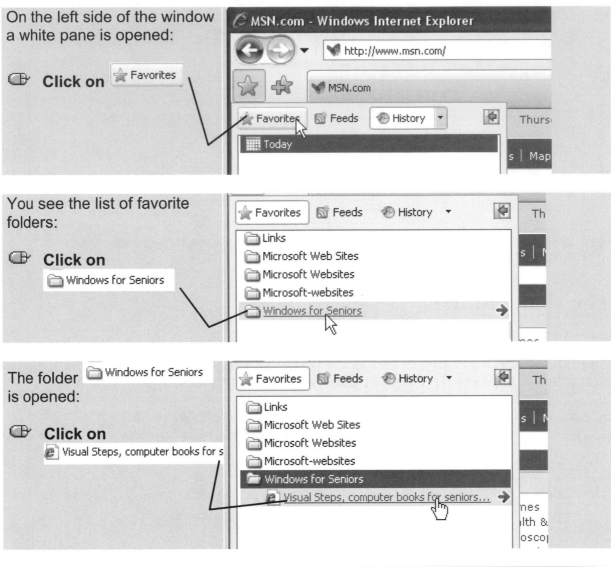

You see the list of favorite folders:

👆 **Click on** 📁 Windows for Seniors

The folder 📁 Windows for Seniors is opened:

👆 **Click on** 🔲 Visual Steps, computer books for s

The saved favorite website appears:

Internet Explorer remembers your Favorites, even after you have closed the program.

Without having to remember complicated web addresses, these references to your favorite websites make it possible to quickly return to them at any given time.

Disconnecting from the Internet

If you have a common analog dial-up connection to the Internet, you have to disconnect each time you stop using the Internet. No other calls can come through to you as long as you're connected to the Internet.
If you have a broadband connection like DSL or cable, you are always connected to the Internet, whether you are using the web or not. You do not have to disconnect.

You can close the *Internet Explorer* window and disconnect this way:

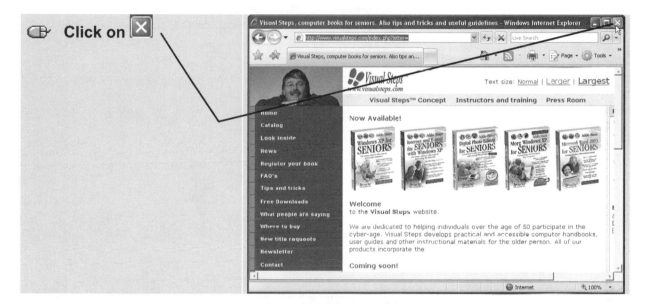

If you have a dial-up connection to the Internet, when you see this window you can disconnect:

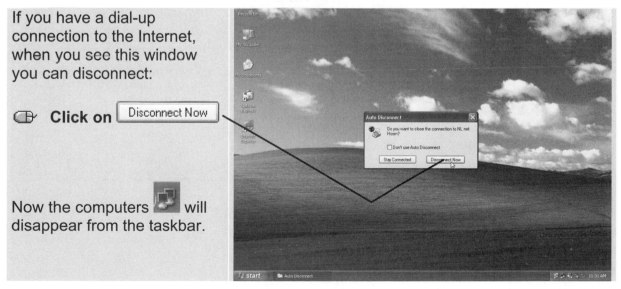

Now the computers will disappear from the taskbar.

If you have a broadband connection such as DSL or cable you will not see a window

like above. You will still see the computers on the taskbar because you are continuously online.

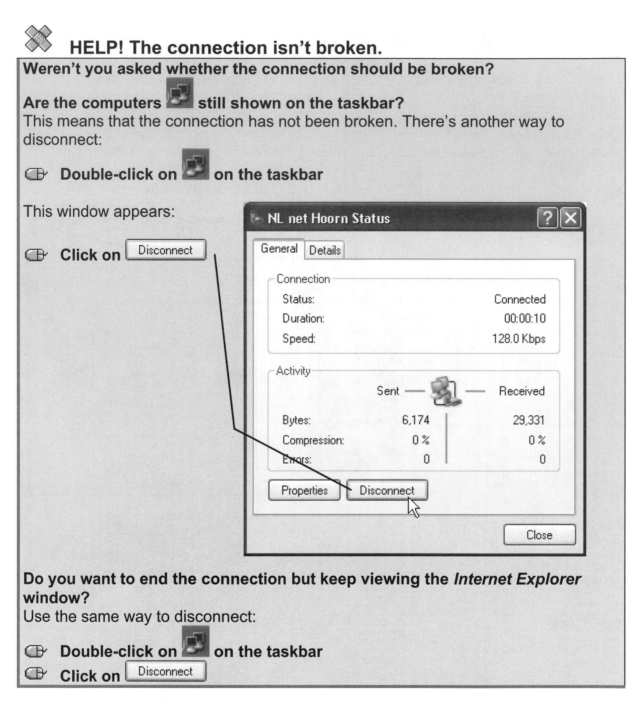

⊗ **HELP! The connection isn't broken.**

Weren't you asked whether the connection should be broken?

Are the computers 🖧 still shown on the taskbar?
This means that the connection has not been broken. There's another way to disconnect:

👆 **Double-click on 🖧 on the taskbar**

This window appears:

👆 **Click on ⌷ Disconnect ⌷**

Do you want to end the connection but keep viewing the *Internet Explorer* window?
Use the same way to disconnect:

👆 **Double-click on 🖧 on the taskbar**
👆 **Click on ⌷ Disconnect ⌷**

You can practice what you've learned with the following exercises.

Exercises

The following exercises will help you master what you've just learned. Have you forgotten how to do something? Use the number beside the footsteps to look it up in the appendix *How Do I Do That Again?*

Exercise: SeniorNet Favorite

In this exercise, you'll open the *SeniorNet* website and add it to your Favorites.

✔ Start *Internet Explorer*. 7.1

✔ If necessary: connect to the Internet. 7.3

✔ Type the Internet address: www.seniornet.org 7.4

✔ Browse through the *SeniorNet* website.

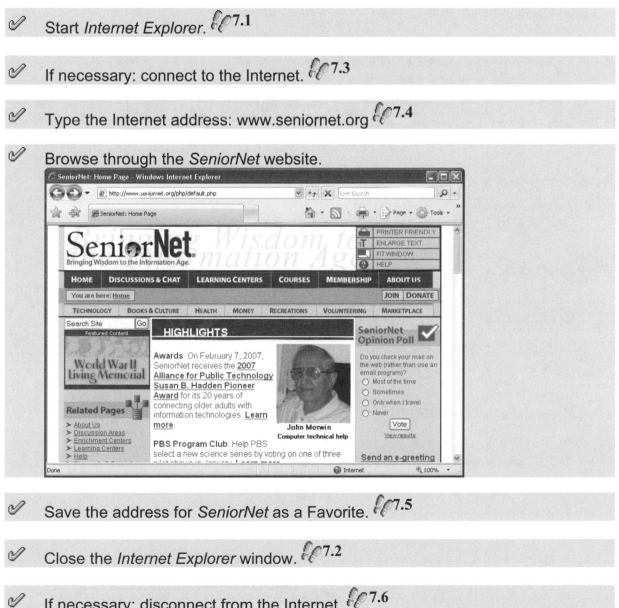

✔ Save the address for *SeniorNet* as a Favorite. 7.5

✔ Close the *Internet Explorer* window. 7.2

✔ If necessary: disconnect from the Internet. 7.6

Exercise: Surfing

Going from one website to another is also called surfing. In this exercise you'll surf among the sites you visited earlier.

✔ Start *Internet Explorer.* 🦶7.1

✔ If necessary: connect to the Internet. 🦶7.3

✔ Using *Favorites,* open the website *visualsteps.com* 🦶7.7

✔ Using *Favorites,* open the website *SeniorNet.* 🦶7.7

✔ Type the address for the Public Broadcasting Service website: *www.pbs.org* 🦶7.4

✔ Now go back to *SeniorNet.* 🦶7.8

✔ Go back to the website *visualsteps.com* 🦶7.8

✔ Now go back to *SeniorNet.* 🦶7.9

✔ Go back to the Public Broadcasting Service website. 🦶7.9

✔ Now go back to the homepage. 🦶7.10

✔ Close *Internet Explorer.* 🦶7.2

✔ If necessary: disconnect from the Internet. 🦶7.6

Background Information

Why do I have to wait so long sometimes?
Sometimes it takes quite a long time for the page you want to be displayed on your screen. How quickly or slowly this goes depends on a number of things:

- Modems can have various speeds. The faster the speed of the modem, the faster the text and pictures are sent. The speed of the connection type also plays an important part. To date, a modem connected via the normal telephone line is the slowest type. Other types of connections, such as cable and DSL, are significantly faster. In this respect, developments are on the verge of giving us a variety of connection types that will make fast transmission possible over the regular telephone line.

- Some websites have more pictures and illustrations than others. Some pages have numerous pictures or various graphic effects. All those dancing figures, revolving text, pop-up assistants and other graphic effects require information to be sent to your computer, and it all has to be sent via the telephone line if that's how you are connected. Receiving pictures takes a particularly long time. The more efficient the web page is designed, the faster it will appear on your screen.

- Sometimes it's extremely busy on the Internet. So many people are surfing at the same time that traffic jams occur. When that happens, you'll have to wait longer than usual.

What can be done about this?
- You don't always have to wait until all the pictures have been received. Sometimes you immediately see the topic you're looking for.

    ☞ **If this is the case, click on** 🔀 **next to the *Address bar***
    No more information is sent and you can click to go to a different page.

- Sometimes a website's opening page will have a button that says :
    Text only.
    If you click on that button, only the text will be sent, not the illustrations. That takes much less time.

Domain Names
A web address is also referred to as a domain name. Every web address has an extension, such as **.com**.

For example: *www.visualsteps.**com***

There are various extensions that can be used. In Europe, for example, the extension is usually an abbreviation for the country:

For example: *www.altavista.**nl***

This site is in the Netherlands. Other country extensions include **.be** for Belgium and **.uk** for the United Kingdom.
In the United States, however, a different system is used. Here, the extension can indicate the type of organization:
.com .... commercial business
.edu .... educational institution
.org .... non-commercial organization

Mini Internet Dictionary
Much jargon is used with reference to the Internet. When you know what the terms mean, they're easy to understand. Below you'll find a short list of jargon that you can expect to run into:

Browser .... The program you use to surf the Internet,
                      such as *Internet Explorer*
Download .... Collect files from the Internet
Homepage .... The first or opening page of a website
HTML .... Programming language used for websites
Hypertext .... A piece of text on which you can click
Log-in name .... Username
Password .... Word that will allow you to continue; a kind of personal key
Provider .... Organization that offers Internet services (ISP)
Server .... The computer that makes the actual connection to the Internet
User ID .... The name by which a user can be identified

Searching on the Internet

When you want to find information on the Internet, you can use a program called a *search engine.*

This is a program that tries to keep track of the contents of millions of web pages on the Internet. You can ask the search engine to find something for you based on a certain key word or phrase. The engine then uses those words to find the web addresses of web pages that include the words or phrase.

Well-known search engines are:

www.google.com
www.altavista.com
www.yahoo.com

You will discover that one search engine will render entirely different results than the other. This is why it's worth the effort to have more than one search engine perform the search.

Searching with Live Search

Internet Explorer has been preprogrammed to use *Live Search* as the default search engine.

In the top right corner of the *Internet Explorer* window, you will see this box:
In this box you can type one or more words that you want to base your search on and then click

If you type more than one word, you will get a list of web pages that contain at least one of the words. However, if you put the words between quotation marks, the list will show only those pages that contain that specific combination.

Tips

💡 Tip

Your History
Internet Explorer also keeps track of all the websites that you have visited. It is easy to display this list:

👆 **Click on** ⭐

👆 **Click on** 🕐 History

👆 **Click on** 🗓 Today

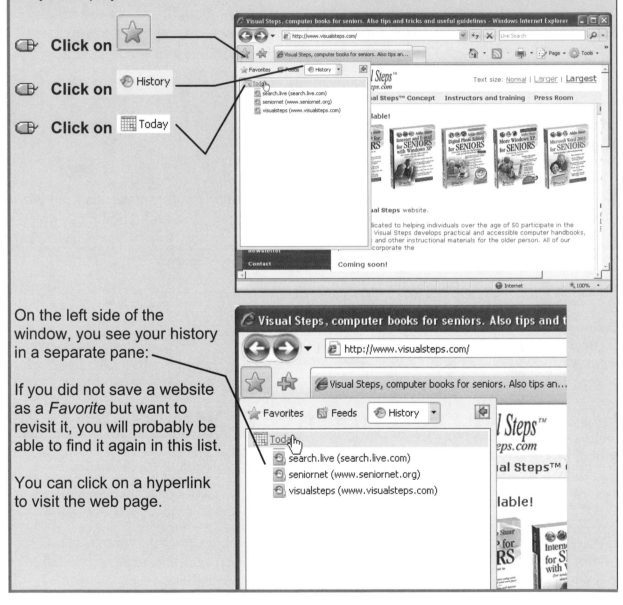

On the left side of the window, you see your history in a separate pane:

If you did not save a website as a *Favorite* but want to revisit it, you will probably be able to find it again in this list.

You can click on a hyperlink to visit the web page.

Tip

Block or Allow Pop-up Windows?
The ability to block pop-up windows is built into *Internet Explorer*. A *pop-up* is a small window that automatically appears when you visit a particular website. The pop-up window opens on top of the regular web page. Pop-ups often contain advertisements, but not always. You can set *Internet Explorer* to show or block these pop-ups.

Click on Tools

A menu appears:

Place the mouse pointer over Pop-up Blocker **and keep it there**

A small menu appears:

The standard setting is to block pop-ups.
You see the following option in the menu: Turn Off Pop-up Blocker

If you click on it, pop-ups will no longer be blocked.

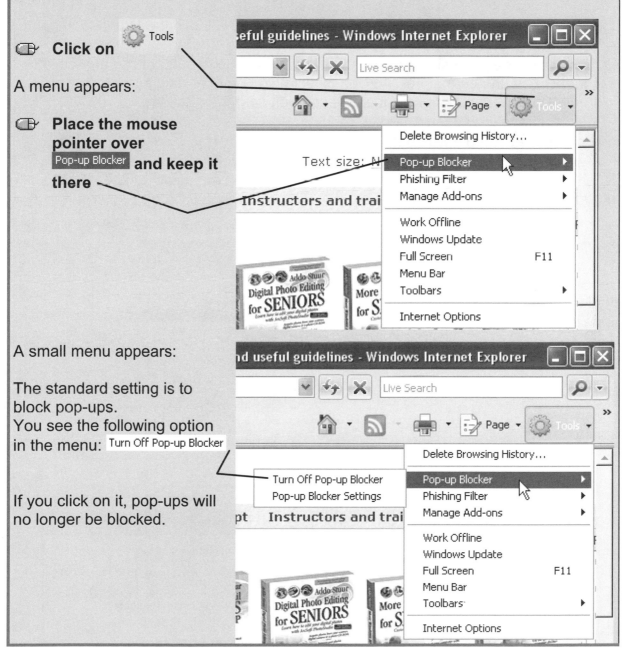

💡 Tip

Information Bar

Sometimes when you are surfing the Internet, an *Information bar* in Internet Explorer is shown. The *Information bar* appears below the *Address bar* and displays information about downloads, blocked pop-up windows, and other activities.

> 📥 To help protect your security, Internet Explorer blocked this site from downloading files to your computer. Click here for options...

If *Internet Explorer* is still using its original settings, you will see the *Information bar* in the following circumstances:

- If a website tries to install an *ActiveX control* on your computer or run an ActiveX control in an unsafe manner. ActiveX is technology for creating interactive web content such as animation sequences or credit card transactions.
- If a website tries to open a pop-up window.
- If a website tries to download a file to your computer.
- If your security settings are below recommended levels.

When you see a message in the *Information bar*, click the message to see more information or to take some action.

Here you see an example of the *Information bar*:

Also a small window appeared:

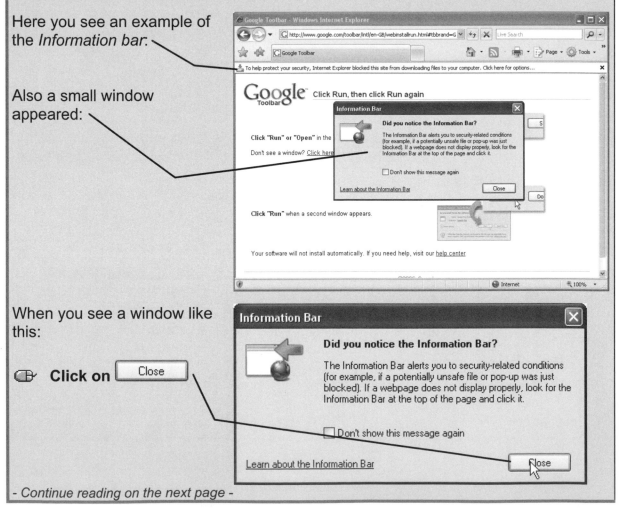

When you see a window like this:

⊞➔ **Click on** ⌈ Close ⌉

- Continue reading on the next page -

To get more information:

☞ **Click on the** *Information bar*

A small menu appears:

☞ **Click on** More information

A new window will be opened and you can read more about the *Information bar.*

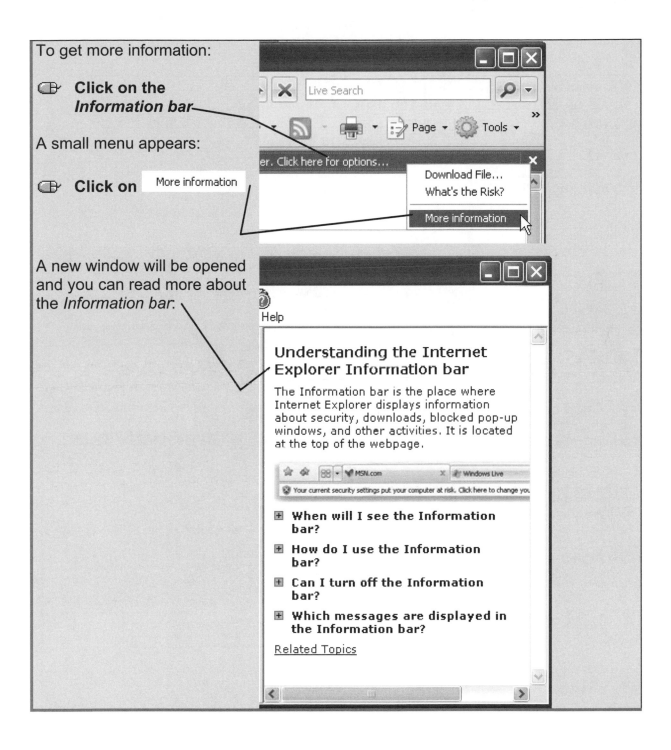

Download File...
What's the Risk?

More information

Help

Understanding the Internet Explorer Information bar

The Information bar is the place where Internet Explorer displays information about security, downloads, blocked pop-up windows, and other activities. It is located at the top of the webpage.

⊞ **When will I see the Information bar?**

⊞ **How do I use the Information bar?**

⊞ **Can I turn off the Information bar?**

⊞ **Which messages are displayed in the Information bar?**

Related Topics

Tip

Tabbed browsing
Tabbed browsing lets you load web pages in separate tabs of a single browser window, so you can switch between them quickly. Here you see the two tabs:

The right tab in this example is empty:

☞ **Surf to www.visualsteps.com**

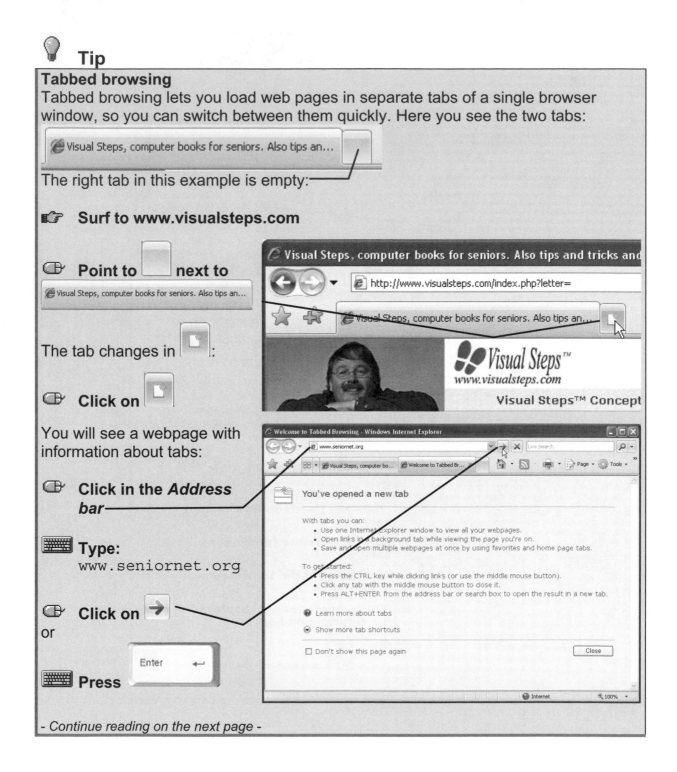

Point to next to

The tab changes in :

Click on

You will see a webpage with information about tabs:

Click in the *Address bar*

Type:
www.seniornet.org

Click on
or

Press Enter

- *Continue reading on the next page -*

The SeniorNet website appears on this tab:

You can open several tabs if you want.
To go to another webpage, that is listed on a tab, just click that tab.

To close a tab:
👉 **Click on** ☒ **on the tab**

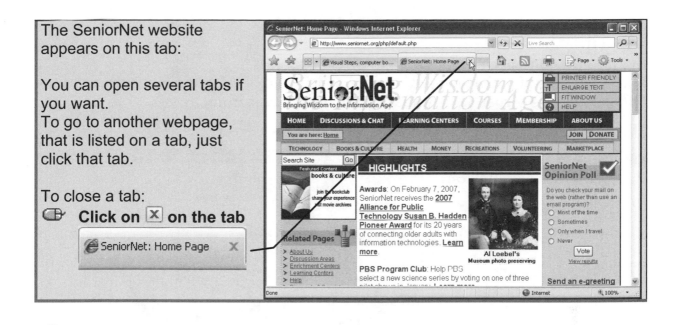

💡 **Tip**

Large icons
If you think the icons in the toolbar of *Internet Explorer* are too small, you can use larger ones:

👉 **Right-click an empty area of the toolbar**

A menu appears:

👉 **Check mark**
Use Large Icons

Now you see large icons:

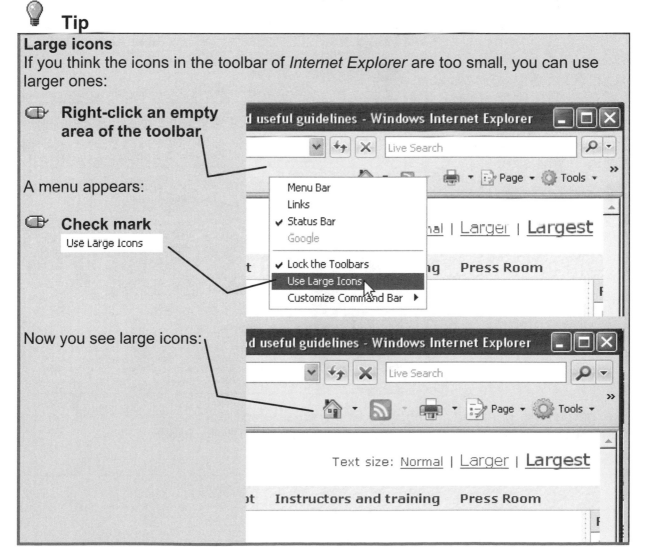

⍟ Tip

Enlarge the font size and/or zoom in on a webpage
Some websites offer the ability to enlarge the font size of the text on the webpage. For example the Visual Steps website **www.visualsteps.com**.

There are three text sizes available: Text size: Normal | Larger | Largest

☞ **Surf to**
    www.visualsteps.com

In the top right corner of the window:

👆 **Click on** Largest

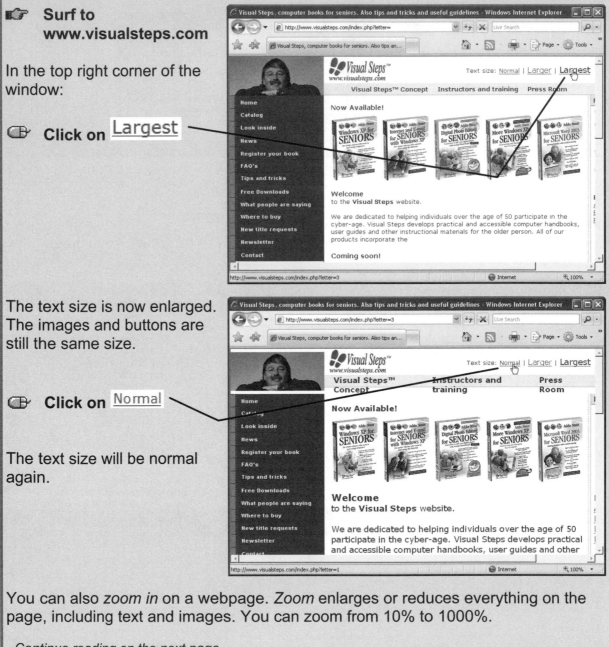

The text size is now enlarged. The images and buttons are still the same size.

👆 **Click on** Normal

The text size will be normal again.

You can also *zoom in* on a webpage. *Zoom* enlarges or reduces everything on the page, including text and images. You can zoom from 10% to 1000%.

- Continue reading on the next page -

In the bottom right corner of the *Internet Explorer* window, there is a zoom button

🔍 100% ▾ :

👆 **Click on** ▾ **next to** 🔍 100%

A menu appears:

👆 **Click on** 200%

The entire page is enlarged, including pictures, buttons and scroll bar:

Try another zoom factor:

👆 **Click on** ▾ **next to** 🔍 200%

👆 **Click on** 125%

This size is better because you can read more information.

Tip:
If you have a mouse with a wheel, hold down the Ctrl key, and then scroll the wheel to zoom in or out.

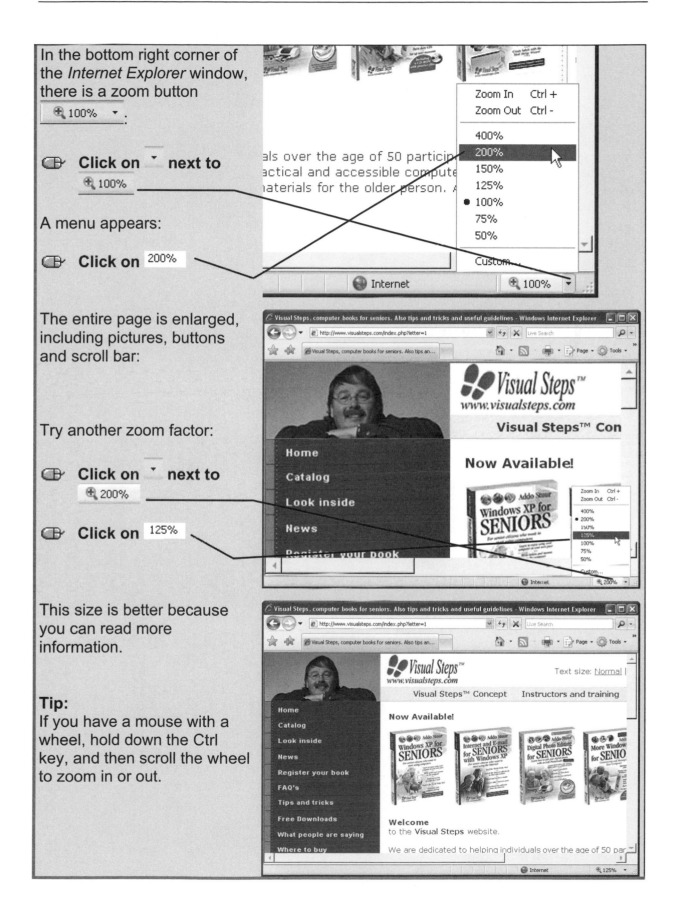

10. E-mail, Your Electronic Mailbox

One of the most widely-used applications on the Internet is electronic mail: e-mail. E-mail uses no pen, paper, envelope or stamp. You type your message into the computer and it is sent via the Internet.

If you have an Internet service subscription, you'll automatically be assigned an *e-mail address*. This e-mail address can be used to send and receive mail. Your Internet Service Provider (ISP) has a kind of post office, also called a *mail server*. Like with regular mail, this post office takes care of all mail traffic.

In order to send an e-mail to someone, the addressee must also have an e-mail address, of course. But it doesn't matter where that person lives. You can send an e-mail to Australia for the same price and just as quickly as you can send one to your next-door neighbor. Unlike stamps on regular mail, there are no direct costs involved per e-mail, except for your Internet subscription. There is no limit to the number of messages that you can send or receive.

Another significant advantage is that you can send all kinds of things with your e-mail, such as a picture that you've made with a digital camera. E-mail has an extensive effect on communication at work: as the use of e-mail increases, the use of the fax and regular telephone decreases.

Windows XP has a simple program, *Outlook Express*, with which you can quickly and easily send and receive electronic "letters". You'll be using that program with this chapter. You'll discover how easy e-mail is: no more stamps to buy and no more trips to the mailbox.

In this chapter, you'll learn how to:

- start *Outlook Express*
- create an e-mail message
- send and receive e-mail
- read an e-mail message
- include an attachment

 Please note:

In order to work through this chapter, you need your own e-mail address and your e-mail program must be properly installed. If this is not the case, you should contact your ISP.

Starting Outlook Express

Windows XP has a program that you can use to send and receive electronic mail. It's called *Outlook Express.* In this chapter you'll learn how use this program to receive and send e-mail. This is how to start the program *Outlook Express:*

Double-click on Outlook Express

Outlook Express will immediately determine whether you are connected to the Internet (online). If you are **offline**, you see a small window like below. You might want to work offline if you want to reduce the amount of time you spend online, either because your Internet Service Provider (ISP) charges you by the hour, or because you have only one phone line and you are not using a broadband connection.

You see this window first if you are offline:

You don't want to connect yet, so:

Click on Cancel

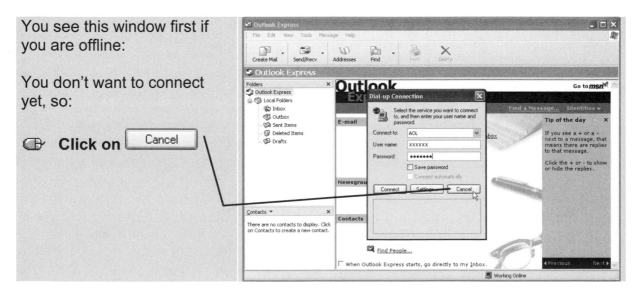

Next you'll see the *Outlook Express* start-up window.

On the left there's a frame with various folders:

On the right you see a summary of the things you can do with the program:

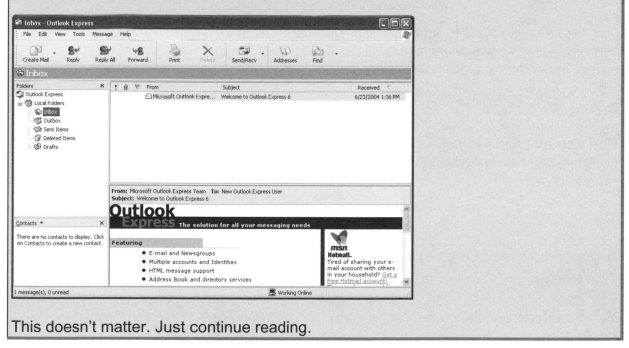

🞕 HELP! My window looks entirely different.

Maybe your *Outlook Express* window looks more like the one shown below:

This doesn't matter. Just continue reading.

The E-mail Address

To practice, you'll be sending a message to yourself. This is an excellent way to learn how to send e-mail. What's more, the message is sent straight to you, so that you can learn how to receive e-mail. This is how to create a new e-mail message:

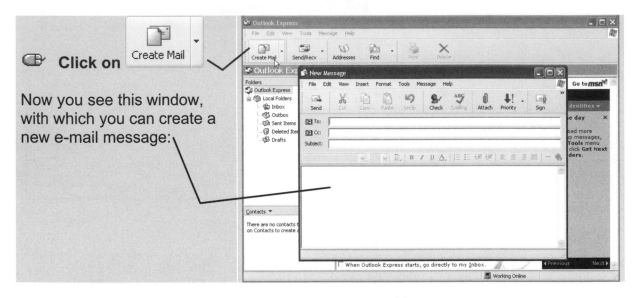

👆 **Click on** Create Mail

Now you see this window, with which you can create a new e-mail message:

The first thing to do is to address your message using an e-mail address. Every e-mail address consists of a number of words, with the familiar symbol @ somewhere in the middle. For example:

name@provider.com

The name of the addressee is located in front of the @. Behind it, the address usually contains the name of the Internet Service Provider from which you received the e-mail address.

💡 **Tip**

E-mail addresses may not contain spaces.

This is why names or words are sometimes separated by a dot (**.**). These dots are extremely important. If you forget one in the address, your message will never arrive. Your mailman usually understands what the sender means if the address isn't completely correct. But a computer doesn't.

Sending an E-mail

The best way to test that your electronic mailbox works as it should is to send a message to yourself.

In the line marked To: **type your own e-mail address**

Every e-mail message is also given a subject.

Click on Subject:

Type: test

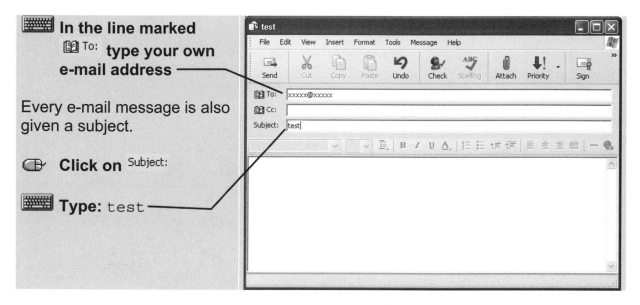

Now you can start typing the actual text of the message.

Click in the large white box

You can type the message here. This window works exactly the same way as a word processor, such as *WordPad*.

Type:
This is a first
e-mail as a test.

When you've finished the e-mail, you can send it.

At the top left, click on

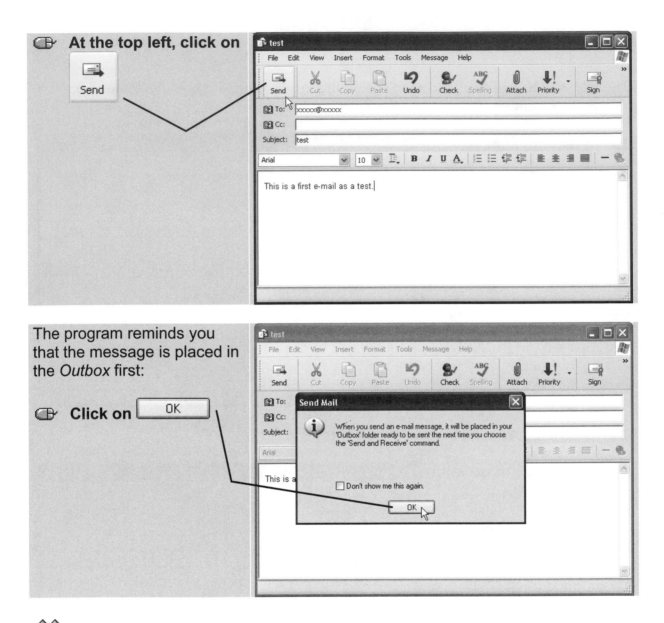

The program reminds you that the message is placed in the *Outbox* first:

Click on OK

HELP! There's no reminder.

Is the reminder about the *Outbox* not shown on your screen?
This means that *Outlook Express* has a different setting, and your e-mail is immediately mailed.

☞ **If this is the case, skip the following section and continue at *Reading a Message***

The Outbox

All of the e-mails you make are collected in the *Outbox* first. Your message will not be sent until you connect to the Internet. This means that you can write all of the e-mails you want, and then send them out all at once.

Now you see the *Outlook Express* window again. There's one message in the *Outbox*:

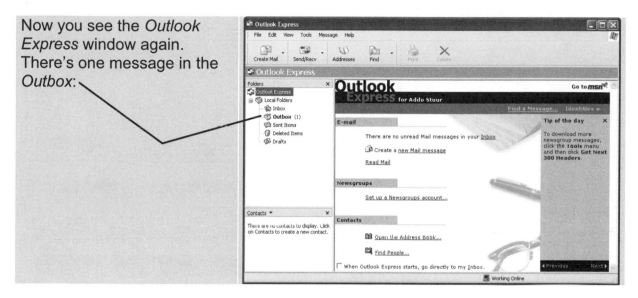

Sending and Receiving

Now you can have the message sent. The program will connect with the Internet to send it.

It's important for you to check to make sure that your modem is ready before you try to connect.

👉 **Make sure your modem is connected to the telephone line or cable**

Do you have an external modem?
👉 **If so, turn the modem on**

Do you have an internal modem?
👉 **Then you don't need to do anything**

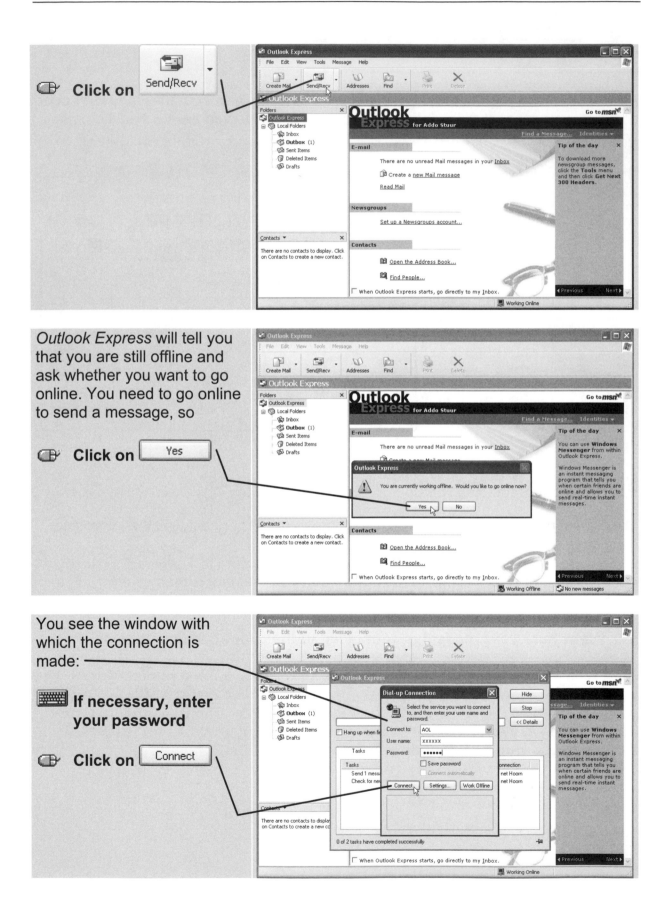

👆 **Click on** Send/Recv

Outlook Express will tell you that you are still offline and ask whether you want to go online. You need to go online to send a message, so

👆 **Click on** Yes

You see the window with which the connection is made:

⌨️ **If necessary, enter your password**

👆 **Click on** Connect

HELP! There's no reminder.

Is the window about the *Dial-up Connection* not shown on your screen?
This means that *Outlook Express* has been given different settings on your computer,

so that the program automatically connects when you click on the button Send/Recv .

☞ **Just continue to read**

A connection is made to your ISP. Next your e-mail message is sent. The program also automatically checks to see if e-mail has been received for you.

You can follow this process
as it proceeds in this window:

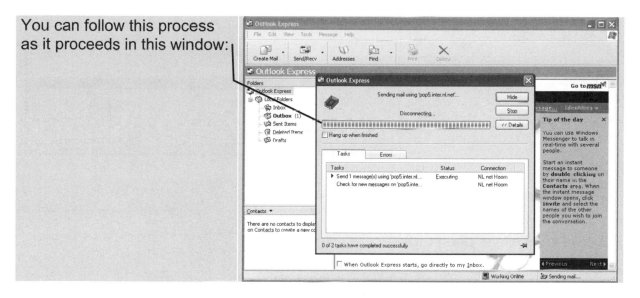

If everything went as it should, your text message was immediately sent to you. Then it's put in the *Inbox*.

Reading a Message

All e-mail messages you receive are placed in a separate folder that is called the *Inbox*.

☞ **Click on** 📧 **Inbox**

At the right, you see your own message:

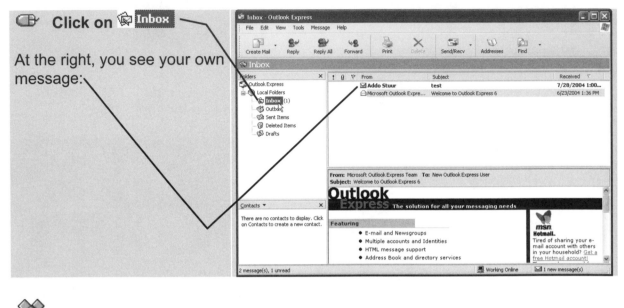

✖ HELP! I don't have any mail.

Is there no message in your *Inbox*?
Perhaps it hasn't yet been received. Try again later:

☞ **Click on** 📧 Send/Recv

You can open the message in a larger window so that you can read it:

☞ **Double-click on your message**

The e-mail message is easy to read in the separate window.

This window has a bar with a variety of handy buttons for replying to e-mail messages:

test							

File Edit View Tools Message Help

Reply   Reply All   Forward   Print   Delete   Previous   Next   Addresses

From: Addo Stuur
Date: Wednesday, July 28, 2004 1:02 PM
To:
Subject: test

This is a first e-mail as a test.

These buttons have the following functions:

Reply
An e-mail to be sent back is made that already has the correct e-mail address. The original e-mail message is included.

Forward
A new e-mail is made from the original message that can be sent to someone else.

Reply All
An e-mail message can be sent to more than one person. This button is used to send a reply to everyone to whom the original e-mail was addressed.

☞ **Close the e-mail message window** 🐾1.4

Including an Attachment

The nice thing about e-mail messages is that you can send all kinds of things with them. You can add a photo, a drawing, or text if you want, for example.

⇨ **Please note:**

To practice, you'll be sending the **Directions** that you made in Chapter 8.

Did you decide not to make these directions?
☞ **Then simply read this section**

Something that you want to send with an e-mail message is called an **attachment**. This is the name it's given in *Windows XP* and on the Internet. This is how to add an attachment to a message:

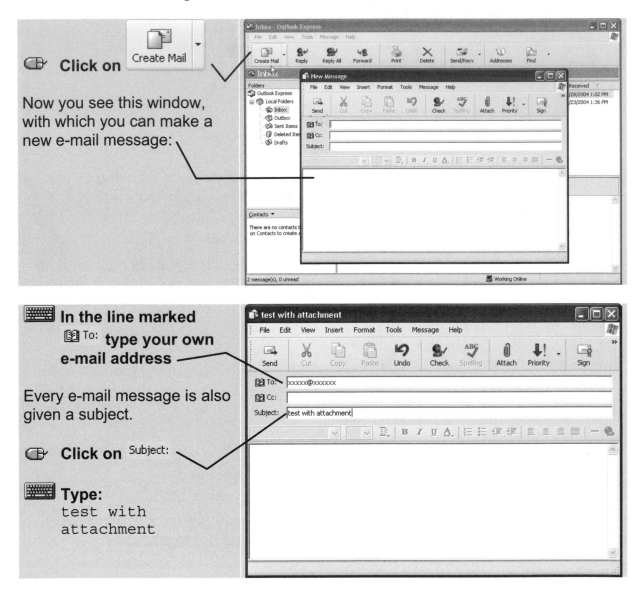

☞ **Click on** Create Mail

Now you see this window, with which you can make a new e-mail message:

⌨ **In the line marked**
📧 To: **type your own e-mail address**

Every e-mail message is also given a subject.

☞ **Click on** Subject:

⌨ **Type:**
test with
attachment

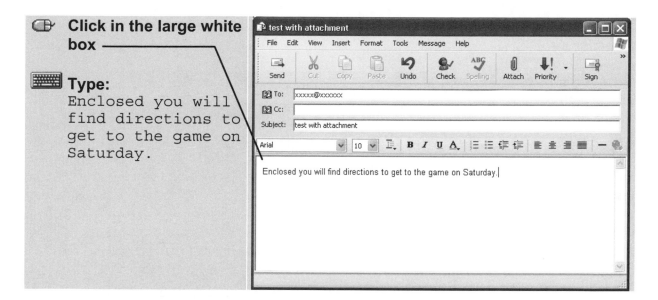

Click in the large white box

Type:
Enclosed you will find directions to get to the game on Saturday.

Now you can add the attachment, in this case the directions.

Click on Insert

Click on File Attachment...

In the folder *My Documents*, select the practice test you made that you named *Directions:*

Now you see this window, with which you can open a folder or file:

☞ **Click on** 🖹 Directions

☞ **Click on** [Attach]

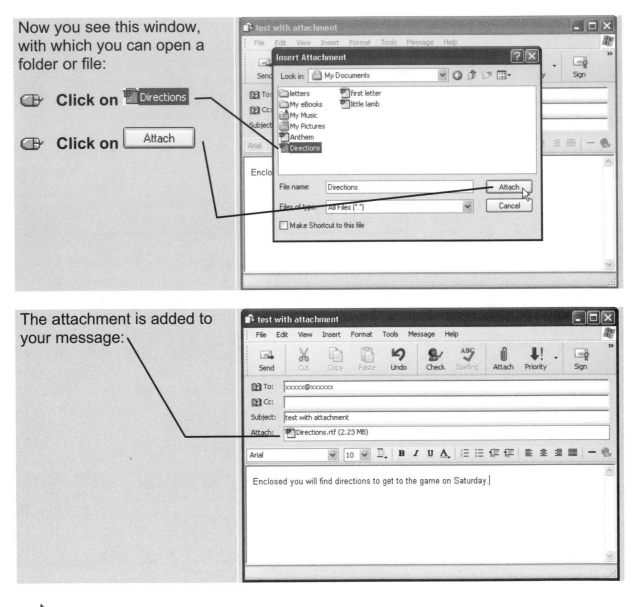

The attachment is added to your message:

⇨ **Please note:**

Sending an e-mail with the directions as attachment takes a bit more time than sending and receiving a "bare" e-mail message. Sending pictures takes a particularly long time. You may decide for yourself whether or not you really want to send this message.
If you don't want to:
☞ **Close the window for the message**
The program will ask whether you want to save the changes.
☞ **Click on** [No]

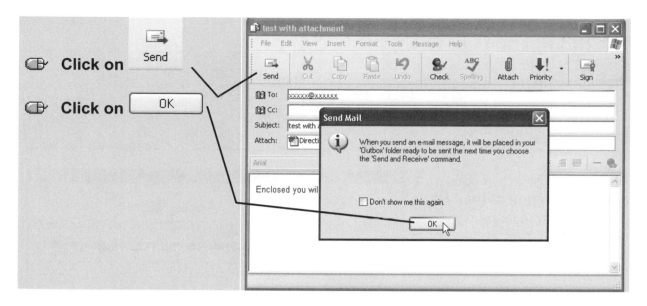

Your message is placed in the *Outbox*. Now you can send it. If all goes well, you'll also immediately receive it:

☞ **Send your e-mail** 7.13

☞ **Connect to the Internet** 7.3

➡ **Please note:**

Sending this e-mail will take quite some time. On the taskbar, you can tell by the blinking computers that information is being sent:

Reading an Attachment

Once your e-mail is sent, it will probably also immediately be received. You can see this in the *Inbox:*

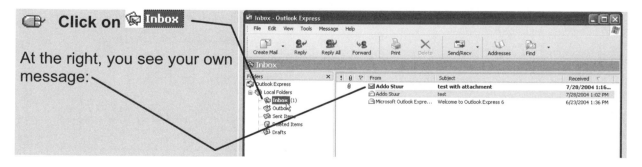

🔖 HELP! I don't have any mail.

Is there no message in your *Inbox*?
Perhaps it hasn't yet been received. Try again later:

☞ **Click on** [Send/Recv ▾]

At the right, you see your own message. In one of the first columns in this list, a paper clip indicates that an attachment has been included:

☞ **Double-click on your message**

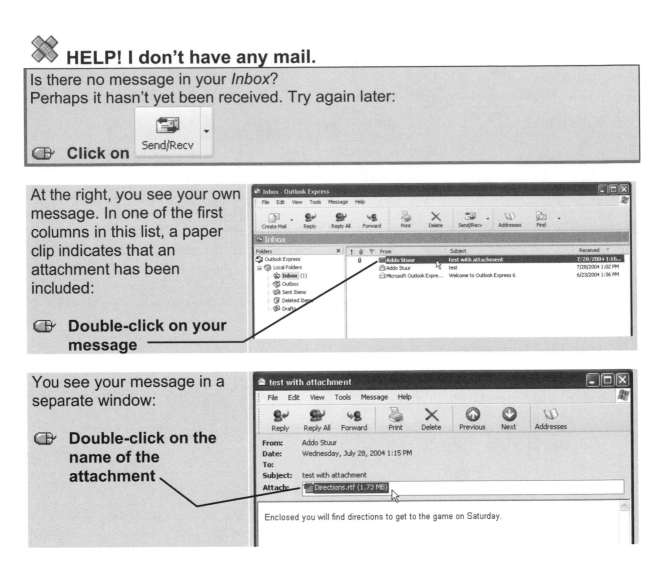

You see your message in a separate window:

☞ **Double-click on the name of the attachment**

If you have *Windows XP* with *Service Pack 2* on your computer, you'll see the following warning:

In this case the attachment is definitely safe, because you sent it yourself:

☞ **Click on** [Open]

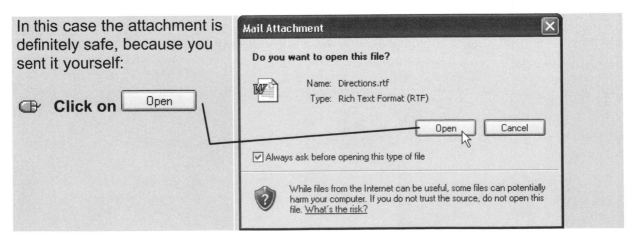

WordPad or *Microsoft Word* is started and the attachment is opened:

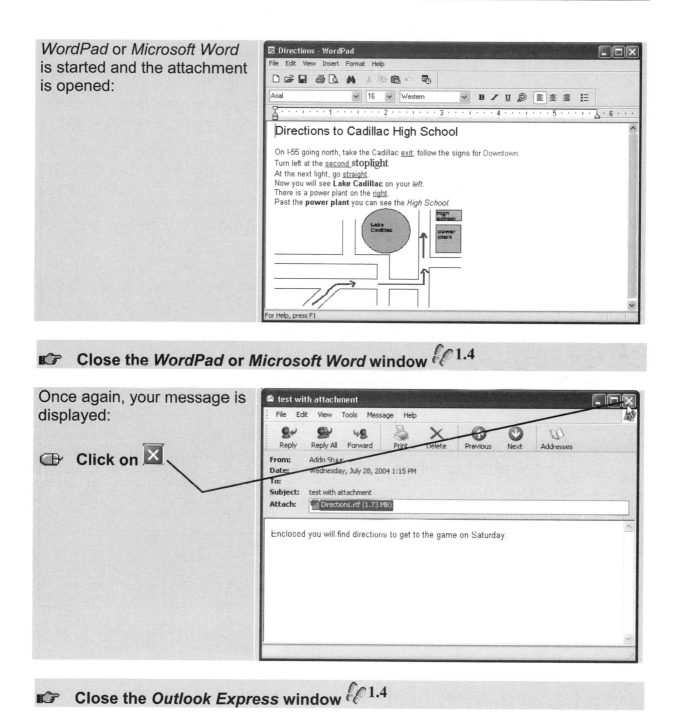

☞ **Close the *WordPad* or *Microsoft Word* window** 🐾 **1.4**

Once again, your message is displayed:

👉 **Click on** ☒

☞ **Close the *Outlook Express* window** 🐾 **1.4**

Now you've learned how to send and receive e-mail messages.
You can practice what you've learned with the following exercises.

Exercises

The following exercises will help you master what you've just learned. Have you forgotten how to do something? Use the number beside the footsteps to look it up in the appendix *How Do I Do That Again?*

Exercise: Creating an E-mail

With this exercise, you can practice writing, sending and receiving a new e-mail message.

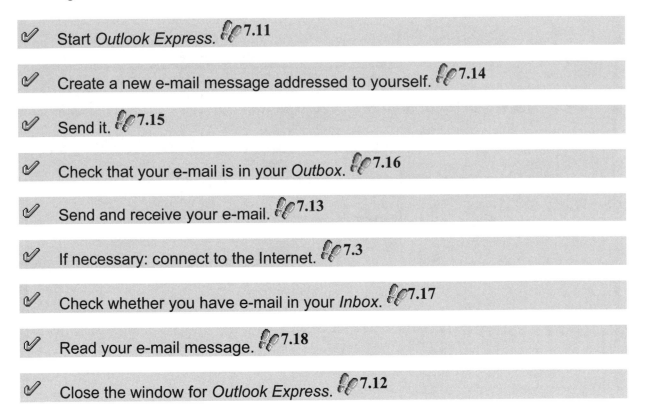

✔ Start *Outlook Express.* 7.11

✔ Create a new e-mail message addressed to yourself. 7.14

✔ Send it. 7.15

✔ Check that your e-mail is in your *Outbox.* 7.16

✔ Send and receive your e-mail. 7.13

✔ If necessary: connect to the Internet. 7.3

✔ Check whether you have e-mail in your *Inbox.* 7.17

✔ Read your e-mail message. 7.18

✔ Close the window for *Outlook Express.* 7.12

Exercise: Is there E-mail?

This exercise is used to practice determining whether or not you've received e-mail messages.

✔ Start *Outlook Express.* 7.11

✔ Send and receive your e-mail. 7.13

✔ If necessary: connect to the Internet. 7.3

✔ Check whether you have e-mail in your *Inbox*. 📖**7.17**

✔ Close the window for *Outlook Express*. 📖**7.12**

Exercise: Sending a Text

With this exercise, you can send another e-mail, this time including the Anthem as an attachment.

⇨ **Please note:**

You typed and saved the Anthem text in Chapter 5. If you didn't, simply attach a different text.

✔ Start *Outlook Express*. 📖**7.11**

✔ Create a new e-mail message addressed to yourself. 📖**7.14**

✔ Add the text *Anthem* in the folder *My Documents* as an attachment. 📖**7.19**

✔ Send it. 📖**7.15**

✔ Check that your e-mail is in your *Outbox*. 📖**7.16**

✔ Send and receive your e-mail. 📖**7.13**

✔ If necessary: connect to the Internet. 📖**7.3**

✔ Check whether you have e-mail in your *Inbox*. 📖**7.17**

✔ Read your e-mail message. 📖**7.18**

✔ Open the attachment. 📖**7.20**

✔ Close the window for *Outlook Express*. 📖**7.12**

Background Information

The Smaller, The Faster
On the Internet, there is one golden rule: the smaller the message, the faster it is sent. The same applies to attachments. If you send a small attachment, such as a small photograph, the transmission will only take a few seconds. If you send a larger drawing, it will take more time and the telephone line will be used longer.

Along with the name of an attachment, such as a text or a picture, its size is always shown, expressed in MB or KB: Directions.rtf (1.73 MB)

The size of a file is always indicated in KB or MB. These are measurements for sizes, just like inches and ounces.

A **Kilobyte** is (about) one thousand bytes.
This means that: 20 Kilobytes is 20,000 bytes. The abbreviation of kilobyte is **KB**.

A **Megabyte** is (about) one thousand kilobytes.
This means that one Megabyte is (about) one million (one thousand times one thousand) bytes. The abbreviation of megabyte is **MB.**

How long does it take to send or receive something?
The speed at which something can be sent or received depends on a number of things, including the speed of your modem, the type of connection and how busy it is on the Internet.
If for example, you are using dial-up networking to connect to the Internet, you can receive **6 KB** per second with a regular modem. This translates into 360 KB or 0.36 MB per minute.

A message that consists of 16 KB therefore takes about three seconds.
The size of the picture attachment you used in this chapter, is 269 KB. It takes about 45 seconds to send or receive.
The directions text as shown in our illustrations measures 1.73 MB and will take about three minutes. As you see, this is quite a long time.

You can send different types of files with an e-mail message. You can even send sounds or video clips! But be careful: sound and video files are usually quite large. It may take a long time to send or receive files of this type.
However, when you are using a broadband connection, for example a DSL line, this will not be a problem. This type of service offers high speed connection to the Internet.

How much fits?
Now you now what a kilobyte and a megabyte are. You can read here how much data fits on various types of data storage devices:

A diskette (floppy): 1.44 MB.
A CD-ROM (CD-R) / CD-Rewritable (CD-RW): 640 MB.

A larger size is used these days for different kinds of data storage: the Gigabyte.
A Gigabyte is (about) one thousand Megabytes, or one billion bytes.
The abbreviation of Gigabyte is **GB.**

A USB stick: 16 MB to 4 GB or even more.
A DVD-ROM (DVD-R) / DVD-Rewritable (DVD-RW): 4,7 GB or more (double layer).

Hard disks on today's computers have a capacity of at least 80 GB or 120 GB.
More powerful computers may have hard disks with 200 GB or even more!

Busy?
Do you connect to the Internet via the telephone line (dial-up networking)? If you are connected to the Internet and someone tries to call you, the caller will get a busy signal. So if you are expecting a call, do not connect to the Internet.

Do you connect by using an ISDN or DSL line? Then you can receive calls while you are connected to the Internet.

Do you have a cable connection? In that case, you can continue regular telephone service because your Internet connection does not interfere with your telephone.

Tips

Tip

Enter password again every time?

Do you have to enter your password every time you connect to the Internet? You can change the settings in this window so that you won't have to.

Type your password

Checkmark the box Save password

Click on Connect

Tip

Immediately connect?

You don't have to connect via this window; you can connect immediately if you want.

This is how:

Check the box Connect automatically

Click on Connect

Tip

Wrong address?
If you make a mistake in the address to which the message is to be sent, it will be returned to you by the *Internet post office*. This post office will return your message as an attachment to a message explaining why it's returning it. This message will be sent to your *Inbox:*

!	0	▽	From	Subject
	0		📩 Mail Delivery Subsystem	Returned mail: see transcript for details

Go to the folder **Messages sent** to see whether you made a typing error in the address. You can make a new message with the correct address.

 Tip

Keeping a List of Addresses
Generally, you'll have to keep track of the e-mail addresses you want to use yourself. There is no book of reference that lists everyone's e-mail address (like a telephone directory for telephone numbers). You can find lists of e-mail addresses on the Internet, but you'd be extremely lucky to find all the addresses you want there.
Outlook Express can help you to keep track of e-mail addresses that you've used,

which can be saved in an address list using the button   📖 Addresses   .
Once an address has been saved, you can enter it without typing the address. This is how:

👉 **Click on** 📖 To:

Now you can select the address you want from the list.

 Tip

Printing an E-mail
Use this button if you want to print out an e-mail message.

🖨 Print

 Tip

If you want to send your e-mail to more than one address, you must type a semi-colon (;) and a space between the addresses. If you select more than one address from your list of addresses, *Outlook Express* will automatically enter these for you.

📖 To: test@visualsteps.com;addo@visualsteps.com

💡 Tip

Security Settings in Outlook Express
When you install *Windows XP Service Pack 2*, a few security settings are automatically activated in *Outlook Express*. You can take a look at these settings:

👉 **Click on** `Tools`

👉 **Click on** `Options...`

You see the *Options* window:

👉 **Click on the tab**
`Security`

On the *Security* tab, you see check marks beside various options:

These security settings ensure that e-mail attachments and images cannot open automatically. You have to give permission at the moment you want to open an e-mail with an image or an attachment. *Outlook Express* notifies you when that occurs.

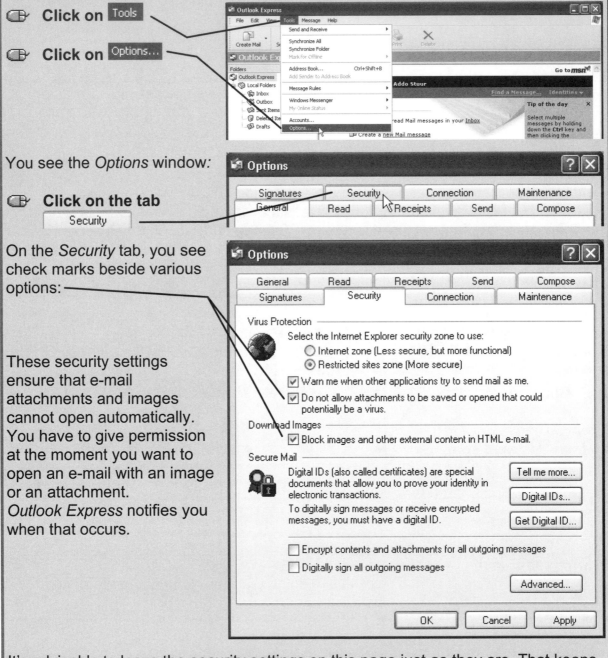

It's advisable to leave the security settings on this page just as they are. That keeps you in control of any undesirable e-mails.
Check whether you trust the content or attachment on a per e-mail basis. If you have any doubts, ask the sender for clarification about the e-mail, or delete it without opening. Don't forget to empty the *Deleted Items* folder afterward.

11. How to Make Working with Your Computer More Pleasant

Now you have more experience with your PC. Nearly every part of your computer can be customized to make working with it more pleasant. You do something similar in a new car before taking it for a drive: First you adjust the seat for the length of your legs and you make sure that all of the mirrors are in the right position.

Customizing your computer is worth the effort not only because this avoids frustration, but also because it prevents negative consequences in the longer term. It's rather easy, for example, to adjust the mouse settings so that you can work easily with it and don't strain your hand or wrist.

This chapter explains which parts of the computer you can change. Particular attention is devoted to aspects that can be important for seniors, requiring you to use your motor skills, your eyesight and your hearing.

Feel free to experiment to determine whether the changes make it more pleasant for you to work with the computer. Remember that all of the changes can just as easily be changed back to the original setting.

In this chapter you will find answers and solutions to the following questions and problems:

- the mouse pointer moves too fast
- I can't double-click with the mouse
- I'm left-handed
- I keep losing the mouse pointer on the screen
- my mouse doesn't move smoothly; it jerks
- I often type double letters
- I can't type apostrophes or accents
- everything on the screen is too small
- the letters on the screen are too small
- *Windows XP* is much too busy and confusing for me
- the sound on my PC is too loud or too soft
- how can I connect a headset or extra speakers to my PC?
- I also want to hear sound signals

The Control Panel

Many of the settings on your computer can be adjusted in a special window: the *Control Panel.* This is how to start it:

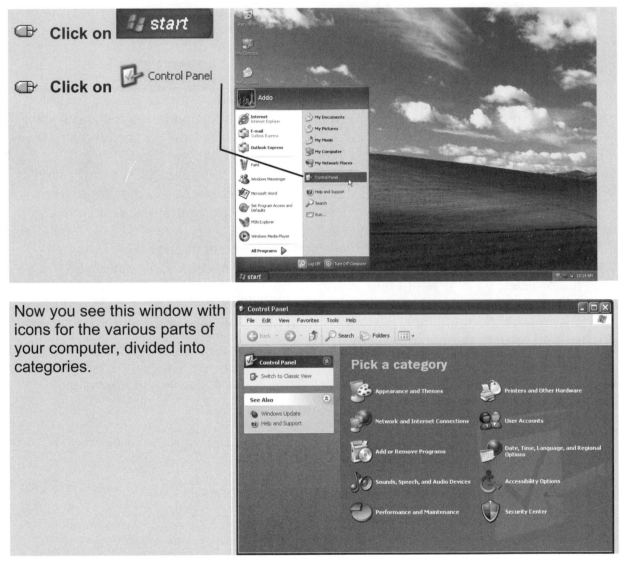

Now you see this window with icons for the various parts of your computer, divided into categories.

You can adjust one of the parts by clicking on the icon.

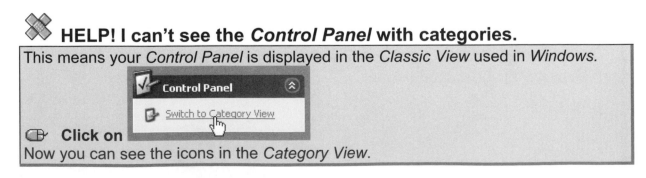

HELP! I can't see the *Control Panel* with categories.

This means your *Control Panel* is displayed in the *Classic View* used in *Windows.*

☞ **Click on**

Now you can see the icons in the *Category View.*

Customizing the Mouse

There are various ways to adjust the settings for your mouse. If you still aren't working comfortably with the mouse despite sufficient practice, you can try changing the settings. You can set:

- the speed
- the double-click speed
- the buttons for left-handed users
- the mouse pointer

All of these settings can be adjusted in the following window.

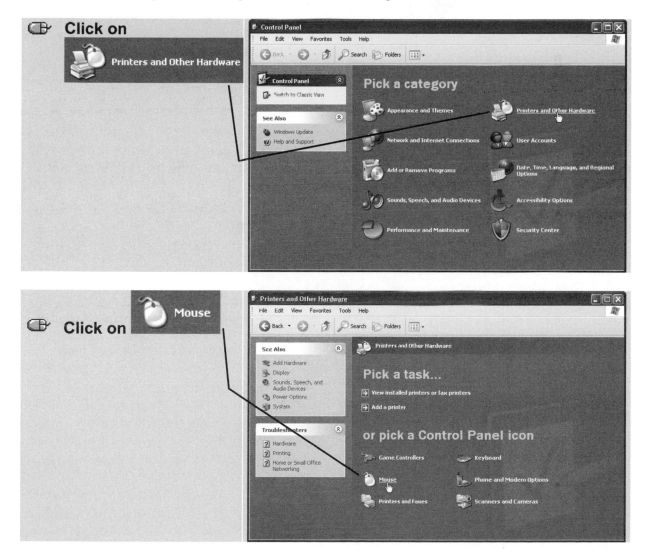

You now see this window:

Please note:
This window may have a different appearance on your screen. Mouse manufacturers sometimes make a modified version of this window for their products.

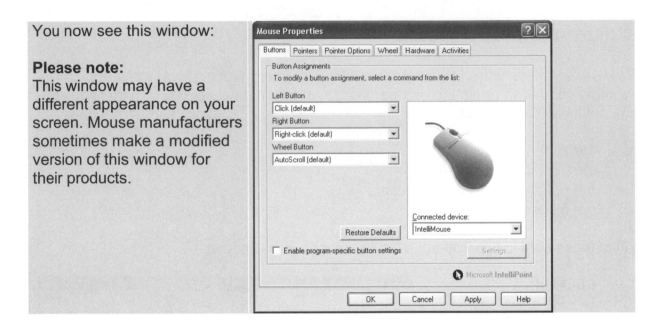

The Speed

The speed of the mouse determines the relationship between a movement made with the mouse over the tabletop and the movement of the mouse pointer on the screen.

> If the mouse speed is **too fast**, when you move the mouse only slightly on the tabletop the **movement on the screen is too large**.
>
> If the mouse speed is **too slow**, when you move the mouse a long way on the tabletop the **movement on the screen is only slight**.

For most people, the mouse speed is correct if a movement with the mouse on the tabletop within the surface of a CD box moves the mouse pointer from one corner of the screen to another corner.

If you still think your mouse is too slow or too fast after practicing, you can try adjusting the speed. This is how:

☞ Click on the tab sheet
  [Pointer Options]

Near Motion you can drag the button more to the left (Slow) or to the right (Fast):

Slow ———◯——— Fast

- Make the setting **faster** if you have to move the mouse over too long a distance on the tabletop.
- Make the setting **slower** if the mouse pointer moves too quickly over the screen.

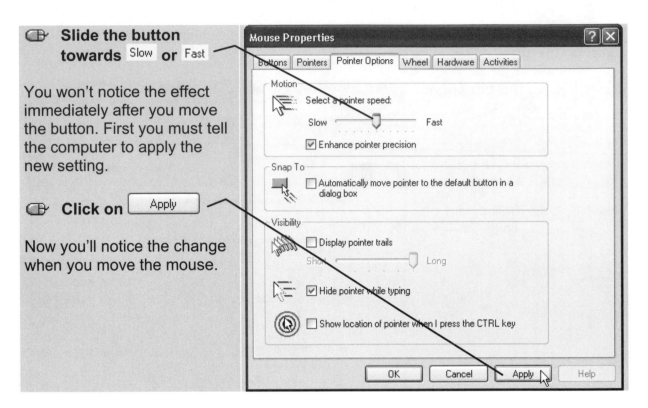

Slide the button towards Slow **or** Fast

You won't notice the effect immediately after you move the button. First you must tell the computer to apply the new setting.

Click on Apply

Now you'll notice the change when you move the mouse.

You can keep changing the position of the button until you've found the setting that works best for you.

The Mouse Pointer

Many computer beginners complain that they regularly lose track of the mouse pointer on the screen. It's very easy to add an effect to the mouse pointer to make it more visible. What you can do is to give the mouse pointer a *tail* or a *pointer trail*. Try it:

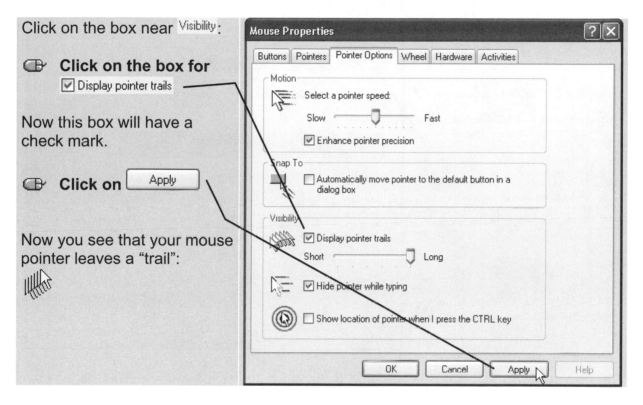

Click on the box near Visibility:

☞ **Click on the box for**
  ☑ Display pointer trails

Now this box will have a check mark.

☞ **Click on** [Apply]

Now you see that your mouse pointer leaves a "trail":

With most mice, you can also adjust the length of the trail. If you don't like this effect, simply click on the box again to remove the check mark.

A Different Mouse Pointer

You can also make the mouse pointer more visible by making it larger or giving it a color. This is done with a different tab:

☞ **Click on the tab** Pointers

Under the box Scheme you probably see that the mouse pointer Windows Default (system scheme) is being used:

Mouse Properties

Buttons | Pointers | Pointer Options | Wheel | Hardware | Activities

Scheme

Windows Default (system scheme)

Save As... | Delete

Customize:

Normal Select

Help Select

Working In Background

Busy

Precision Select

☑ Enable pointer shadow   Use Default   Browse...

OK   Cancel   Apply   Help

You can opt for a larger mouse pointer. It might be easier for you to see. This is how:

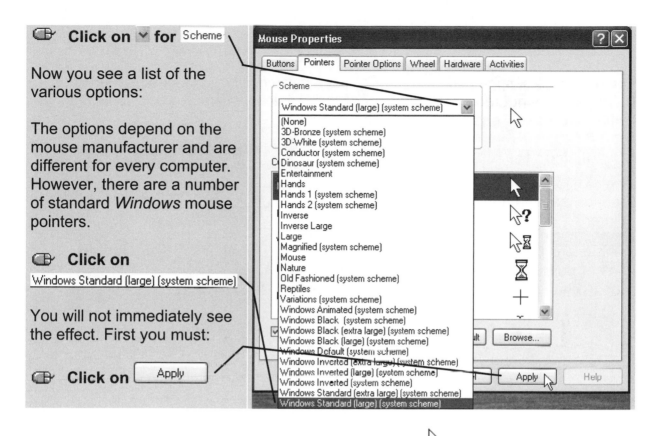

☞ **Click on** ❤ **for** Scheme

Now you see a list of the various options:

The options depend on the mouse manufacturer and are different for every computer. However, there are a number of standard *Windows* mouse pointers.

☞ **Click on**

Windows Standard (large) (system scheme)

You will not immediately see the effect. First you must:

☞ **Click on** Apply

Now you see that you have a very large mouse pointer:
If you like it, you can leave the setting as it is. If not, you can select the regular *Windows Standard* scheme or you can try one of the other options.

A Black Mouse Pointer

In the list, you will also a see a number of options with which the **mouse pointer is colored black**:

For some people, the black version is easier to follow on the screen. Try this setting to see if you like it.

✖ HELP! Nothing changes.

When you select a different setting, you must always first tell the computer to apply it:

☞ **Click on**

The Double-Click Speed

The double-click speed can also be adjusted. If you don't double-click fast enough, *Windows* does not recognize your two clicks as a double-click. Perhaps changing the setting will make it easier for you to double-click.

Click on the tab
Activities

Under the section Double-Click Speed you see another button that you can slide to change the speed:

Slow ———————— Fast

Mouse Properties

Buttons | Pointers | Pointer Options | Wheel | Hardware | Activities

Double-Click Speed
Double-click the folder to test your setting. If the folder does not open, try using a slower setting.

Test Area

Slow ——————— Fast

Orientation
Improves pointer movement according to the way you hold and move the pointing device.

Set Orientation...

Use Default

ClickLock
Enables you to highlight or drag without holding down the button. To set, briefly hold down the primary button. To release, click the button again.

☐ Turn on ClickLock   Settings...

Microsoft IntelliPoint

OK | Cancel | Apply | Help

- Make the setting **slower** if you have trouble double-clicking.
- You can make the double-click speed **faster** once you've mastered the technique of clicking in rapid succession.

HELP! I'm having trouble with double-clicking.

You can use the following trick:
Click once on the icon
The icon will turn blue to show that it has been clicked on.

Enter ↵

Press
The window will be opened.

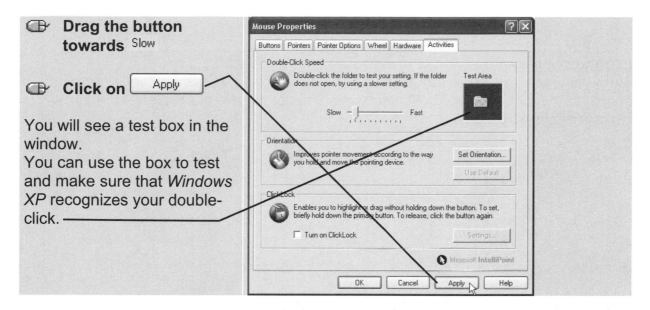

☞ **Drag the button towards** Slow

☞ **Click on** Apply

You will see a test box in the window.
You can use the box to test and make sure that *Windows XP* recognizes your double-click. —

If you're left-handed, you may be interested in the following. If not, you can skip the following section and continue with *Has the Mouse Been Customized?*

Left-Handed Users

If you're left-handed, you should also customize the mouse so that you can use it in your left hand.
Naturally, you will place the mouse to the left of your keyboard. But you can also switch the mouse buttons so that you can click with the pointing finger on your left hand:

☞ **Click on the tab** Buttons

☞ **Click on** ▾ **for** Left Button

☞ **Click on** Right-click

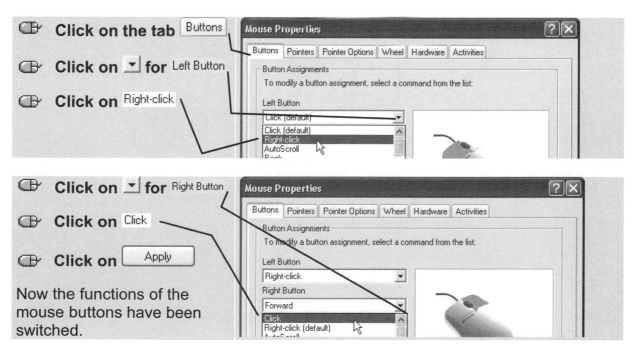

☞ **Click on** ▾ **for** Right Button

☞ **Click on** Click

☞ **Click on** Apply

Now the functions of the mouse buttons have been switched.

💡 **Tip**

Ergonomic mice?
Many mice are shaped to ergonomically fit into the hand. However, these are often only suitable for users who are right-handed. Other mice are universal and can be used in either hand.

ergonomic right-handed   *universal*

The mouse is the part of the computer that gets the most intensive use. Make sure you use a suitable mouse. Some manufacturers also have ergonomically-shaped mice for users who are left-handed.

Has the Mouse Been Customized?

Once you've customized the mouse to suit your preferences, you can close the window with the mouse properties.

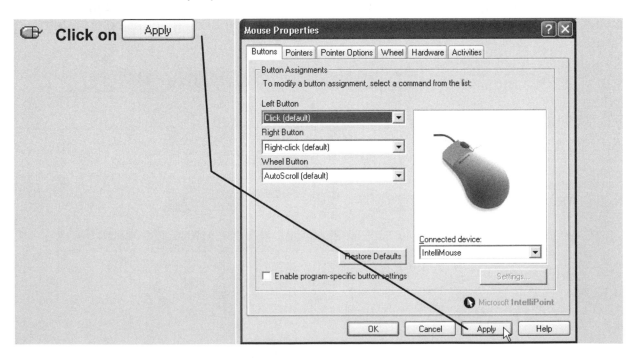

All of the changes that you have made to the settings will be saved and you'll return to the *Control Panel*.

Tips for Using a Mouse

 Tip

Prevent RSI

People who use a mouse often run the risk of getting RSI (Repetitive Strain Injury). This can be prevented with the proper posture. Make sure that your lower arm, wrist and hand are in a horizontal position. Your wrist and hand rest lightly on the tabletop. It's also important to regularly take a break and change your position.

Tip

Cleaning Your Mouse

Because of the way they're constructed, sooner or later every mouse will become dirty and not work as it should. The mouse's sliding surfaces are dirty in no time, but the ball inside the mouse also collects dirt. This dirt prevents the mouse from working precisely. It's as if the mouse jerks. You should therefore regularly clean the mouse with a cloth, cotton swabs and a de-greasing cleaning agent, such as *Windex*.

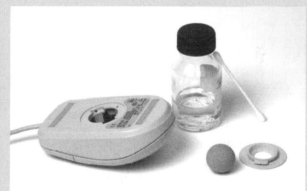

This is how:

☞ **Clean the sliding surfaces on the underside of the mouse**
☞ **Twist the round ring to release the ball**
☞ **Take out the ball and clean it thoroughly**
☞ **On the inside, use cotton swabs to clean the three little wheels**
☞ **Put the mouse back together**

Tip

A Mouse Pad

A mouse will only work properly on a flat, hard surface. Is your mouse clean but does it still seem to jerk?
You might consider using a special mouse pad. These are available from computer stores.

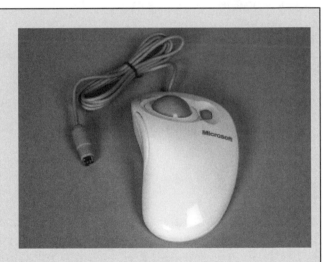

 Tip

The Trackball

If you're still having trouble using the mouse, you might consider using what is known as a *trackball*.
A trackball is actually kind of like an upside-down mouse. The trackball remains on a single spot on the tabletop. You use your thumb to turn the ball in order to move the mouse pointer.
The trackball also has the same buttons as a regular mouse.
The newest trackballs also have a wheel that is handy for on the Internet.

Some computer users like using a trackball much more than a mouse. The trackball is also often used by people who have difficulty with their motor skills.

💡 Tip

Double-Clicking with a Special Mouse Button

Mice that have multiple buttons also offer the possibility of "programming" the extra buttons. You can assign the function of "double-clicking" to one of these buttons.

You can do this in the *Control Panel*. Once you've done this, you only have to press this button once in order to double-click.

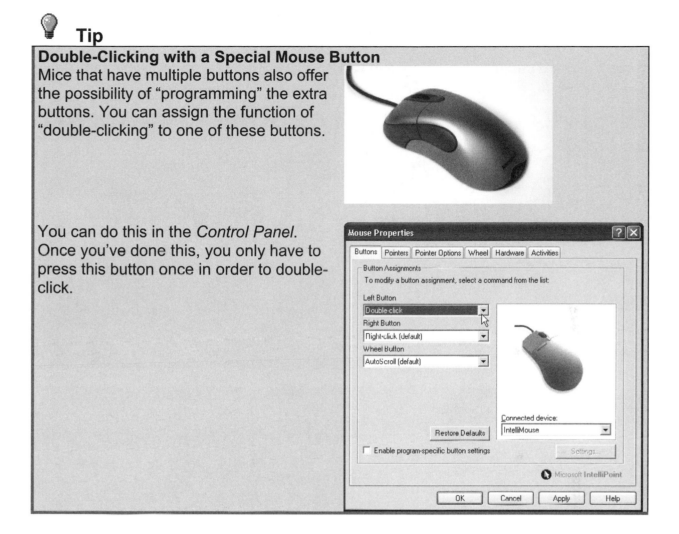

Customizing the Keyboard

Your keyboard can also be changed in various ways. This is also done with the *Control Panel*.

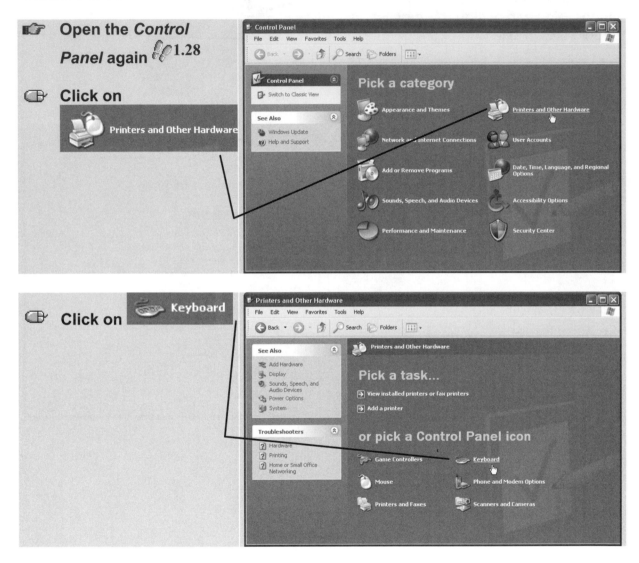

☞ **Open the *Control Panel* again** 🐾 1.28

🖰 **Click on**   Printers and Other Hardware

🖰 **Click on**   Keyboard

Now you see the window for customizing the keyboard:

☞ **Click on the tab** ⌷ Speed

Your Keystroke

Perhaps you accidentally type double letters often. This happens when you press a key for too long. You can adjust the keyboard to reduce the chance of a repeated keystroke.

In the Repeat delay: section you see a button that you can slide towards Long or Short:

If you want a longer delay before *Windows XP* repeats the letter, slide the button to the left.

☞ **Click on** ⌷ Apply

Now you won't type double letters accidentally as often as before.

💡 Tip

Slanting the Keyboard

Nearly every keyboard has two supports on the bottom with which the keyboard can be slanted.

Support

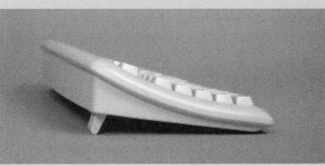

Keyboard with the supports in use

You can flip the supports out and try the slanted position. You'll immediately notice whether this makes your wrists feel more relaxed.

💡 Tip

Ergonomically-Shaped Keyboards

In recent years a wide variety of ergonomically-shaped keyboards have been introduced. The positions of the keys on these keyboards are adjusted to fit the natural position of the hands and wrists.

The rows of keys on these keyboards have been moved to suit the natural hand position, so that the wrists are not forced as closely together. These keyboards take some getting used to. But especially if you've learned how to type properly, they can be very pleasant to use.

Customizing the Display

Many older users complain about the poor legibility of the screen. The standard letters used in *Windows XP* for buttons and menus are too small for them. Luckily, this can be changed in a variety of ways. You can experiment to find out what you like best.

☞ **Open the *Control Panel*** 𝒆𝒆1.28

☞ **Click on**

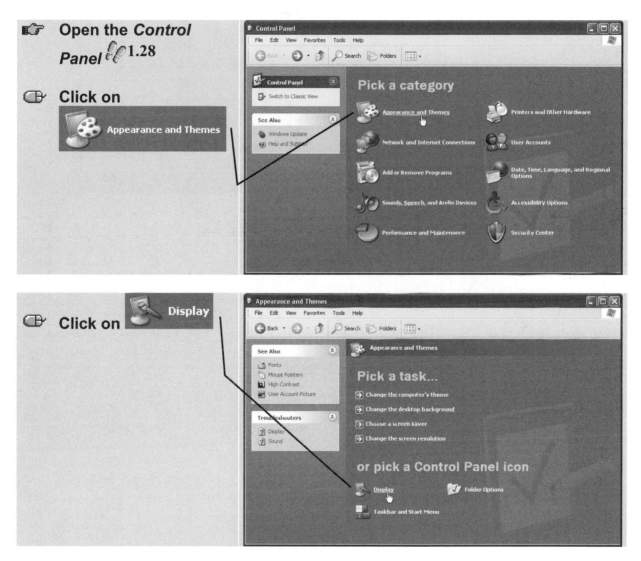

You can change the following settings for your screen:

- the size of the letters
- the background used with *Windows XP*
- the screen saver
- the standby mode

Larger Text

You can start by making the letters and the buttons a bit larger. This is how:

Click on the tab
Appearance

In Windows and buttons: you
probably see Windows XP style :

You can select a different font size that has larger letters.

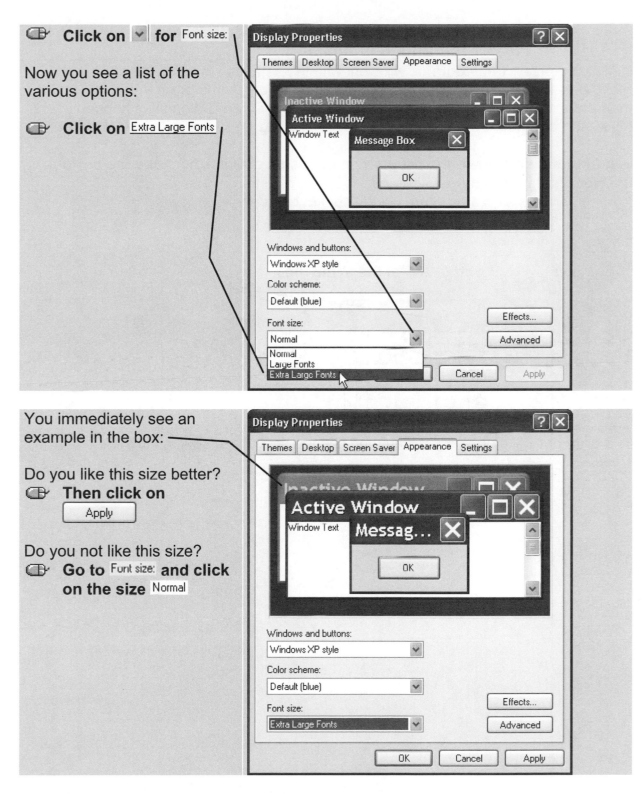

Click on ⌄ **for** Font size:

Now you see a list of the various options:

Click on Extra Large Fonts

You immediately see an example in the box:

Do you like this size better?
Then click on
Apply

Do you not like this size?
Go to Funt size: **and click on the size** Normal

There are various font sizes, including a number that make everything in *Windows XP* extra large. You can experiment to find out what you like best. If necessary, you can always change back to the original settings.

HELP! Part of the image is missing.

Nine out of every ten programs will work with the settings *Windows XP style (Large fonts)* and *Windows XP style (Extra large fonts)*. Sadly, some programs don't, and then parts of the program are not displayed on your screen. When this happens, you must stop the program and select the original setting *Windows XP style (Normal)*.

Is it impossible to stop the program in the usual manner because the buttons are not displayed on your screen?
You can always stop a program using your keyboard.

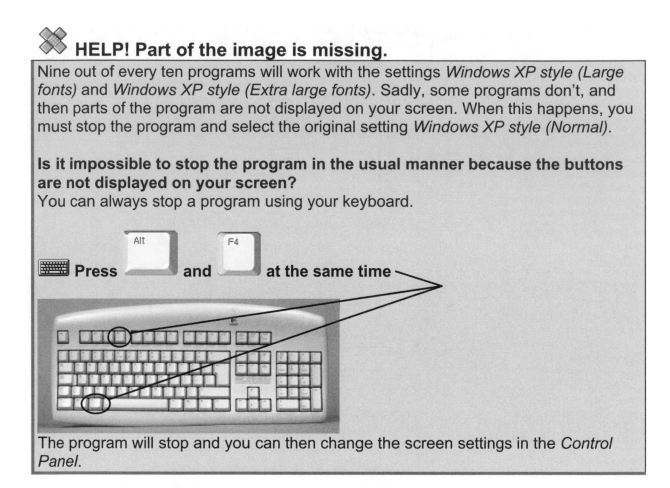

Press `Alt` **and** `F4` **at the same time**

The program will stop and you can then change the screen settings in the *Control Panel*.

A Different Background

Working with the computer is pleasant when the background on the desktop is peaceful. Perhaps the background on your desktop is brightly colored, or a cloudy sky, or a variety pattern. Or maybe you think your background is boring, or you just want to try something new. It's very easy to select a different background.

👈 **Click on the tab** Desktop

Under Background: you see a list of patterns to choose from:

☞ **Remember which pattern was originally selected on your computer**

In the list, this setting will be colored.

The setting at the top of the list ⊘ *(None)* is the most peaceful, giving a solid background:

👈 **Click on** ⊘ (None)

On the image of the display on your screen, you can see what the background will look like:

Do you like this background?
👈 **Then click on**
Apply

Do you not like this background?
👈 **Then click on the original background or try another pattern**

The Screen Saver

Perhaps a moving pattern appears on your screen if you haven't used your computer for a while. This is the *screen saver*. The screen saver prevents your screen from "burn-in". Burn-in happens if the same motionless image is on the screen for a long period of time. You can set the screen saver yourself in *Windows XP*. And the screen saver is not only functional: it can be fun to watch. Some of the options are very surprising.

Click on the tab
Screen Saver

Under Screen saver you see a list of various screen savers:

Display Properties

Themes | Desktop | Screen Saver | Appearance | Settings

Screen saver
Windows XP   Settings   Preview
Wait: 10 minutes On resume, password protect

Monitor power
To adjust monitor power settings and save energy, click Power.
Power...

OK   Cancel   Apply

Click on ⌄ for
Screen saver

Click on 3D Pipes , for
instance

Take your hands from
the mouse and the
keyboard

If you wait for a bit, the image
of the display on your screen
will show an example:

Do you like this choice?
Then click on
Apply

Do you not like it?
Then click on the
original screen saver,
try another or select
(None)

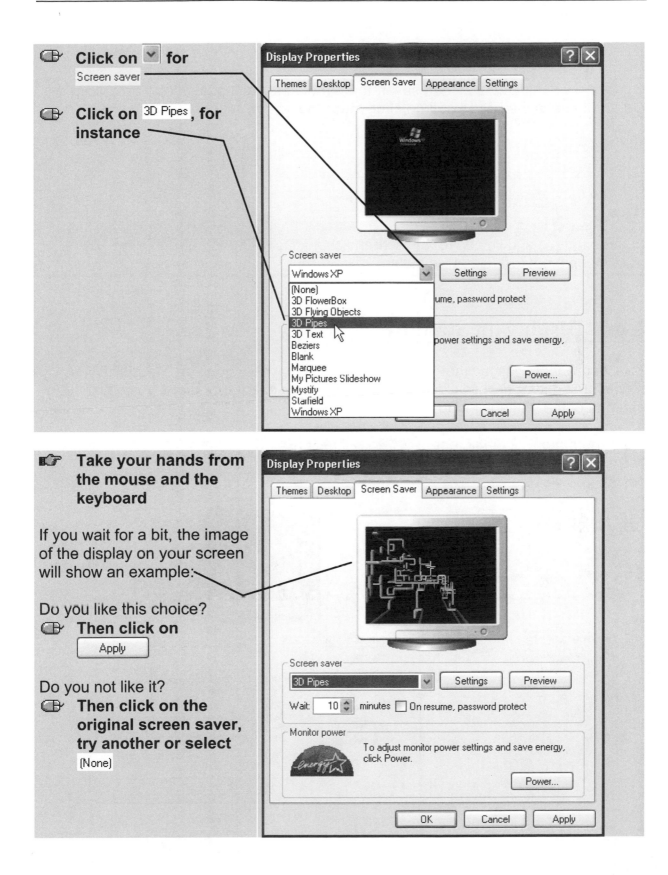

💡 Tip

Once you've selected a screen saver, there are other settings that can be changed. One of these is the period of time after which the screen saver is activated:

Screen saver
3D Pipes ▾   [Settings]   [Preview]
Wait: 60 ⬍ minutes ☐ On resume, password protect

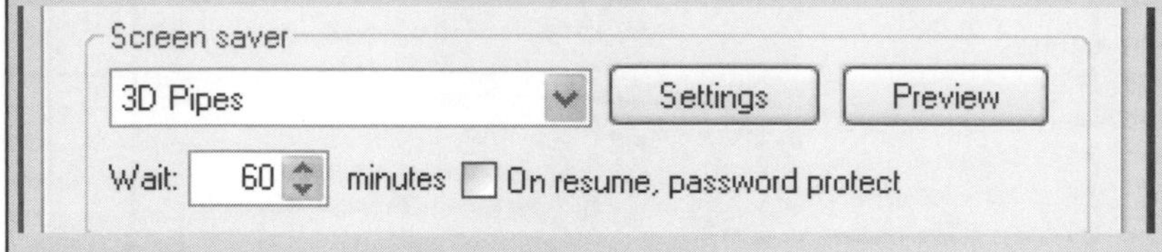

In the example shown above, the screen saver is activated after 60 minutes, but most people opt for 10 or 15 minutes.

Your Display on Standby

You've probably noticed that your computer automatically goes on *Standby* if you haven't used it for a while. This is done to conserve energy. You can customize the settings of the standby mode.

Near the bottom of the screen you see a frame called *Monitor power:*

👆 **Click on** [Power...]

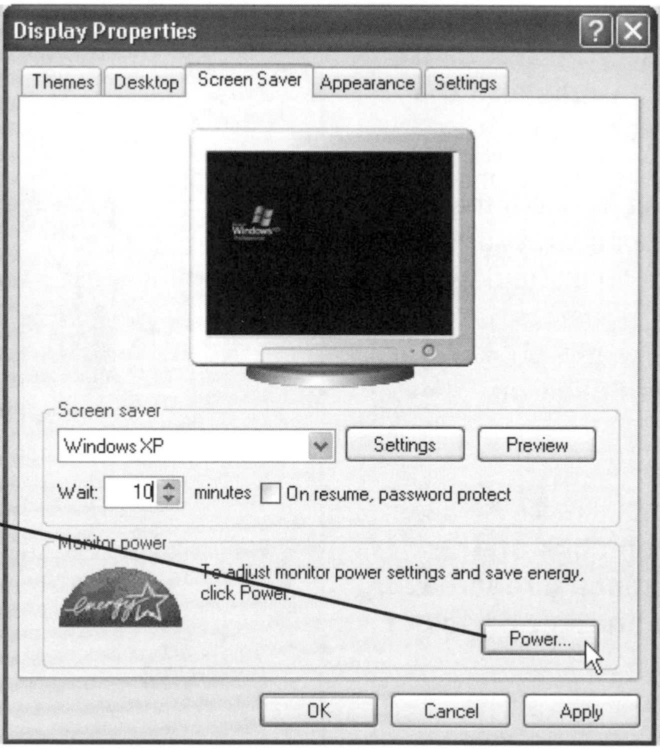

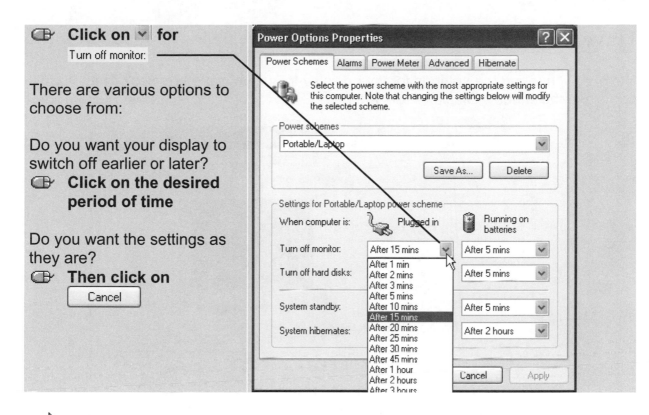

Click on ⌄ for

Turn off monitor: ————

There are various options to choose from:

Do you want your display to switch off earlier or later?

☞ **Click on the desired period of time**

Do you want the settings as they are?

☞ **Then click on**

Cancel

⇨ **Please note:**

In the window shown above, you can see that there are other energy-conserving settings that you can activate, such as having the entire computer system switch to *standby*. These options are not discussed in this book because we've discovered that they don't function properly on every computer.

Have You Customized the Display?

Have you changed the settings for your display to suit your preferences? Then you can close the window *Display Properties*.

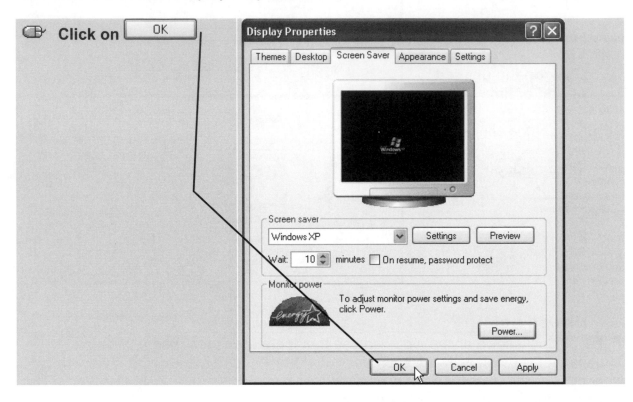

All of the changes that you've made to the settings will be saved and you'll return to the *Control Panel*.

Tips for the Display

 Tip

The Position of the monitor

According to OSHA guidelines, you should place your monitor directly in front of you, about 20 to 40 inches from your face. The top of the screen should be level with your eyes. However, if you have half-shaped reading glasses or multi-focus lenses, the monitor may be lower.

 Tip

Your Reading Glasses and the Screen

The distance from your face to the screen is a bit longer than the distance for which your reading glasses were made. Reading glasses are made for a reading distance of 15 - 20 inches. In theory, you should be able to easily read the letters on your screen with the distance viewing section of the bifocal glasses.

However, if you can only read the letters with the reading section of the lenses, you can move the monitor a bit closer. You can also position the monitor as low as possible so that you don't have to strain to look through the reading part of the lenses, with your face turned upward. This would quickly make your neck feel tired. If you can't read the letters on the screen easily with the distance viewing section of the glasses, please contact your optician. Special "computer glasses" are available that are intended for an intermediate screen distance.

 Tip

Adjusting the Screen

Like most television sets, your monitor has buttons for adjusting settings such as brightness and contrast.

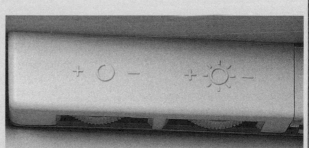

It's also often possible to change the position of the image on the screen. This is important, for example, if parts of the *Windows* screen are located just off the screen. On some displays, these buttons are hidden behind a cover:

Take the time to optimally adjust your display. If necessary, consult the instructions that came with it.

Customizing the Sound

The term *multimedia* refers to software in which (moving) images and sound play important parts. If you have a program that uses many voices or sounds, you must be able to hear these.
To begin with, you should adjust the sound level on your computer to suit your taste. There are two ways to do this:

- in *Windows XP* itself
- with the volume knob on the computer, the speakers or the monitor

It's a matter of experimenting. If the sound in *Windows XP* is very low or off, you'll still hear nothing even if you set the volume knob on the computer or speakers wide open. If this is the case, you'll have to set the sound level in *Windows XP* first.
A speaker icon ◀: is shown on the taskbar for this purpose.

☞ Minimize the *Control Panel* window ⟋ℓ 1.1

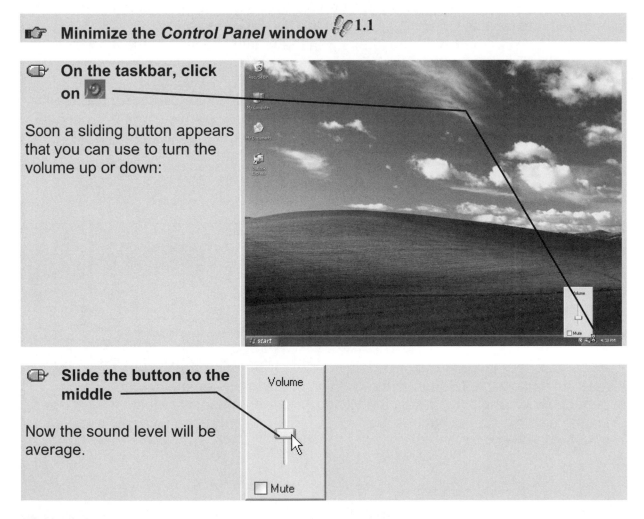

☞ **On the taskbar, click on** ⟟

Soon a sliding button appears that you can use to turn the volume up or down:

☞ **Slide the button to the middle**

Now the sound level will be average.

This is how to set the sound level in *Windows XP*. The best way to further adjust the sound level is to play some music on your computer. You need a music CD to do so.

Music as a Test

Your computer can play regular music CDs. This is a good way to adjust the sound level to suit your taste. It's also sometimes pleasant to listen to music while you're working.

You need a music CD for this section, for example:

How Do I Insert a CD in the CD-ROM Drive?

Most CD-ROM players have a drawer into which the CD must be inserted:

☞ **Press the button <u>on the right</u> on the CD-ROM drive**

☞ **After it opens, insert the CD in the drawer**

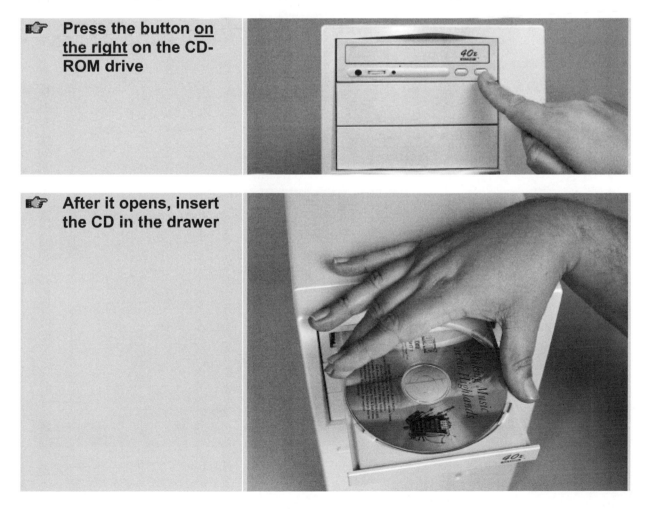

☞ **Now gently push the drawer to close it**

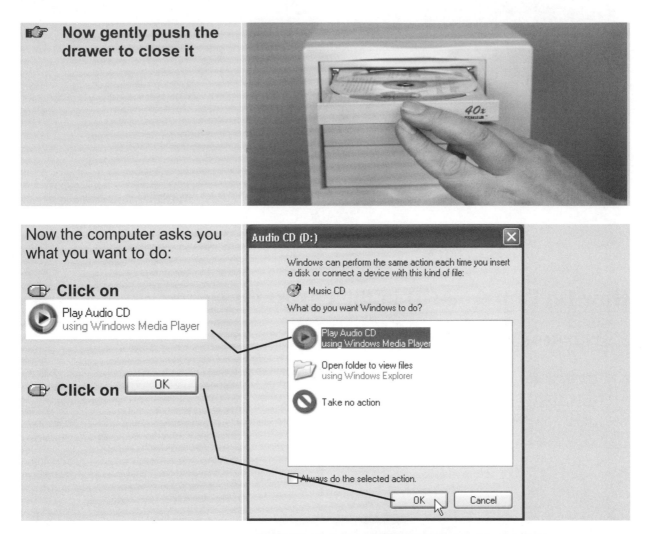

Now the computer asks you what you want to do:

⊕ **Click on**

▶ Play Audio CD
using Windows Media Player

⊕ **Click on** [OK]

Audio CD (D:) ☒

Windows can perform the same action each time you insert a disk or connect a device with this kind of file:

🎵 Music CD

What do you want Windows to do?

> ▶ Play Audio CD
> using Windows Media Player

> 📁 Open folder to view files
> using Windows Explorer

> 🚫 Take no action

☐ Always do the selected action.

[OK] [Cancel]

The *Windows Media Player* starts and you can hear music.

Windows Media Player has its own volume slider

🔊 ▬▬▬▬▬○▬ :

If you can not hear the music:
⊕ **Drag** 🔲 **to the right**

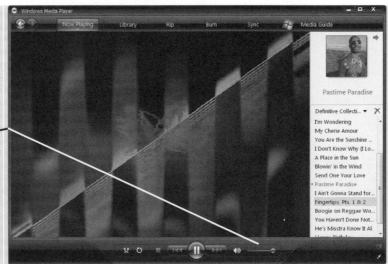

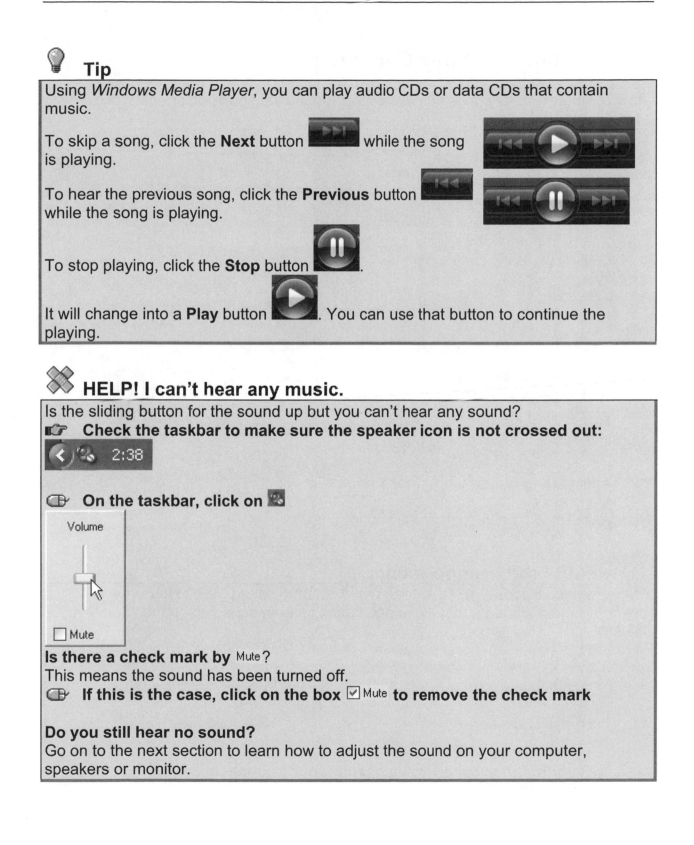

Tip

Using *Windows Media Player*, you can play audio CDs or data CDs that contain music.

To skip a song, click the **Next** button ▶▶| while the song is playing.

To hear the previous song, click the **Previous** button |◀◀ while the song is playing.

To stop playing, click the **Stop** button ⏸.

It will change into a **Play** button ▶. You can use that button to continue the playing.

HELP! I can't hear any music.

Is the sliding button for the sound up but you can't hear any sound?
☞ **Check the taskbar to make sure the speaker icon is not crossed out:**

🔊 2:38

🖱 **On the taskbar, click on** 🔊

Volume

☐ Mute

Is there a check mark by Mute?
This means the sound has been turned off.
🖱 **If this is the case, click on the box** ☑ Mute **to remove the check mark**

Do you still hear no sound?
Go on to the next section to learn how to adjust the sound on your computer, speakers or monitor.

Sound Knobs on Your Computer

Most computers have knobs somewhere for turning the sound up or down, on or off.

The knobs are on the computer itself sometimes, as is the case with a *laptop*:

With other computers, the knobs will be on the speakers:

However, if the speakers are built into the display, you'll find the knobs on the monitor:

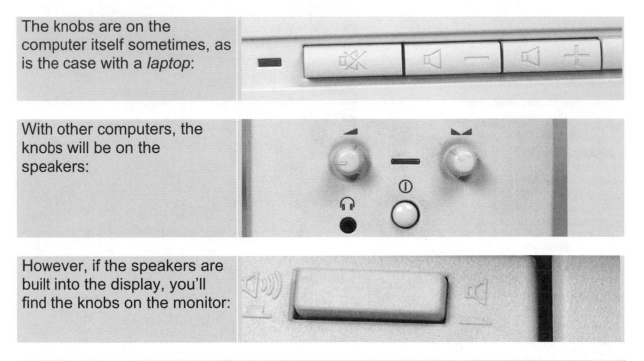

☞ **Adjust the volume using these knobs**

Now you should be able to hear the sound.

✖ HELP! I still hear no sound.

Check on the *Windows XP* taskbar to make sure the sound hasn't been muted. Next check to make sure that the sound hasn't been switched off on the computer itself.

Some computers, displays or speakers have a knob that can be used to turn the speakers completely off:

☞ **Turn the sound on**

Do you still hear no sound?

☞ **Make sure the speakers have been properly connected or consult your computer supplier**

Customizing Sound Signals

Windows XP has a wide variety of sounds built in that work as warning signals. In some situations, it's handy to have a sound signal warn you about something. In situations in which something may go wrong, for example. Perhaps you've already noticed that your computer makes noises, for example when *Windows XP* is started or stopped. But there are more sound signals that you can customize.

Open the *Control Panel* 𝓵𝓵1.28

Click on

Sounds, Speech, and Audio Devices

Click on

Sounds and Audio Devices

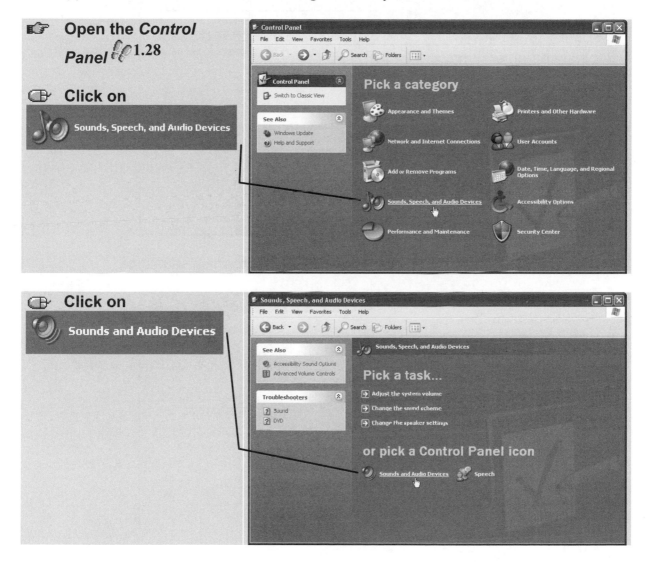

Now a window appears in which various settings can be selected.

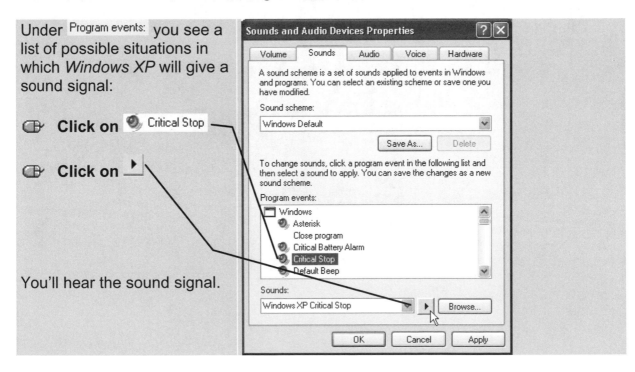

☞ **Click on the tab**
  Sounds

Under Sound scheme: you see a list of sound schemes to choose from:

Does your computer not make any sound, or do your hear other sounds on your computer?

☞ **Then click on the scheme** Windows Default

You can determine which sound signals will be heard in which situations.

Under Program events: you see a list of possible situations in which *Windows XP* will give a sound signal:

☞ **Click on** 🔊 Critical Stop

☞ **Click on** ▶

You'll hear the sound signal.

It's worth the effort to test and see if you like the sound signals. When you start or stop *Windows XP*, you'll also hear a brief tune.
If you don't like this setting, you can always select a different scheme or *No sounds* in the window shown above.

Have You Customized the Sound?

Now you can save the changes you made to the sound settings.

👆 **Click on** [Apply]

👆 **Click on** [OK]

Sounds and Audio Devices Properties [?][X]

| Volume | Sounds | Audio | Voice | Hardware |

A sound scheme is a set of sounds applied to events in Windows and programs. You can select an existing scheme or save one you have modified.

Sound scheme:

[Windows Default] [v]

[Save As...] [Delete]

To change sounds, click a program event in the following list and then select a sound to apply. You can save the changes as a new sound scheme.

Program events:

- 🖥 Windows
  - 🔊 Asterisk
  - Close program
  - 🔊 Critical Battery Alarm
  - 🔊 **Critical Stop**
  - 🔊 Default Beep

Sounds:

[Windows XP Critical Stop] [v] [▶] [Browse...]

[OK] [Cancel] [Apply]

The window is closed and you'll return to the *Control Panel*.

👉 **Close the *Control Panel* window**

Tips for the Sound

 Tip

Connecting Additional Speakers
If you aren't satisfied with the sound quality of your computer, you might consider connecting extra speakers or "heavy-duty" speakers to your computer.

Computer speakers

Every computer has three contact points for the sound: a microphone, a headset and extra speakers. Sometimes these will be marked OUT:

Three contact points

It's easy to plug in the speakers. Computer speakers can be found in a wide variety of types and sizes in computer stores.

 Tip

Connecting a Headset
Undoubtedly, you'll hear best if you use a headset. You can adjust the volume to any level you want without bothering others. Nearly every type of headset can be connected to the computer. You don't need a special computer headset.

Naturally, the plug has to fit. Some computers have a separate plug for the headset that's specially marked. If your computer doesn't have this, you can connect the headset to one of the three contact points shown in the previous tip.

More about Windows XP

The book **Windows XP for SENIORS** has taken you through the basics of computing and *Windows XP*. Now you can write a letter, surf the internet, send an e-mail and personalize *Windows XP*.
Interested in gaining more skills?
Try the following Visual Steps books in the **Windows XP for SENIORS series**:

More Windows XP for SENIORS
ISBN: 978 90 5905 114 0

Like all Visual Steps books it is a learn-as-you-go-book:
- easy step-by-step approach
- screen shots illustrate every step

You will learn how to:
- maintain and manage your computer
- safeguard your computer with *Windows Security Center*
- adjust more *Windows* settings
- set up User Accounts
- make backups and perform a System Restore
- burn data CDs and compress files

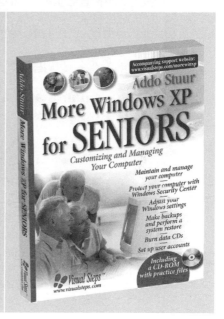

Do you want to know more about e-mail and surfing the Internet?
This Visual Steps book will be an excellent choice:

Internet and E-mail for SENIORS with Windows XP
ISBN: 978 90 5905 054 9

Like all Visual Steps books it is a learn-as-you-go-book:
- easy step-by-step approach
- screen shots illustrate every step

You will learn how to:
- search the Internet more effectively
- prevent virus attacks
- download free software from the internet
- personalize your e-mail
- send, receive, open and save attachments
- save e-mail addresses

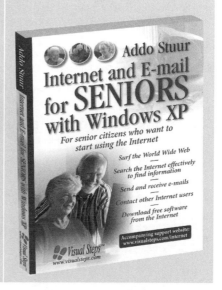

Tips

💡 Tip

The Visual Steps Newsletter
Do you want to be informed about the release date of our new books? You can subscribe to the **free Visual Steps Newsletter**. We will send out periodic e-mails to inform you of our product releases, tips & tricks, special offers, free guides, etc.

☞ **Open *Internet Explorer* and surf to the website www.visualsteps.com**

👆 **Click on Newsletter**

☞ **Fill in your name and e-mail address in the box**

👆 **Click on Submit**

Please be sure that we will not use your e-mail address for any purpose except to send you the information you have requested and we will not share this address with any third-party.

💡 Tip

Test Your Knowledge
You are at the end of this Visual Steps book. Now you can test your knowledge about the computer and *Windows.* Visual Steps offers online a series of multiple-choice quizzes over a range of different topics created specifically for seniors.
A special certificate is available to all individuals who can successfully answer the questions.

☞ **Surf to the website: www.ccforseniors.com**

👆 **Click on one of the quizzes**

👆 **Click on the right answers**

If a sufficient score is achieved you will be able to receive your **Computer Certificate** by e-mail.

This service is free for all participants.

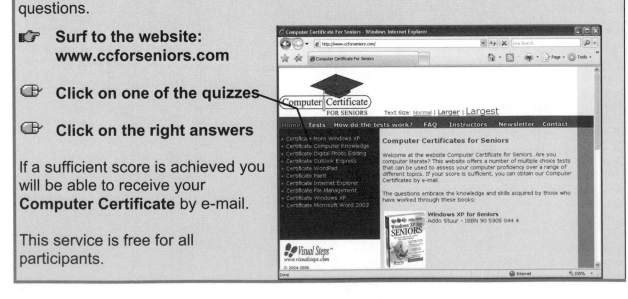

Appendix A. Clicking, Dragging and Double-Clicking in Solitaire

The card game *Solitaire* is not only very popular among computer users, but also an extremely pleasant way to practice working with the mouse. The game requires a lot of clicking and dragging. This section describes how to play the game.

Starting Solitaire

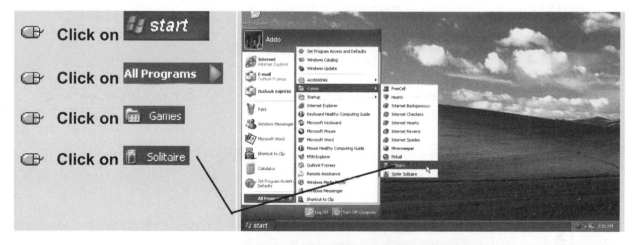

☞ **Click on** start

☞ **Click on** All Programs

☞ **Click on** Games

☞ **Click on** Solitaire

You now see this window with seven piles of cards:

This is how to play the game: At the top left there is a pile of cards with the face down, called the deck. You can turn over the cards in this pile by clicking on it.

☞ **Click on the deck**

The top three cards are turned over:

You can place a card in the correct spot by dragging it with the mouse.

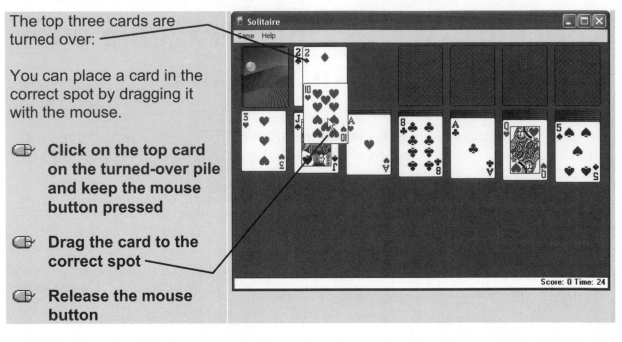

- ☞ **Click on the top card on the turned-over pile and keep the mouse button pressed**

- ☞ **Drag the card to the correct spot**

- ☞ **Release the mouse button**

You can move the card to one of the seven lower piles, called "row stacks". There you release the mouse button.

- If the card can be played here, it will remain there.
- If the card cannot be played here, it will automatically go back to the turned-over pile.

Do you already know how to play this version of the card game *Solitaire*?
Then you really already know how to play: try to play all of the cards and get them all up to the suit stacks.

Do you not know how to play this version of the card game *Solitaire*?
Then you can read the objective of the game and the rules below.

The Rules for Solitaire

The Objective

○ The objective of this game is to play all of the cards in proper order on the suit stacks at the top right. Next to the deck, you see the empty spaces for the four suit stacks:

○ The first card that you can play on these piles is the ace; then you must play the two, three, four, and so on, up to the king.

○ Spades, clubs, diamonds and hearts each have their own pile.

Some of the cards are divided over seven stacks: —

The rest of the cards are in the deck at the top left.

The Beginning

You must try first to play cards on the seven playing stacks.

You can take a card from these stacks by *dragging* it with your mouse:

⇨ **Please note:**

A card can only be played on these seven stacks if it is the next descending card of the opposite color: red eight on black nine, black jack on red queen, and so on.
In *Solitaire*, the **king** is the **highest** card and the **ace** is the **lowest**.

The Seven Stacks

You can play a card from one of the playing stacks to a different playing stack:

This can only be done if the card fits.

Once you've played the top card from a stack, you can click on the stack to turn over the next card:

In this way you must try to turn over all of the cards and play them on one of the row or suit stacks.
But there are a few more things you need to know:

If there is a stack of cards that fits onto a different stack, you can move the entire stack by dragging the first card in the stack:

If one of the seven playing stacks at the bottom is emptied, you can only start it again by placing a **king** there:

Once your entire deck has been turned over, you'll see a circle in the empty space.
You can turn back the pile of cards from the deck that couldn't yet be played by clicking on the circle:

Playing Suits

You can also play cards by suit. There's a space for each of the four suits at the top right of the screen.

If an **ace** has turned up, you should start the suit stacks by moving it to one of the four spaces, as illustrated here with the ace of spades. You can move cards to a suit stack not only by dragging them, but also by double-clicking with the left mouse button:

If a two of spades turns up later, you can play it on top of the ace of spades:

End of the Game

You've **won the game** if you succeed in completing all of the four suit stacks, one for clubs, one for diamonds, one for hearts and one for spades.

The cards will be so happy for you that they'll jump all over your screen:

A New Game

You're "stuck" if you can no longer turn over cards from the deck or move any of the cards in the stacks. The best thing to do when this happens is to start a **new game**. This is how to start a new game:

Click on Game

Click on Deal

Now the cards will be shuffled and redealt. You can start playing the game again.

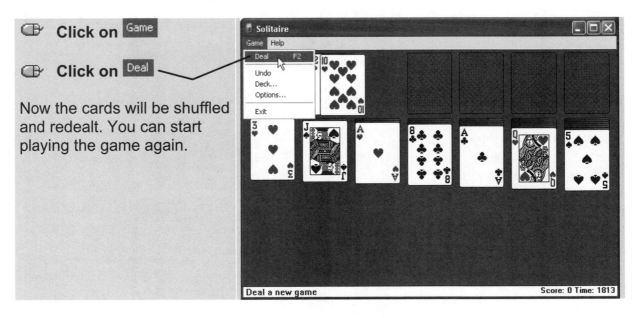

Tips

 Tip

Paying Attention and a Bit of Luck!
Solitaire is game in which you must pay attention. You have to continually look carefully to see if a card can be played somewhere. But you also need a bit of luck. Even the very best players can't win every game.

 Tip

Always pay attention to the following:
- Always turn over cards that are face down first.
- Then look to see if a card can be played on one of the seven row stacks.
- Check to see if you can play a card on one of the four suit stacks.
- Don't turn cards over from the deck until you have played all of the cards that you can.

 Tip

Do you want a different deck of cards?
You can change the deck as follows:

Click on Game

Click on Deck...

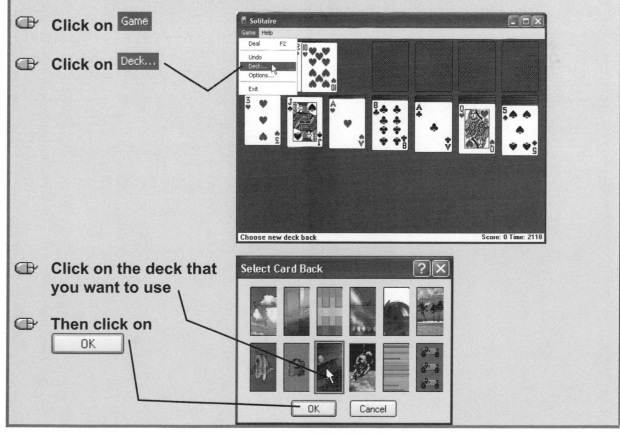

Click on the deck that you want to use

Then click on OK

Appendix B. How Do I Do That Again?

In this book you'll find many exercises that are marked with footsteps. x.x
In this appendix, use the number next to the footsteps to see how to do something.

1. Windows Programs

The most-frequently used actions for *Windows* programs are listed below.

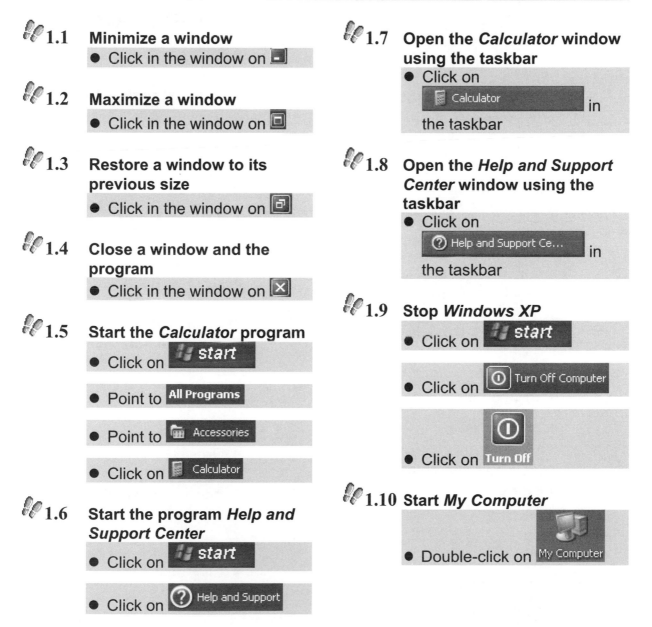

1.1   Minimize a window
- Click in the window on

1.2   Maximize a window
- Click in the window on

1.3   Restore a window to its previous size
- Click in the window on

1.4   Close a window and the program
- Click in the window on

1.5   Start the *Calculator* program
- Click on   start
- Point to   All Programs
- Point to   Accessories
- Click on   Calculator

1.6   Start the program *Help and Support Center*
- Click on   start
- Click on   (?) Help and Support

1.7   Open the *Calculator* window using the taskbar
- Click on   Calculator   in the taskbar

1.8   Open the *Help and Support Center* window using the taskbar
- Click on   (?) Help and Support Ce...   in the taskbar

1.9   Stop *Windows XP*
- Click on   start
- Click on   Turn Off Computer
- Click on   Turn Off

1.10   Start *My Computer*
- Double-click on   My Computer

1.11 Drag a window
- Place the mouse pointer on the title bar at the top
- Drag with the mouse

1.12 Change the size of a window
- Place the mouse pointer on the edge of the window. The pointer changes to ↔, ↕ or ↖
- Drag with the mouse

1.13 Scroll text
- Place the mouse pointer on the scrollbar
- Drag with the mouse

1.14 Start the program *WordPad*
- Click on `start`
- Point to `All Programs`
- Point to `Accessories`
- Click on `Wordpad`

1.15 Stop the program *WordPad*
- Click on `File`
- Click on `Exit`

1.16 Start a new file (text or drawing)
- Click on `File`
- Click on `New`

1.17 Start a new file - save changes
- Click on `File`

- Click on `New`

Question: Save Changes?

- Click on `Yes`

1.18 Start a new file - <u>do not</u> save changes
- Click on `File`
- Click on `New`

Question: Save Changes?

- Click on `No`

1.19 Print a text or drawing
- Click on `File`
- Click on `Print...`
- Click on `Print`

1.20 Viewing the contents of *Help and Support Center*
- Click on the tab sheet 🏠

1.21 View the index of *Help and Support Center*
- Click on the tab sheet `Index`

1.22 View subsections
- Click on ⊞

1.23 Read the information
- Click on ⊡

1.24 Read the information
- Click on the key phrase, for example `2004, year date settings`
- Click on `Display`

1.25 Copy a selection

- Click on Edit

- Click on Copy

1.26 Paste a selection

- Click on Edit

- Click on Paste

1.27 Cut a selection

- Click on Edit

- Click on Cut

1.28 Open the *Control Panel*

- Click on start

- Click on Control Panel

1.29 Open a window using the taskbar

- On the taskbar, click on the button for the program

1.30 Open the index

- Click on Index

1.31 Read about a subject

- Click on the subject

- Click on Display

1.32 Go back to the homepage of *Help and Support Center*

- Click on Back

2. Save File / Save As

This command is used to save your work. The commands are the same in all *Windows* programs, such as *WordPad, Paint* and *MS Word.*

2.1 Save a new file
- Click on `File`
- Click on `Save`
- At `File name:`, type the name of your file:

  File name: test2
- Click on `Save`

2.2 Save an existing file
- Click on `File`
- Click on `Save`

2.3 Save a new file in the folder *My Documents*
- Click on `File`
- Click on `Save`
- At `File name:`, type the name of your file:

  File name: test2
- At `Save in:`, select the folder `My Documents`
- If this folder is still closed, first click on `Open`
- If the folder is already open, click on `Save`

2.4 Save on floppy disk or USB stick
- Click on `File`
- Click on `Save`
- At `File name:`, type the name of your file:

  File name: test2
- At `Save in:`, select `3½ Floppy (A:)` or `Removable Disk (E:)`
- Click on `Save`

2.5 Save with a different name
- Click on `File`
- Click on `Save As...`
- At `File name:`, type the new name of your file:

  File name: new test
- If applicable, at `Save in:` select the folder in which you want to save the new file:

  Save in: Adults
- If this folder is still closed, first click on `Open`
- If the folder is already open, click on `Save`

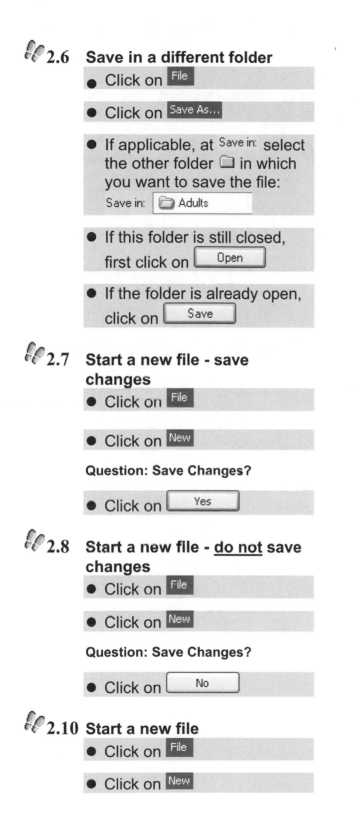

2.6   Save in a different folder

● Click on File

● Click on Save As...

● If applicable, at Save in: select
  the other folder 🗀 in which
  you want to save the file:

  Save in: 🗀 Adults

● If this folder is still closed,
  first click on ⬛ Open

● If the folder is already open,
  click on ⬛ Save

**2.7   Start a new file - save
changes**

● Click on File

● Click on New

Question: Save Changes?

● Click on ⬛ Yes

**2.8   Start a new file - do not save
changes**

● Click on File

● Click on New

Question: Save Changes?

● Click on ⬛ No

2.10 Start a new file

● Click on File

● Click on New

3. Open File

These commands are used to open a file so that you can work on it. The commands are the same in all *Windows* programs, such as *WordPad, Paint* and *MS Word.*

3.1 Open a file
- Click on `File`
- Click on `Open...`
- Click on the name of the file
- Click on `Open`

3.2 Open a file in the folder *My Documents*
- Click on `File`
- Click on `Open...`
- Click at `Look in:` on
  `My Documents`
- Click on the name of the file
- Click on `Open`

3.3 Open a file from a floppy disk or USB stick
- Click on `File`
- Click on `Open...`
- Click at `Look in:` on
  `3½ Floppy (A:)` or
  `Removable Disk (E:)`
- Click on the name of the file
- Click on `Open`

3.4 Open a file in a different folder
- Click on `File`
- Click on `Open...`
- Click at `Look in:` on the relevant folder
- Click on `Open`

When the folder is open:
- Click on the name of the file
- Click on `Open`

4. Word Processing

The commands are the same in all word-processing programs, such as *WordPad, WordPerfect* and *MS Word 2002/2003.*

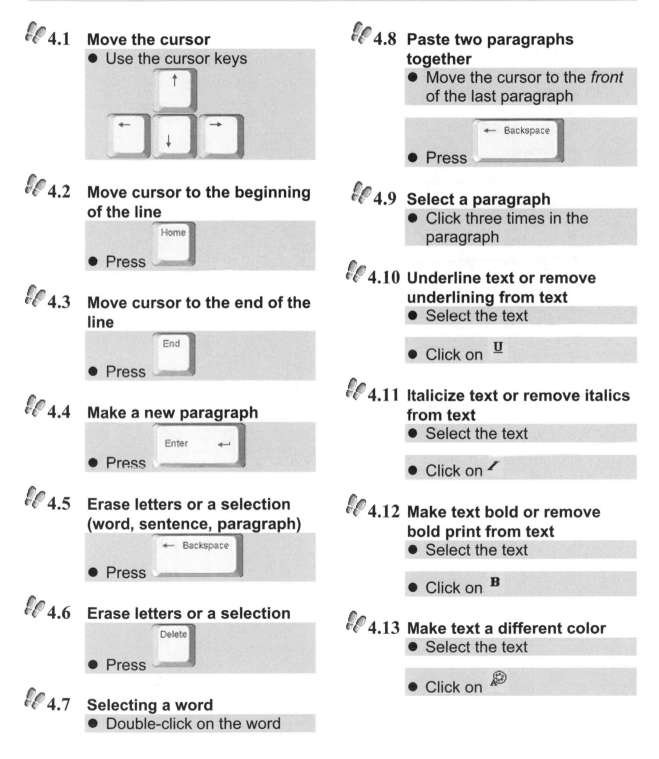

4.1 Move the cursor
- Use the cursor keys

4.2 Move cursor to the beginning of the line
- Press [Home]

4.3 Move cursor to the end of the line
- Press [End]

4.4 Make a new paragraph
- Press [Enter]

4.5 Erase letters or a selection (word, sentence, paragraph)
- Press [Backspace]

4.6 Erase letters or a selection
- Press [Delete]

4.7 Selecting a word
- Double-click on the word

4.8 Paste two paragraphs together
- Move the cursor to the *front* of the last paragraph
- Press [Backspace]

4.9 Select a paragraph
- Click three times in the paragraph

4.10 Underline text or remove underlining from text
- Select the text
- Click on U

4.11 Italicize text or remove italics from text
- Select the text
- Click on I

4.12 Make text bold or remove bold print from text
- Select the text
- Click on B

4.13 Make text a different color
- Select the text
- Click on

4.14 Change text font

- Select the text

- Click on 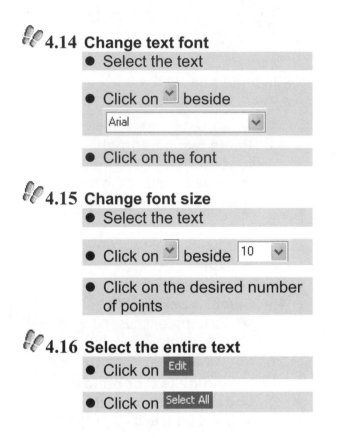 beside

  Arial

- Click on the font

4.15 Change font size

- Select the text

- Click on ⌄ beside 10 ⌄

- Click on the desired number of points

4.16 Select the entire text

- Click on Edit

- Click on Select All

5. Folders and Files

These actions can be performed in the *My Documents* window.

5.1 Open *My Documents*
- Double-click on My Documents

5.2 Open the folder *letters*
- Double-click on

  Letters

5.3 Open a folder one level higher
- Click on ← Back

5.4 Make a new folder
- Click on File
- Click on New ▶
- Click on 🗀 Folder
- Type the name of the folder
- Press Enter ↵

5.5 Open a folder
- Double-click on the folder

5.6 Copy a file to a folder
- Select a file by clicking on it
- Click on 📄 Copy this file
- Click on the correct folder
- Click on Copy

5.7 Rename a file
- Select a file by clicking on it
- Click on 🖼 Rename this file
- Type the new name
- Press Enter ↵

5.8 Delete a file
- Select a file by clicking on it
- Click on ✕ Delete this file
- Click on Yes

5.9 Copy a file to a floppy disk or USB stick
- Select a file by clicking on it
- Click on 📄 Copy this file
- Click on 💾 3½ Floppy (A:) or 💾 Removable Disk (E:)
- Click on Copy

6. Paint

These actions can be performed in the drawing program *Paint*.

6.1 Start *Paint*
- Click on 🏁 start
- Point to All Programs
- Point to 🗂 Accessories
- Click on 🖌 Paint

6.2 Draw using the mouse
- Click on ✏
- Move the mouse pointer to the white box
- Press the mouse button and keep it pressed
- Move the mouse
- Release the mouse button

6.3 Draw a square
- Click on ▢
- Move the mouse pointer to the white box
- Drag with the mouse

6.4 Draw a line
- Click on ＼
- Move the mouse pointer to the white box
- Drag with the mouse

6.5 Select a color
- Click on ▦

6.6 Draw an oval
- Click on ⬭
- Move the mouse pointer to the white box
- Drag with the mouse

6.7 Type text
- Click on A
- Move the mouse pointer to the white box
- Drag a dotted rectangle with the mouse
- Type the text in this rectangle

6.8 Select a section of a drawing
- Click on ⬚
- Move the mouse pointer to the white box
- Drag a dotted rectangle with the mouse

6.9 Copy a section of a drawing
- Click on ⬚
- Move the mouse pointer to the white box
- Drag a dotted rectangle with the mouse
- Click on Edit
- Click on Copy

7. Internet

These actions are performed in the programs *Internet Explorer* and *Outlook Express*.

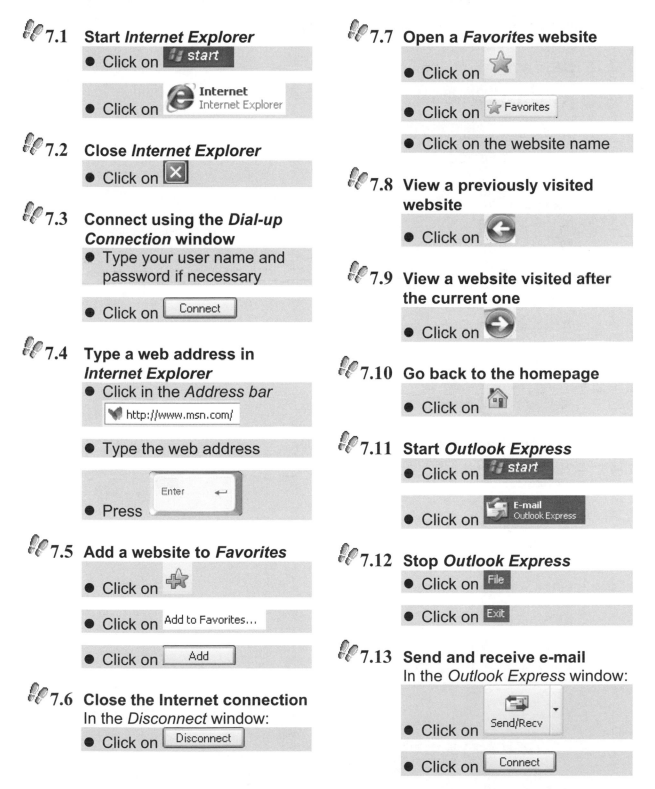

7.1   Start *Internet Explorer*
- Click on **start**
- Click on **Internet** Internet Explorer

7.2   Close *Internet Explorer*
- Click on ☒

7.3   Connect using the *Dial-up Connection* window
- Type your user name and password if necessary
- Click on **Connect**

7.4   Type a web address in *Internet Explorer*
- Click in the *Address bar*

  http://www.msn.com/

- Type the web address
- Press **Enter ↵**

7.5   Add a website to *Favorites*
- Click on ✛
- Click on **Add to Favorites...**
- Click on **Add**

7.6   Close the Internet connection
In the *Disconnect* window:
- Click on **Disconnect**

7.7   Open a *Favorites* website
- Click on ★
- Click on **☆ Favorites**
- Click on the website name

7.8   View a previously visited website
- Click on ←

7.9   View a website visited after the current one
- Click on →

7.10   Go back to the homepage
- Click on 🏠

7.11   Start *Outlook Express*
- Click on **start**
- Click on **E-mail** Outlook Express

7.12   Stop *Outlook Express*
- Click on **File**
- Click on **Exit**

7.13   Send and receive e-mail
In the *Outlook Express* window:
- Click on **Send/Recv**
- Click on **Connect**

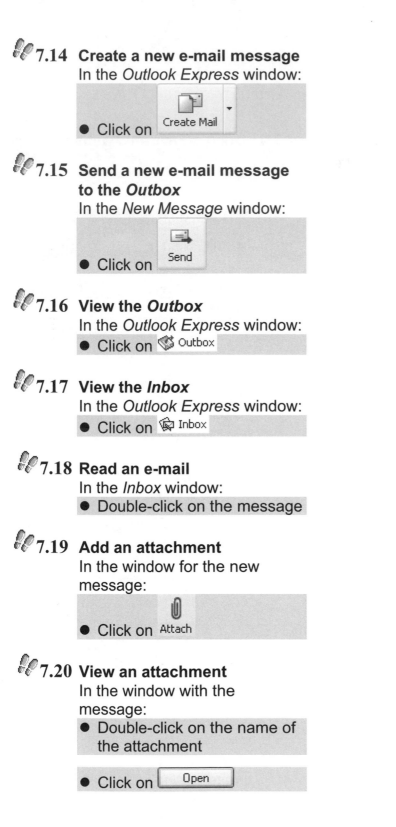

7.14 Create a new e-mail message
In the *Outlook Express* window:

● Click on Create Mail

**7.15 Send a new e-mail message
to the *Outbox***
In the *New Message* window:

● Click on Send

7.16 View the *Outbox*
In the *Outlook Express* window:
● Click on Outbox

7.17 View the *Inbox*
In the *Outlook Express* window:
● Click on Inbox

7.18 Read an e-mail
In the *Inbox* window:
● Double-click on the message

7.19 Add an attachment
In the window for the new
message:

● Click on Attach

7.20 View an attachment
In the window with the
message:
● Double-click on the name of
the attachment

● Click on Open

Appendix C.
Changing Your Keyboard Settings

If you'd like to be able to type foreign letters such as ñ, á, ö, and ç, you might need to change your keyboard settings. You can do this using the *Control Panel*.

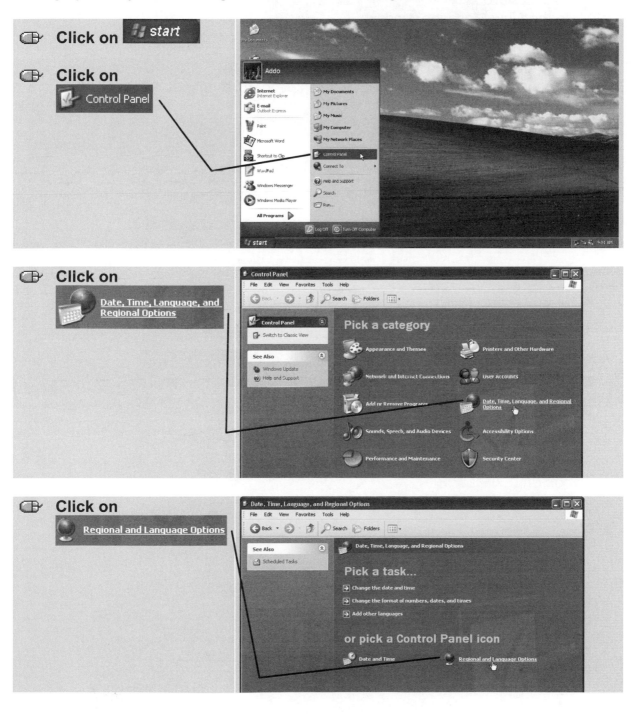

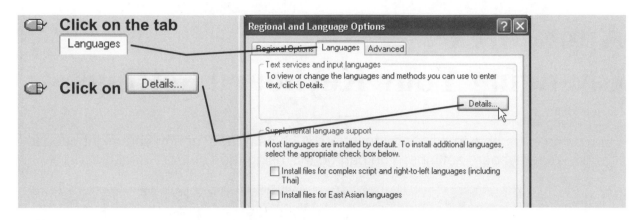

Click on the tab [Languages]

Click on [Details...]

You'll see a small window with several language settings. To type foreign letters on a QWERTY keyboard, choose an international keyboard setting as follows:

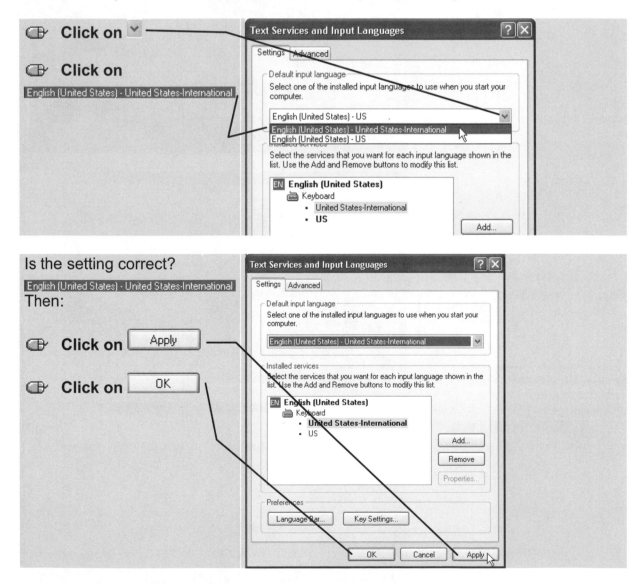

Click on ⌄

Click on [English (United States) - United States-International]

Is the setting correct? [English (United States) - United States-International]
Then:

Click on [Apply]

Click on [OK]

Now you can type accents and umlauts just as we've described in this book.

Appendix D. Index